Algonquians, Hurons and Iroquois
Champlain Explores America
1603-1616

Samuel de Champlain

Brook House Press
2000

Algonquians, Hurons and Iroquois Champlain Explores America 1603-1616

being

The Voyages and Explorations of Samuel de Champlain (1604-1616). Narrated by himself. Translated by Annie Nettleton Bourne. Together with The Voyage of 1603, reprinted from Purchas His Pilgrimes. Edited with introduction and notes by Edward Gaylord Bourne, professor of history in Yale University. Illustrated. Two Volumes. New York, A.S. Barnes & company, 1906.

Reformated into
One Unabridged Volume

Brook House Press
Dartmouth, Nova Scotia

Brook House Press
102 Windmill Rd.
Dartmouth, Nova Scotia
Canada B3A 1E1

Copyright © 2000, Dale McClare

Canadian Cataloguing in Publication Data

Champlain, Samuel de, 1567-1635
    Algonquians, Hurons, and Iroquois : Champlain explores America, 1603-1616 : being The voyages and explorations of Samuel de Champlain (1604-1616)

Originally published in 2 v., New York : A.S. Barnes, 1906.
"Reformated into one unabridged volume."
Translation of Les voyages de la Nouvelle France.
Includes bibliographical references.
ISBN 1-896986-01-3

    1. Champlain, Samuel de, 1567-1635. 2. Indians of North America—Canada. 3. America—Discovery and exploration—French. 4. Canada—History—To 1763 (New France) I. Bourne, Edward Gaylord, 1860-1908. II. Bourne, Annie Nettleton III. Title. IV. Title: Voyages de la Nouvelle France. V. Title: Voyages and explorations of Samuel de Champlain, 1604-1616.

FC332.A3 1999   971.01'13
C99-901147-2
F1030.1.C435 1999

Cover Illustration: *Champlain in Huronia*, by Rex Woods. Champlain and Brûlé, with Huron and Algonquin warriors, on eve of campaign against the Iroquois of Lake Oneida, September 1615.
From the Confederation Life Gallery of Canadian History. Courtesy of Rogers Communications Inc.

INTRODUCTION

SAMUEL DE CHAMPLAIN was the first explorer to make a detailed examination of the coast of New England and Nova Scotia and to prepare a full and accurate report of his observations. To him, likewise, we are indebted for our earliest exact accounts of the Indians of New England, eastern Canada and New York. To the Canadian he is more than the explorer and the acute observer of the native life; he is the founder of New France and at the same time the chief of its early historians. To the student of history to-day, in addition to all this, he stands forth as perhaps the ablest of the earlier makers of America, a leader of indefatigable energy and sterling character, a Frenchman who devoted his life to extending the name and power of France and the civilizing influences of the Church. His fame is impregnably established and grows with the lapse of time and the extension of knowledge of his work.

In view of all these facts it is surprising that his writings have to so slight a degree been accessible to the English reader. His earliest account of the Indians of the St. Lawrence River region, published in Paris in 1604 under the title *Des Sauvages, ou, Voyage de Sammuel Champlain de Brouage faict en la France Nouvelle, l'an mil six cens trois*, was made English and published in *Purchas His Pilgrimes*, London, 1625. In 1859 the Hakluyt Society brought out an English version of his *Brief Discours des choses plus remarquables que Sammuel Champlain de Brouage à reconneues aux Indes Occidentalles au voiage qu'il en a faict en iceles en l'année mil V^c. IIII^{xx}XIX & en l'année mil Vi^c I (1598-1601)*, under the title *Narrative of a Voyage to the West Indies and Mexico, 1599-1602*. The original remained unpublished until 1870, when the Abbé Laverdière published his *Oeuvres de Champlain*.

It was not until 1878, some 270 years after his exploration of the New England coast, that New Englanders and others unfamiliar with French could read the earliest descriptions of the shores since so rich in historic associations, whose picturesque variety of scenery and invigo-

INTRODUCTION

rating air have rendered them familiar and even dear to thousands of fortunate sojourners from every part of our country who have only this transitory connection with New England. In that year the Prince Society began the publication, under the learned editorial care of Reverend Edmund F. Slafter, of an English translation of all of Champlain's narratives of explorations on the New England coast, in New York, and in Canada down to the year 1617, when his activity in exploration gave place to efforts to build up Quebec. The translation was entrusted to a highly competent scholar, the late Charles Pomeroy Otis, at that time Professor of Modern Languages in the Massachusetts Institute of Technology. The translation, the editorial notes and the biography of Champlain by Mr. Slafter, formed a whole which was highly honorable to American scholarship and imposed lasting obligations upon every student of Champlain's career. Yet the edition was strictly limited and is now to be found only in the richer public or private collections of Americana. Equally scarce and expensive is Laverdière's collected edition of Champlain's works in the original.

It remains true, then, even after all the loving labors that Laverdière, Slafter and Otis have devoted to the publication and elucidation of Champlain's writings, that they are still a closed book to that rapidly growing body of readers who are interested in the original narratives of the explorers, the earliest observations of the Indians as yet uncontaminated by contact with Europeans, and the local history of New England and Canada. No more fitting addition, therefore, to The Trailmakers' Series could be made than a satisfactory popular edition of Champlain's own narrative of his explorations. In such an edition the translation should be both accurate and readable, and the notes should be as brief and clear as possible. To fulfill these requirements, the translator and the editor have made an earnest effort.

The Prince Society Edition of *Champlain's Voyages* contains translations: 1, of the narrative entitled, *Des Sauvages, ou, Voyage de Sammuel Champlain de Brouage faict en la France Nouvelle, en l'an mil six cens trois,* etc., i. e., the voyage of 1603, with its description of the Indians; 2, of the narrative of 1613, entitled, *Les Voyages du Sieur de Champlain Xaintongeois, Capitaine ordinaire pour le Roy en la Marine, Devisez en deux livres, ou Journal tres-fidele des Observations faites és descouvertures de la Nouvelle France; tant en la description des terres, costes, rivières, ports, havres, leurs hauteurs et plusieurs declinaisons de la guide aymant; qu'en la creance des peuples, leur superstitions, façon de vivre & de guerroyer,* etc.,

INTRODUCTION

Paris, MDCXIII; 3, *Quatriesme Voyage du Sr de Champlain, Capitaine ordinaire pour le Roy en la Marine & Lieutenant de Monseigneur le Prince de Condé en la Nouvelle France, fait en l'année 1613* (2 and 3 were published in the same volume in 1613); and 4, *Voyages et Descouvertures faites en la Nouvelle France depuis l'année 1615, jusques à la in de l'année 1618. Par le Sieur de Champlain, Capitaine ordinaire pour le Roy en la mer du Ponant,* Paris, 1619.

As the authorities of the Prince Society were unwilling to consent to have their translation reissued in a popular form, two courses were open for those who had in hand the preparation of a popular edition: either these narratives could be translated over again without the expectation of making any considerable improvement on Mr. Otis's work, or an English version could be undertaken of that portion of Champlain's own final edition of his works which relates to his explorations. This final edition was published in 1632 under the title: *Les Voyages de la Nouvelle France Occidentale dicte Canada, faits par le Sr de Champlain, Xainctongeois, Capitaine pour le Roy en la Marine du Ponant & toutes les Descouvertures qu'il à faites en ce pais depuis l'an 1603, jusques en l'an 1629,* etc. The latter course was chosen, for two reasons. First, this compilation, although hastily prepared, is in a very definite sense a revised and final edition by the author of his earlier publications. This is shown by the frequent corrections in estimates of distances and in the character of the omissions. Second, in this edition Champlain appears not only as a narrator of his own explorations, but as the historian of the earlier French discoveries and as the earliest French writer on colonization. His criticisms and judgments on the various aspects of the colonial experiments that he records help us to understand his point of view and the French point of view in regard to a number of important questions of colonial policy in regard to which the English practice was different.

The narrative of 1632, then, contains all the essentials of the earlier narratives, arranged in a systematic historical form, and, in addition, a sketch of the earlier French explorations and many interesting reflections on colonial policy. It is true the Abbé Laverdière was inclined to think that this narrative was edited by a hand unfriendly to the Recollect friars and favorable to the Jesuits, because so many particulars related to the Recollects in the earlier narratives are omitted in the narrative of 1632. I have examined each omission and am convinced that this conclusion is erroneous. In dovetailing several narratives of successive voyages into a history, Champlain had it in mind to present a continu-

INTRODUCTION

ous story of explorations, and he omitted details unessential for that purpose. A very competent scholar who has made extensive critical researches into the early literature of New France writes of this opinion of Laverdière, "I cannot find any grounds for accepting it."[1]

Again, the statement in the preface to the translation in the Prince Society edition, I, 219, that the narrative of 1632 "is an abridgment, and not a second edition in any proper sense. It omits for the most part personal details and descriptions of the manners and customs of the Indians, so that very much that is essential to the full comprehension of Champlain's work as an observer and explorer is gone," is most misleading and can only be accounted for on the ground that the writer had not carefully studied the 1632 edition, and had been unduly influenced by the summary way in which Champlain treated the voyage of 1603. In the present edition attention is called in the notes to nearly all the cases where the narrative of 1632 omits interesting details found in the earlier narratives.

The voyage of 1603 is very briefly recounted in this final narrative to avoid needless repetition. The geographical features of the St. Lawrence were more fully and accurately described in Champlain's later voyages, and his observations upon the Indians in 1603, so far as they were confirmed by later study, he incorporated with his later descriptions.

In this edition, however, it has been thought best to include Purchas's version of the voyage of 1603, even at the risk of some repetition, in order to place before the modem reader Champlain's first impressions, unrevised, of the Indians of the St. Lawrence, and the geographical details of this first voyage, especially when it could be done in so fine an example of early seventeenth century prose. This will be relished, I am sure, not only for its own beauty, but also because it lends Champlain's story the antique flavor which his own writing has for the modern Frenchman.

The translation of that part of the 1632 edition of Champlain's *Voyages* here given (Laverdière, *Voyages, 1632*, I, pp. 1-309) was undertaken by my wife, who devoted herself assiduously to the task. As editor, I have gone over the text, carefully comparing it with the original for verification and occasional revision. That it is entirely free from misconceptions or mistakes cannot be expected, nor will such expectations be

---

[1] See H. P. Biggar, *The Early Trading Companies of New France*, 279-280, where the case is gone into in some detail.

INTRODUCTION

entertained by any who have had experience in preparing translations. We have, however, made especial efforts to reduce such slips to the minimum.

In the preparation of the translation much help was derived from Mr. Otis's work, but in the same way that a translator to-day of Herodotus or Thucydides could and would legitimately be aided by the versions of Rawlinson or Jowett. As the texts used by Mr. Otis and by Mrs. Bourne are often almost identical for pages at a time, the versions unavoidably have much in common. For innumerable French sentences in direct narrative prose there is a natural English equivalent that would occur to independent translators in substantially identical form. In such cases, to give a studiedly varied form of expression would be most unprofitable, and such a practice would place a progressively heavy handicap on each successive translator.

In preparing the notes, the voluminous commentaries of the Abbé Laverdière and Mr. Slafter have been freely drawn upon, but in most cases the source of the note has been indicated by the initial L. or S. Help has also been derived from Dr. Samuel E. Dawson's valuable *History of the St. Lawrence Basin* and from Professor Ganong's admirable monograph on *Dochet* (St. Croix) *Island* (Transactions of the Royal Society of Canada, 2d Ser., VIII, sec. IV, 127-231), and also from Professor Ganong's *Champlain's Narrative of the Exploration and First Settlement of Acadia* (Acadiensis, IV, 179-216). That every modern student of Champlain's career owes a debt to Francis Parkman, both for kindling his interest and extending his knowledge, goes without saying.

The proper purposes of an Introduction to this edition of Champlain's *Voyages* would not be met without a sketch of the great explorer's life.

Samuel Champlain was born at Brouage, a small seaport town in the old province of Saintonge, southeast of Rochefort and opposite the island of Oléron, about the year 1567. The once excellent harbor has long since been filled in by the sea, and the little peasant village now lies nearly two miles inland. Although Champlain was interested from early youth in the art of navigation, his first known voyage was one to Spain in 1598 with his uncle, who was in command of a French ship chartered by the Spanish authorities. Early in 1599, Champlain was given command of this ship for the voyage to the West Indies and New Spain with the annual fleet. His observations on this voyage, which lasted two years, he recorded in his *Brief Discours des Choses plus remarquables . . . reconneues aux Indes Occidentallas*, the earliest French account that we have of New

INTRODUCTION

Spain. To this journey may be safely attributed the beginnings of Champlain's interest in colonization, and through it he alone of all the great leaders in the colonization of North America had the privilege of observing and studying a European colony before he tried to found one. Soon after his return to France, Champlain was enlisted by Aymar de Chastes, the Governor of Dieppe, to make a reconnoissance of the St. Lawrence in company with the merchant and fur trader, Francis Gravé, Sieur du Pont, a citizen of the Breton seaport, St. Malo. De Chastes had secured a patent from King Henry IV and had formed a trading company under whose patronage a settlement was to be made on the St. Lawrence. Champlain and Pontgravé (as he is more commonly called) explored the St. Lawrence as far as the rapids above Montreal, and later the country about Gaspé. Champlain's account of this voyage, published in 1604, he entitled, *Des Sauvages, ou Voyage de Samuel Champlain de Brouage, fait en la France Nouvelle l'an mil six cens trois*. This is the earliest detailed description we have of the Algonquin Indians of eastern Canada.[2]

When Champlain and Pontgravé returned they learned that De Chastes had died. His place as the promoter of a French colony in the New World was taken by Pierre du Gua (or Guast), Sieur de Monts, and the site selected was the milder region to the south of the mouth of the St. Lawrence. De Monts secured a charter from Henry IV similar to the later English proprietary charters, which granted him all the region between the fortieth and forty-sixth degrees of north latitude, or from Philadelphia to Cape Breton Island.[3] De Monts was also granted the monopoly of the fur trade from Tadoussac southward. It is not necessary here to go into the history of this enterprise which provided Champlain the opportunity to make the first careful exploration of the coast of Nova Scotia and New England. After following the shore line of Nova Scotia round into the Bay of Fundy and exploring its more shel-

---

[2] See vol. II, pp. 151-229 [pp. 201-238 present edition]. The attention of the reader may here he called to the fact that while the English followed the Spanish usage started by Columbus, of calling the aborigines of the New World "Indians," i. e., people of the Indies, the early French writers adopted the simple descriptive name of *Sauvages*, which, in the seventeenth century, had the primary meaning "wild," e. g., as in *herbes sauvages*, "weeds," or the English, "wild animals."

[3] De Monts's charter is given in English translation in the *Maine Hist. Soc. Collections*, 2d series, VII, 2-6. Three years later James I of England granted the Plymouth Company the right to establish a colony in the same region, completely ignoring the prior grant of the French king and the rights of De Monts under it.

INTRODUCTION

tered waters, De Monts and his associates selected Dochet Island in the St. Croix River as the most suitable place for their settlement, in July, 1604. During August and September, Champlain explored the coast of Maine as far west as Monhegan Island, almost to the mouth of the Kennebec, when prudence dictated a return to the settlement. A winter of tragic misery bereft the little colony of half its numbers, and in June, 1605, De Monts, encouraged by the return of his associate, Poutrincourt, with supplies, undertook a further exploration of the coast to find a more desirable location for the colony. The new ground covered in this reconnoissance was the shores of Maine, New Hampshire and Massachusetts, around Cape Cod as far as Nauset Harbour. In this region, in August, 1605, came their first clash with the Indians. Upon their return to the St. Croix, the explorers found that Pontgravé had arrived from France with reinforcements. It was then decided to remove the colony across the Bay of Fundy to the more sheltered location of Annapolis Basin. It was now given the name Port Royal. In the fall De Monts returned to France.

In September, 1606, another attempt was made, this time by Poutrincourt and Champlain, to find a more favorable site for the colony. So much of the time at their disposal, however, was consumed in following, contrary to Champlain's advice, along the coast already explored, that the only real addition to their previous exploration was the short stretch from Nauset Harbour to Wood's Hole, where they gave the name of River Champlain to the tidal passage; a name which should be restored to that tortuous channel, as a memorial of the explorer, to mark the limit of his explorations in New England, and to remind the thousands who pass the spot every summer of his services to American history and geography. In 1607, De Monts's monopoly of the fur trade was taken away, and the colony had to be given up for lack of resources to meet expenses. After a brief exploration of the Basin of Mines, Champlain and his fellow-colonists returned to France, arriving at St. Malo, October 1, 1607.

From this time the scene of Champlain's labors and plans for a New France is the St. Lawrence Basin. In April, 1608, he set sail for Canada in company with Pont Gravé, to carry on the further exploration of the St. Lawrence as the lieutenant of De Monts, to whom King Henry IV granted a monopoly of the Indian trade for one year, to meet the expenses of the expedition. After a brief excursion up the Saguenay, Champlain began the voyage up the St. Lawrence from Tadoussac, June

INTRODUCTION

30, 1608. The foundations of a settlement at Quebec were laid on July 3. Hardly was this work begun when Champlain was apprised of a plot to murder him and sell the new station to the Basques. The ringleader was hanged and three accomplices were sent to France for punishment when Pont Gravé returned in September. The first winter at Quebec was a repetition of the cruel hardships which Cartier had suffered there. Ten of the little company died of scurvy and five of dysentery. Of the miseries to which the Indians were reduced in the long Canadian winter, Champlain has given a most vivid picture.

In the summer of 1609, Champlain, to cement his friendship with the Algonquins, which he regarded as an indispensable requisite for a successful settlement at Quebec, joined in one of their war parties against the Iroquois. They proceeded up the St. Lawrence to the mouth of the Richelieu, which was then followed to the beautiful lake to which Champlain gave his own name after a victorious encounter with the Iroquois at Ticonderoga. In September, 1609, Champlain returned to France to report to De Monts and to the King.

The early spring of 1610 found him again on his way to New France, where he again joined a war party against the Iroquois, who were ensconced in a barricade at the mouth of the Richelieu. His reasons for such participation in these Indian wars he gives at length in his narrative. This year saw no new exploration, and Champlain returned to France in the fall.

In the spring of 1611, after his arrival in Canada, Champlain went up the St. Lawrence to Montreal to meet the band of Algonquins with whom he had left, for the winter, one of his men, presumably Etienne Brulé to make observations. On this occasion Champlain had the thrilling experience of shooting the Lachine Rapids in a canoe. He was the second European to accomplish this feat, in which he was anticipated only by Brulé a few days earlier. In August, 1611, Champlain returned to France, where he remained until 1613, when he undertook one of his most important explorations, that up the Ottawa to verify the reports of the mendacious voyageur named Nicholas de Vignaud, who asserted that he had been to the sea on the north (Hudson Bay). The incident of the discovery of De Vignaud's deceit is one of the most dramatic in Champlain's narratives. Although he was profoundly disappointed not to reach the sea, as he had hoped, he explored the Ottawa beyond the site of the present city of that name, as far as Allumette Island, and made

INTRODUCTION

some of the most interesting observations of Indian manners and customs that his works contain.

During these years the work of the explorer was constantly impeded by the contending interests of rival fur traders. Champlain felt that the only practical way to deal with the Indians and to advance the interests of a settlement was through the agency of a responsible monopoly, and that free, unregulated competition in dealing with Indians by rival traders would be demoralizing to all concerned. On the other hand, every grant of a monopoly called forth a storm of protests and accusations from the traders not admitted to these privileges, which, they asserted, should belong to all Frenchmen in common. The year 1614 Champlain spent in France, trying to adjust these matters and arranging for the establishment of missions among the Indians. In April, 1615, he set sail for New France with four Recollect friars, who thus began one of the most wide-reaching and imposing missionary enterprises of modem times.

It was an eventful year also in Champlain's experience, for it was marked by the discovery of Lake Huron and Lake Ontario, an attack on the Iroquois in central New York, and a winter in an Indian village. Following his route of 1613, up the Ottawa, he continued his exploration westward to Lake Nipissing and thence to the shores of Lake Huron. The Huron Indians that he found in this region, familiar now to many holiday-seekers as the Muskoka Lake country, were planning an expedition against one of the home strongholds of the Iroquois, far to the south, across Lake Ontario. Champlain embraced the opportunity to accompany them to see something of the region which the Dutch fur traders were penetrating by way of the Hudson. The attack upon the Iroquois fort, which was situated not many miles from the present city of Syracuse, was repulsed, owing to the flighty, undisciplined fighting of the assailants, whom Champlain in vain tried to steady. The lateness of the season precluded his being accompanied to Quebec, and he had to spend the winter with the Indians. He joined in their fall hunting, and during four tedious months he had an unequaled opportunity to study Indian life as yet uncontaminated by association with Europeans. Of their villages, preparation of food, marriage customs, funeral ceremonies, religious usages, their pow-wows and medicine men, he has given us not only one of the earliest, but one of the best descriptions that we have.

This expedition of 1615-16 was the last work of exploration which Champlain accomplished, and with it the portion of the narrative of

INTRODUCTION

1632, selected for this edition, closes. The rest of it, a little more than half, belongs to the history of Quebec and of Canada, and not to the story of American exploration. It is the record of Champlain's devotion to his great design of establishing a New France in America, and of the obstacles arising from the lack of real vital interest in the work in the minds of the ruling powers in France and from the jealousies of rival traders and companies. In the years 1628 and 1629, to internal dissensions the new peril of outside hostility was added, and the prospects of a New France were temporarily eclipsed by the English attack upon and capture of Quebec. In the years immediately following, Champlain labored in France in the interest of the colony. Most important among the varied activities in its behalf was the preparation of a revised narrative of his explorations and of the history of New France down to 1629. This work was the *Voyages* of 1632.

Canada had now been restored to France, and in 1633 Champlain returned to Canada under a new commission as Governor. But little over two years of life remained, and these, like the thirty of ceaseless activity that had preceded them, were devoted to restoring the colony from the ravages of war. The end came on Christmas Day, 1635, after an illness of nearly three months.

Champlain left no children. He did not marry until over forty years of age. In 1610 he entered into a contract of marriage with Hélène Boullé, then a girl of twelve, who, by agreement, was to live two years more with her parents before joining he husband. She went to Quebec with him in 1620 and lived there four years. After that their lives drew apart and Madame de Champlain lived by herself in Paris, and later asked her husband to allow her to enter a convent of Ursuline nuns. Champlain refused, but some years after his death she carried out her wish and founded an Ursuline monastery in Meaux.

In his first two publications, Champlain is plain "Samuel Champlain of Brouage," but some time later and before the issue of his narrative of 1613 he was raised to noble rank and henceforth became the Sieur de Champlain.

Of Champlain no authentic portrait is known to exist. Those hitherto reproduced have been shown by Victor Hugo Paltsits to be all derived from a lithograph, the work of a nineteenth century artist, Louis César Joseph Ducornet, which was given to the public in 1854.[4] Yet

---

[4] *A Critical Examination of Champlain's Portraits.* Acadiensis, Vol. IV (1904), pp. 306-312.

INTRODUCTION

although we have no physical likeness of the man, his moral image is ineffaceably stamped upon the memory of every student of his writings. The more familiar one becomes with these narratives, the more solid and permanent is the impression of a singularly well-rounded character, full of strength, dignity and sweetness.

If we compare him with the other explorers and founders of that age he stands above them all in the range of his achievement. The explorations of De Soto and Coronado surpass those of Champlain in the extent of territory covered and in magnitude, but the results fall short of his in accuracy of detail and in permanent positive contribution to knowledge. The figure of La Salle is more brilliant on the page of the historian, but he was inferior to Champlain as a leader, and, like De Soto and Coronado, he ranks as an explorer only; Champlain, on the other hand, was not only an explorer who "threw light into the dark places of American geography and brought order out of chaos of American cartography,"[5] he was also the historian of his expeditions and of the early days of Quebec, and in addition to that the most indefatigable promoter of French colonization and the first French writer to discuss the principles of colonial policy. In France, he undertook the work to which Raleigh and Hakluyt in England devoted themselves with such assiduity. Of the English explorers who were also writers, Captain John Smith has attained the widest celebrity. That his explorations should rank with Champlain's will hardly be pretended by his most enthusiastic admirers. On the other hand, his writings are too full of the air of romance, if not of its substance, for him to be taken as a serious historian of his own career; and his services as an administrator in Virginia, considerable as they were, extended over too short a time to rival Champlain's at Quebec. Of English founders and governors of colonies who have also recorded the history of such beginnings, William Bradford and John Winthrop unquestionably stand first in this period, and a comparison of their work with that of "The Father of New France" suggests itself. In literary quality Bradford's *History of Plimouth Plantation* surpasses anything that Champlain wrote, and the community over which Winthrop presided so many years and whose story he told with such candor has played a far larger part in American history and life than fell to the fortune of the people of New France, yet the outlook and range of Champlain's achievements are far more comprehensive than those of either

---

[5] Parkman, *Pioneers of France in the New World,* 256.

INTRODUCTION

Bradford or Winthrop. Neither of them was an explorer, nor did either become a sympathetic and observing student of Indian life. Thus, in some one or two of the many fields of his activity, others have surpassed Champlain, but no other Frenchman and no Spaniard or Englishman has attained his high level and wide range. His fame is steadily increasing, and the two races who dwell in the scene of his labors, however antagonistic in other things, unite in a friendly rivalry in rendering homage to his name.

EDWARD GAYLORD BOURNE.

New Haven, June, 1906.

CONTENTS

VOLUME I

BOOK I

Introduction. Edward Gaylord Bourne v
Index of Chapters xvii
Dedication to Cardinal Richelieu xxv
Champlain's Map of 1632 xxviii

INDEX OF CHAPTERS

CHAPTER I

Extent of New France and the excellence of its soil. Reasons for establishing Colonies in the New France of the West. Rivers, lakes, ponds, woods, meadows and islands of New France. Its fertility. Its peoples 01

CHAPTER II

That Kings and great Princes ought to take more pains to spread the knowledge of the true God and magnify His glory among barbarians than to multiply their states. Voyages of the French to the New World since the year 1504 05

CHAPTER III

Voyage to Florida under the reign of King Charles IX by Jean Ribaut. He has a fort built, called Fort Charles, on the River of May. Albert, the Captain, whom he leaves there, has no provisions, and is killed by the soldiers. They are taken to England by an Englishman. Voyage of Captain Laudonnière. Narrowly escapes being killed by his own men; has four of them hanged. Is pursued by famine. Recompense from the Emperor Charles to those who discovered the Indies. The French driven from the River of May by the Spaniards. They attack Laudonnière. The French killed and hanged with inscriptions 08

CONTENTS

CHAPTER IV

The King of France feigns to take no notice for a time of the injury that he has received from the Spaniards in the cruelty that they showed to the French. Vengeance for it was reserved for Sieur Chevalier de Gourgues. His voyage; his arrival on the coast of Florida. Is attacked by some Spaniards whom he defeats and treats as they did the French 12

CHAPTER V

The voyage that Sieur de Roberval despatched. Sends Alphonse of Saintonge to Labrador. His departure. His arrival. Return on account of the ice. The voyages of foreigners to the North, to go to the West (?) Indies. Voyage of the Marquis de la Roche without result. His death. Noticeable defect in his undertaking 19

CHAPTER VI

Voyage of Sieur de Saint Chauvin. His plan. Remonstrances made with him by Pont Gravé. Sieur de Monts goes with him. Return of Saint Chauvin and Du Pont to France. Second voyage of Chauvin: his plan 22

CHAPTER VII

Fourth undertaking in New France by the Commander de Chaste. Sieur du Pont Gravé chosen for the voyage to Tadoussac. The author undertakes the voyage. Their arrival at the Great Sault St. Louis. Their difficulty in passing it. Their retreat. Death of this commander, which breaks up the sixth voyage 24

CHAPTER VIII

Voyage of Sieur de Monts. Wishes to continue the plan of the late Commander de Chaste. Obtains a commission from the king to make discoveries farther south. Forms a company with the merchants of Rouen and Rochelle. The author goes with him. They reach Cape Héve. They discover several harbors and rivers. Sieur de Poutrincourt goes with Sieur de Monts. Complaints of this Sieur de Monts. His commission revoked 27

BOOK II

CHAPTER I

Description of La Héve. Of Port Mouton. Of Cape Negro. Of the Cape Sable and Sable Bay. Of Cormorant Island. Of Cape Fourchu. Of Long Island. Of

CONTENTS

Bay Saint Mary. Of Port Saint Margaret, and of all the remarkable things that there are along the coast of Acadie 33

CHAPTER II

Description of Port Royal, and its peculiarities. Of High Island. Of the Harbor of Mines. Of the Great French Bay. Of the River Saint John, and what we have noticed between the Harbor of Mines and this place. Of the island called by the savages Manthane. Of the Etechemins River, and several beautiful islands in it. Of Saint Croix Island, and other conspicuous things on this shore 36

CHAPTER III

Of the coast, peoples, and River of Norembegue 41

CHAPTER IV

Discovery of the Quinibeguy River, which is on the coast of the Almouchiquois, as far as latitude 42°, and the particulars of the voyage. How the men and women pass the time during the winter 46

CHAPTER V

The Choüacoet River. Places that the author discovered there. Cape of Islands. Canoes of the people made of birch bark. How the savages of that country revive those who faint away. Use stones instead of knives. Their chief honorably received by us 51

CHAPTER VI

Continuation of the discoveries along the coast of the Almouchiquois, and what we specially noticed there 55

CHAPTER VII

Continuation of these explorations as far as Port Fortuné, some twenty leagues from there 60

CHAPTER VIII

Discovery from Cape la Héve to Canseau, very much in detail 64

BOOK III

CHAPTER I

Voyages of Sieur de Poutrincourt in New France, where he left his son, Sieur de Biencourt. The Jesuit fathers who were sent there, and their progress in making the Christian faith flourish 67

CHAPTER II

Second undertaking of Sieur de Monts. Advice that the author gave him. Obtains commission from the King. His departure. Buildings that the author makes in Quebec. Outcries against Sieur de Monts 78

CHAPTER III

Departure of the author, to go to settle the great River St. Lawrence. Description of the harbor of Tadoussac; of the River Saguenay; of the Isle of Orleans 81

CHAPTER IV

Discovery of the Hare Island; of the Island of Coudres, and of the Falls of Montmorency 83

CHAPTER V

Arrival of the author at Quebec, where he made his place of abode. Habits of the savages of that country 85

CHAPTER VI

Planting of vines at Quebec by the author. His kindness to the poor savages 88

CHAPTER VII

Journey from Quebec to the Island of St. Eloi, and the meeting that I had with some Algonquin and Ochataiguin savages 90

CHAPTER VIII

Return to Quebec, and then continuation with the savages to the Rapids of the River of the Iroquois 93

CONTENTS

CHAPTER IX

Departure from the rapids of the Iroquois River. Description of a large lake. Of the encounter with the enemy that we had at this lake, and of the manner in which they attacked the Iroquois 96

CHAPTER X

Return from the battle, and what happened on the way 103

CHAPTER XI

Defeat of the Iroquois near the mouth of this River Iroquois 106

CHAPTER XII

Description of whaling in New France 111

CHAPTER XIII

Departure of the author from Quebec. Mont Royal and its cliffs. Islands where potter's clay is found. Island of Ste. Hélène 113

CHAPTER XIV

Two hundred savages return the Frenchman who had been entrusted to them, and take back the savage who had returned from France. Various remarks by the author 117

VOLUME II

BOOK IV

CHAPTER I

Departure from France; what took place up to the time of our arrival at St. Louis Rapids 123

CHAPTER II

Continuation. Arrival at Tessoüat's, and the kind reception he gave me. Character of their cemeteries. The savages promise me four canoes to continue my way. Soon afterward they refuse me them. Speech of the savages to dissuade me from

CONTENTS

my undertaking, showing the difficulties. Response with regard to these difficulties. Tessoüat accuses my guide of lying, and of not having been where he said he had. The guide maintains that what he says is true. I urge them to give me some canoes. Several refusals. My guide convicted of lying, and his confession...132

CHAPTER III

Our return to the Rapids. False alarm. Ceremony at the Chaudière Falls. Confession of our liar before each one. Our return to France 140

CHAPTER IV

The author goes to Sieur de Monts, who gives him the authorization to join the company. This he shows to the Count de Soissons. The commission that he gives him. The author addresses himself to the Prince, who takes him under his protection 143

CHAPTER V

Departure of the author for New France. New discoveries in the year 1615 150

CHAPTER VI

Our arrival at Cahiagué. Description of the beauty of the country; character of the savages who inhabit it, and the inconveniences that we suffered 158

CHAPTER VII

How the savages traverse the ice. Concerning the Tobacco People. Their way of living. People called the Neutral Nation 171

THE VOYAGE OF 1603

Title Page of the Voyage of 1603 199

CHAPTER I

Short account describing the voyage from Honfleur, in Normandy, to the Port of Tadoussac, in Canada 201

CONTENTS

CHAPTER II

Kind reception of the French by the great Sagamo of the savages of Canada; their feasts and dances; the war they carry on with the Iroquois; how and of what their canoes and cabins are made; with a description of St. Matthew's Point 203

CHAPTER III

The rejoicing which the savages make after they have been victorious over their enemies; their disposition, suffering from hunger, ill-will; their beliefs and false ideas; they speak to devils; their clothes, and how they walk on the snow; with their marriage customs and the burial of their dead 206

CHAPTER IV

The River Saguenay and its source 212

CHAPTER V

Departure from Tadoussac, to go to the Rapids; description of Hare Island, Isle du Coudre, Isle D'Orleans and many other islands, and of our arrival at Quebec 213

CHAPTER VI

Point St. Croix, the River Batiscan; the rivers, rocks, islands, lands, trees, fruits, vines and the fine region beyond Quebec up to Three Rivers 215

CHAPTER VII

The length, breadth and depth of a lake, and of the rivers which flow into it; the islands in it; the soil one sees in the country; the river of the Iroquois, and the stronghold of the savages who wage war with them 218

CHAPTER VIII

Arrival at the Rapids. Description of them and the remarkable sights there, with the account given by the savages of the upper end of the great river 220

CHAPTER IX

Return from the Rapids to Tadoussac, with the comparison of the reports of several savages as to the length and source of the great River of Canada, the number of rapids and lakes that it traverses 226

CONTENTS

CHAPTER X

Voyage from Tadoussac to Isle Percée. Description of the Bay of Codfish; of Bonaventure Island; of Chaleur Bay; of many rivers, lakes and regions where there are various kinds of mines 229

CHAPTER XI

Return from Isle Percée to Tadoussac, with the description of the coves, harbors, rivers, islands, rocks, points, bays, and shallows which are along the northern coast 232

CHAPTER XII

The ceremonies of the savages before going to war. The Almouchicois savages and their monstrous shape. Narrative of the Sieur de Prevert, of St. Malo, on the discovery of the coast of Acadie 234

CHAPTER XIII

A frightful monster, which the savages call Gougou. Our short and safe return to France 237

To

Monseigneur, the most illustrious Cardinal, Duke de Richelieu, Head, Grand Master and Superintendent-General of the Commerce and Navigation of France.

MONSEIGNEUR:

These narratives are offered to you as the one to whom they are chiefly due, not only because of your eminent power in the Church and in the State, as well as in the command of all navigation, but also that you may be promptly informed of the greatness, the fertility, and the beauty of the places that they describe. For it may be assumed that it was not without great and vital reasons that the Kings who were predecessors of His Majesty, and he also, not only raised the standard of the Cross in that land, in order to establish the faith there, as they did, but also wished to attach to it the name of New France. You will find here the great and dangerous voyages that have been undertaken thither; the discoveries that followed upon them; the extent of these lands, no less than four times as large as France; their situation; the facility with which a safe and important commerce can be carried on there; the great profit to be derived from it; the fact that our Kings have taken possession of a large part of the country; the missions that they have instituted there of various religious orders; their progress in the conversion of a good many savages; [the account of] the clearing of certain tracts of land, by which you will discover that they in no way fall short of the soil of France in fertility; and, finally, the settlements and forts which have been built there in the name of France. The fact that I have been assiduously engaged in the preservation of these beginnings, as well as in a large number of these discoveries, for the last thirty years, both by the authority of our viceroys, and by that of your Grace, will be my excuse, Monseigneur, if you please, for the liberty that I take in offering you this little treatise, feeling confident that it will not be disagreeable to you; not out of consideration for myself, but only out of consideration for the public, who already make your name resound on the shores of every sea throughout the habitable earth, with their acclamations of the results of which the continuation of your glorious deeds gives promise. And since your Grace has raised them to the utmost height on land, by the peace that you have established in this Kingdom after so many and

DEDICATION

such fortunate victories, you will not be less inclined to call forth admiration during the peace in the matters that concern it: above all, in the re-establishment of the commerce of France in the most remote countries, as the most assured way that she has of reviving it under your favorable auspices. But among these foreign peoples those of New France are foremost in extending their hands to you; believing, with all France, that, since God, on the one hand, has constituted you a Prince of the Church, and, on the other hand, has raised you to the pre-eminent dignities that you hold, you will not only bestow upon them the light of the faith which they long for continually, but will also assist and support the possession of this new land, by the settlements and colonies that will be found necessary there; and that, in fine, since God has expressly chosen you among all men for the perfection of this great work, it will be entirely accomplished by your hands. This is my constant wish, and I add to it the offer of my remaining years, which I shall regard as very happily and usefully employed in so glorious a design if, in addition to all my past labors, I may still be honored by the commands that I await from your Grace,

MONSEIGNEUR:

Your very humble and very affectionate servant,

CHAMPLAIN.

[Overleaf]

Champlain's Map of New France
1632

Champlain's M
National Archi

The Voyages of Sieur de Champlain

VOLUME I—BOOK I

CHAPTER I

Extent of New France and the excellence of its soil. Reasons for establishing Colonies in the New France of the West. Rivers, lakes, ponds, woods, meadows and islands of New France. Its fertility. Its peoples.

THE labors that Sieur de Champlain has endured in discovering several countries, lakes, rivers, and islands of New France, during the last twenty-seven years,[1] have not made him lose courage because of the difficulties that have been encountered; but, on the contrary, the dangers and risks that he has met with, instead of lessening, have redoubled his courage. And two very strong reasons in particular have decided him to make new voyages there. The first is that under the reign of King Louis the Just,[2] France should become enriched and increased by a country of which the extent exceeds sixteen hundred leagues in length and nearly five hundred in breadth; the second, that the richness of the soil and the useful things that can be derived from it, whether for commerce or to make life pleasant in that country, are such that one cannot estimate the advantage that the French would gain from it some day, if the French colonies that may be established there should be protected by the favor and authority of His Majesty.

The new discoveries led to the purpose of establishing colonies, which, though at first of little account, have nevertheless in course of time, by means of commerce, become equal to the states of the greatest kings.

[1] I. e., from 1603 to 1630.
[2] Louis XIII.

ALGONQUIANS, HURONS AND IROQUOIS

One may put in this class several cities that the Spaniards have founded in Peru and other parts of the world within the last hundred and twenty years, which were nothing to begin with. Europe can offer the example of the city of Venice, which was originally a refuge for poor fishermen. Genoa, one of the most superb cities of the world, was built in a region surrounded by mountains, very wild, and so sterile that the inhabitants were obliged to have soil brought from outside to cultivate their garden plots, and their sea is without fish. The city of Marseilles, which formerly was nothing but a great marsh, surrounded by rugged hills and mountains, nevertheless in the course of time made its land fertile, and has become famous and an important seat of commerce. Similarly, many small colonies which had the convenience of ports and harbors have increased in wealth and in reputation.

It must be said also that the country of New France is a new world, and not a kingdom; perfectly beautiful, with very convenient locations, both on the banks of the great river St. Lawrence (the ornament of the country) and on other rivers, lakes, ponds and brooks. It has, too, an infinite number of beautiful islands, and they contain very pleasant and delightful meadows and groves where, during the spring and the summer, may be seen a great number of birds which come there in their time and season. The soil is very fertile for all kinds of grain; the pasturage is abundant; and a network of great rivers and lakes, which are like seas lying across the countries, lend great facility to all the explorations of the interior, whence one could get access to the oceans on the west, the east, the north, and even on the south.

The country is filled with immense tall forests composed of the same kinds of trees that we have in France. The air is salubrious and the water excellent in the latitudes corresponding to ours. The benefit that can be derived from this country, according to what Sieur de Champlain hopes to demonstrate, is sufficient to make the enterprise worth considering, since this country can supply for the service of the King the same advantages that we have in France, as will appear from the following account.

In New France there are a great many savage peoples; some of whom are sedentary, fond of cultivating the soil, and having cities and villages enclosed with palisades; others are roving tribes which live by hunting and fishing, and have no knowledge of God. But there is hope that the clergy who have been sent there and who are beginning to establish themselves and to found seminaries will be able in a few years to make great progress in the conversion of these peoples. This is the first care of

SAMUEL DE CHAMPLAIN

His Majesty, who, turning his eyes toward Heaven rather than toward the earth, will support, if it is his good pleasure, such founders as engage to transport clergy to work at this sacred harvest, and propose to establish a Colony as being the only way of making the name of the true God recognized, and of establishing the Christian religion there: such founders, too, as would oblige the French who go there to work, first of all, at tilling the soil, in order to have the necessaries of life on the spot, without being forced to bring them from France. That done, the country will furnish in abundance all that can be wished in life, whether to satisfy needs or pleasures, as will be shown hereafter.

If one cares for hawking, one can find in these places all sorts of birds of prey in as great numbers as one could wish: falcons, gerfalcons, sakers, tassels, sparhawks, goshawks, marlins, muskets, two kinds of eagles, little and big owls, great horned owls of exceptional size, pyes, woodpeckers. And there are other kinds of birds of prey, less common than those named, with grey plumage on the back and white on the belly, as fat and large as a hen, with one foot like the talon of a bird of prey, with which it catches fish; the other like that of a duck. The latter serves for swimming in the water when he dives for fish. This bird is not supposed to be found except in New France.[3]

For hunting with setters, there are three kinds of partridges: some are true pheasants, others are black, and still others white. These last come in winter and have flesh like wood-pigeons, of a very excellent flavor.

As for hunting for other game, river birds abound there; all sorts of ducks, teal, white and grey geese, bustards,[4] little geese, woodcock, snipe, little and big larks, plover, herons, cranes, swans, divers of two or three kinds, coots, ospreys, curlews, thrushes, white and grey sea gulls; and on the coasts and shores of the sea, cormorants, sea parrots, sea pyes, and others in infinite numbers which come there in their season.

In the woods and in the country which is inhabited by the Iroquois, a people of New France, there are many wild turkeys, and at Quebec a quantity of turtle-doves throughout the summer; also blackbirds, linnets, sky larks, and other kinds of birds of varied plumage, which in their season sing very sweetly.

---

[3] The belief that this bird, which was probably the bald buzzard or sea eagle, has one foot webbed is a bit of folk-lore.

[4] The brant goose was called *outarde* (bustard) by the early French explorers. On these birds cf. J. P. Baxter, *Jacques Cartier, 158*, n.

ALGONQUIANS, HURONS AND IROQUOIS

After this kind of hunting may be mentioned another not less pleasant and agreeable, but more difficult. There are in this same country, foxes, common wolves and spotted lynxes, wild cats, porcupines, beavers, muskrats, otters, sables, martens, varieties of badgers, hares, bears, moose, stags, deer, caribous as big as wild asses, kids, flying squirrels, and other kinds of animals which we do not have in France. They can be caught either by lying in wait or with a trap, or, if one suddenly shouts on the islands where they resort most often, one can kill them easily as they throw themselves in the water when they hear the noise; or they can be caught in any other way that the ingenuity of those who take pleasure in it may suggest.

If one is fond of fishing, whether with the line, nets, warrens, weels or other inventions, there are rivers, brooks, lakes and ponds in as great number as one could desire, with an abundance of salmon; very beautiful trout, fine and large, of every kind; sturgeon of three sizes; shad; very good bass, some of which weigh twenty pounds. There are carp of all kinds and some of them are very large; and pike, some of them five feet long; turbot without scales, two or three kinds, big and little; white fish a foot long; gold fish, smelts, tench, perch, tortoises, seal, of which the oil is very good even for frying; white porpoises, and many others that we do not have and that are not found in our rivers and ponds. All these varieties of fish are found in the great river St. Lawrence; besides, cod and whales are caught on the coasts of New France in nearly all seasons.

Thus one can judge of the pleasure that the French will have when once they are settled in these places; living a sweet, quiet life, with perfect freedom to hunt, fish, and make homes for themselves according to their desires; with occupation for the mind in building, clearing the ground, working gardens, planting them, grafting, making nurseries, planting all kinds of grains, roots, vegetables, salad greens and other potherbs, over as much land and in as great quantity as they wish. The vines there bear pretty good grapes, even though they are wild. If these are transplanted and cultivated they will yield fruit in abundance. And he who will have thirty acres of cleared land in that country, with the help of a few cattle, and of hunting and fishing, and trading with the savages in conformity to the regulations of the company of New France, will be able to live there with a family of ten as well as those in France who have an income of fifteen or twenty thousand livres.

SAMUEL DE CHAMPLAIN

CHAPTER II

That Kings and great Princes ought to take more pains to spread the knowledge of the true God and magnify His glory among barbarians than to multiply their states. Voyages of the French to the New World since the year 1504.

THE most illustrious palms and laurels that kings and princes can win in this world are contempt for temporal blessings and the desire to gain the spiritual. They cannot do this more profitably than by converting, through their labor and piety, to the catholic, apostolic and Roman religion, an infinite number of savages, who live without faith, without law, with no knowledge of the true God. For the taking of forts, the winning of battles, and the conquests of countries, are nothing in comparison with the reward of those who prepare for themselves crowns in heaven, unless it be fighting against infidels. In that case, war is not only necessary, but just and holy, since the safety of Christianity, the glory of God and the defence of the faith are at stake. These labors are, in themselves, praiseworthy and very commendable, besides being in conformity to the commandment of God, which says, *That the conversion of an infidel is of more value than the conquest of a kingdom.*[1] And if all this cannot move us to seek after heavenly blessings at least as passionately as after those of the earth, it is because men's covetousness for this world's blessings is so great that most of them do not care for the conversion of infidels so long as their fortune corresponds to their desires, and everything conforms to their wishes. Moreover, it is this covetousness that has ruined and is wholly ruining the progress and advancement of this enterprise, which is not yet well under way, and is in danger of collapsing, unless His Majesty establishes there conditions as righteous, charitable and just as he is himself; and unless he himself takes pleasure in learning what can be done to increase the glory of God and to benefit his state, repelling the envy of those who should support this enterprise, but who seek its ruin rather than its success.

It is nothing new for the French to make sea voyages for conquest. We know very well that the discovery of new countries and noble enterprises on the sea were begun by our forefathers.

---

[1] Possibly a confused and vague recollection of "For what shall it profit a man if he shall gain the whole world and lose his own soul?" Mark viii, 36.

ALGONQUIANS, HURONS AND IROQUOIS

It was the Bretons and Normans who, in the year 1504, were the first Christians to discover the grand bank of the Codfish[2] and the islands of the New World, as is noted in the histories of Niflet and of Antoine Maginus.[3]

It is also very certain that in the time of King Francis I, in the year 1523, he sent Verazzano, a Florentine, to discover the lands, coasts and harbors of Florida, as the accounts of his voyages bear testimony; where, after having explored the coast from latitude 33° to latitude 47°, just as he was thinking of making a home there, death put an end to his life and his plans.[4]

After that, the same King Francis, persuaded by Messire Philip Chabot, Admiral of France, sent Jacques Cartier to discover new lands, and for this purpose he made two voyages in the years 1534 and 1535. In the first he discovered the Island of Newfoundland and the Gulf of Saint Lawrence, with several other islands in this gulf, and he would have gone farther had not the severe season hastened his return. This Jacques Cartier was from the city of St. Malo. He was thoroughly versed and experienced in seamanship; the equal of any one of his times. And St. Malo is under obligation to preserve his memory, for it was his greatest desire to discover new lands. At the request of Charles de Mouy, Sieur de la Mailleres,[5] at that time Vice-Admiral, he undertook the same voyage for the second time; and in order to compass his purpose and to have His Majesty lay the foundation of a colony to increase the honor of God and his royal authority, he[6] gave his commissions with that of the aforesaid Sieur Admiral, who had the direction of this embarkation and contributed all he could to it. When the commissions had been prepared, His Majesty put this same Cartier in charge, and he set sail with two vessels on May 16, 1535. His voyage was so successful that he arrived at the Gulf of Saint Lawrence, entered the river with his ships of 800 tons burden,[7] and even got as far as an island a hundred and twenty leagues up the river, which he called the Isle of Orleans. From there he

---

[2] The words of the original are "le grand Banc des Moluques." The last word should be "Morues."

[3] The reference is to Wytfliet's *Descriptionis Ptolemaicae Augmentum,* as translated into French by Antoine Magin. Douay, 1611. See Parkman, *Pioneers of France,* 190.

[4] On Verazzano, see Bourne, *Spain in America,* 143-145.

[5] Meilleraye. L.

[6] I. e., the Vice-Admiral.

[7] A copyist's or printer's error. The narrative of Cartier's second voyage gives the tonnage of his three vessels as 100-120, 60 and 40, respectively. –(L.)

went some ten leagues farther up the same stream to winter on a small river which is almost dry at low tide. This he named St. Croix, because he arrived there on the day of the Exaltation of the Holy Cross.[8] The place is now called the St. Charles River and at present the Recollect fathers and the Jesuit fathers are stationed there to found a seminary for the instruction of youth.

From there Cartier went up the river some sixty leagues, as far as a place which was called Ochelaga in his time and is now called Grand Sault St. Louis.[9] It was inhabited by savages who were sedentary and cultivated the soil. This they no longer do, because of the wars that have made them withdraw into the interior.

When Cartier, according to his account, perceived the difficulty of passing up the rapids and that it was impossible, he returned where his vessels were; and the weather and the season were so urgent that he was obliged to winter on the St. Croix River, in the place where the Jesuits live now, on the border of another little river which empties into the St. Croix, called the Jacques Cartier River, as his narratives testify.

Cartier was made so unhappy in this voyage, particularly by the ravages of scurvy, of which the larger part of his men died, that when spring came he returned to France, saddened and disturbed enough at this loss and at the little progress that he thought he had made. He came to the conclusion, as a result of his winter's experience with the scurvy, which he called the disease of the country, that the climate was so different from our own that we could not live in it without great difficulty.

So when he had made his report to the King and to the Sieur Admiral and De Mailleres,[10] who did not go deeply into the matter, the enterprise bore no fruit. But if Cartier could have understood the cause of his sickness, and the beneficial and certain remedy for its prevention, although he and his men did receive some relief from an herb called *aneda*,[11] just as we did when we were in the same plight, there is no doubt that the King from that time would not have neglected to forward the plan, as he had already done: for at that time the country was more peopled with sedentary tribes than now. It was this last fact that led His Majesty to have this second voyage made and the undertaking carried on, for he had a holy desire to send colonists there. This was what came of it.

[8] September 14.
[9] The modern Lachine Rapids.
[10] I. e., De Meilleraye, the Vice-Admiral.
[11] Apparently a spruce or arbor vitae. Parkman, *Pioneers of France,* 214.

This affair might well have been undertaken by some others than Cartier, who would not have been so soon daunted and would not, on that account, have abandoned an enterprise so well begun. For, to tell the truth, those who are the leaders of explorations are oftentimes those who can put an end to the execution of a praiseworthy project, if people stop to consider their reports. For, if they are believed, it is thought that the enterprise is impossible or so involved in difficulties that it cannot be brought to completion without almost unendurable outlay and trouble. This is the reason why this enterprise did not achieve success. Besides, there are sometimes affairs of so much importance in a state as to cause others to be neglected for awhile; or it may be that those who would gladly have gone on with them, die, and so the years pass with nothing done.

CHAPTER III

Voyage to Florida under the reign of King Charles IX by Jean Ribaut. He has a fort built, called Fort Charles, on the River of May. Albert, the Captain, whom he leaves there, has no provisions, and is killed by the soldiers. They are taken to England by an Englishman. Voyage of Captain Laudonnière. Narrowly escapes being killed by his own men: has four of them hanged. Is pursued by famine. Recompense from the Emperor Charles to those who discovered the Indies. The French driven from the River of May by the Spaniards. They attack Laudonnière. The French killed and hanged with inscriptions.

UNDER the reign of Charles IX and the leadership of Admiral de Chastillon,[1] Jean Ribaut set sail on February 18, 1562, with two ships equipped with all that he needed to found a colony. Passing by the islands of the Gulf of Mexico, he sailed close to the coast of Florida, where he explored a river which he called the River of May.[2] There he built a fort, to which he gave the name of Charles, leaving in command of it Captain Albert, whom he supplied with all that he thought necessary. This done, he returned to France on July 20. He was nearly six months on the voyage.

But Captain Albert did not take the trouble to have land cleared and planted, so as to prevent want, and they ate their provisions without the system that is necessary in such matters, with the result that they found themselves so short that the scarcity was extreme. Thereupon, as the

---

[1] Admiral Coligny, who was Lord of Châtillon.
[2] The St. John's.

soldiers and others in subjection to him did not wish to obey him, he had one of them hanged for a very small matter. This brought about, within a few days, a mutiny so violent and disobedience so great, that they killed their captain and made another man, Nicolas Barré their leader. When they saw that no help was coming from France, they built a little boat to return there, and set sail with very few provisions. History tells us that their hunger was so cruel that they ate one of their companions. But God pitied this miserable crew and had mercy upon them, and they were picked up by an Englishman who came to their aid and took them to England, where they revived. This shows how little pains was taken to bring relief to the colonists, on account of the war that was going on between France and Spain.

Nevertheless, it was very cruel to let men die of hunger and be reduced to the point of eating one another, to save risking a small vessel at sea, which could bring them relief. This delayed the founding of a colony and foreboded a worse end, since the beginning had been badly conducted in every respect.

Peace was made between France and Spain, which gave leisure to enter upon new plans and expeditions. The same Sieur Admiral de Chastillon had other vessels equipped, under the charge of Captain Laudonnière, who was supplied with everything for his emigrants. He left on April 22, 1564, and reached the coast of Florida in latitude 32°, at the River of May. There he landed all his companions and supplies and had a fort built, which he called Caroline.

While the ships were at this place, conspiracies were formed against Laudonnière, which were discovered. When everything was straightened out, Laudonnière decided to send back his ships to France, and he let Captain Bourdet command them. He set out on the voyage, leaving Laudonnière with his companions, some of whom were so rebellious that they threatened to kill their captain if he did not let them cruise for plunder in the direction of the Islands of the Virgins and Santo Domingo; and he had to give his permission and let them go. They got into a small vessel, made prey of some Spanish ships, and, after they had sailed all about all these islands, they were obliged to return to Fort Caroline. Upon their arrival, Laudonnière had four of the principal mutineers seized and put to death.

After these misfortunes, as the provisions were coming to an end, they suffered much until May, without any help from France. And when they had been obliged, for six weeks, to go in search of roots in the woods, they at last resolved to build a boat and have it ready by the month of August to return to France.

The famine, however, increased more and more, and these men became so weak and debilitated that they were scarcely able to complete their work. This led them to look for provisions among the savages, who treated them badly, charged them much more for their provisions than they were worth, laughing at and making fun of the Frenchmen, who endured these jeers grudgingly. Laudonnière pacified them as gently as he could, but, do what he would, it was necessary to fight the savages, in order to get something to live on. They were so successful that they got some Indian corn, which gave them courage to finish their ship. That done, they began to pull down and demolish the fort, so as to return to France. While they were engaged in this they descried four sail. At first they feared that they were Spanish, but at last recognized them as English, and they, when they saw that the Frenchmen were in need, aided them with supplies and even fitted up their vessel. This remarkable courtesy was offered by the leader of this expedition, whose name was Jean Hanubins[3] [Hawkins]. When he had assisted them to the best of his ability, he weighed anchor and set sail to carry out the purpose of his voyage.

As Laudonnière was about to set sail with his companions, he sighted some vessels out at sea, and, while he was in suspense as to who they were, it was discovered that it was Captain Ribaut, who had come to bring aid to Laudonnière. The rejoicing on both sides was great, for now they saw the revival of their hope that before had seemed absolutely lost. But they were very sorry that the fort had been pulled down. Ribaut told Laudonnière that several bad reports had been made concerning him, which he recognized to be false, and that, if they had been true, he should have had reason to do what he had been ordered.

It is always the rule that virtue is oppressed by the slander of the wicked, which, in the end, reveals them for what they are and causes them to be despised by every one. It is well known how much trouble this made in the conquest of the Indies, both for Christopher Columbus and later for Ferdinand Cortez and others, who, blamed unfairly, justified themselves in the end to the Emperor.

This is why one should not believe anything thoughtlessly, before matters have been thoroughly examined into; but one should always

[3] That Hawkins appears in the text disguised as Hanubins is one of the many indications that Champlain did not see the proofs of his book.

recognize the merit and worth of the generous courage which sacrifices itself for God, for king and for country, as did these men just mentioned, to whom the Emperor accorded recognition, in spite of envy, and whom he honored with wealth and fine, honorable commissions, in order to give them courage to do well, in order to inspire others to imitate them, and the wicked to reform.

While Laudonnière and Ribaut were consulting about having their provisions unloaded, they sighted, on September 4, 1565, six sails which seemed to be big vessels and which they recognized as Spanish. They dropped anchor in the harbor where Ribaut's four ships were and assured the French of their friendship. Then, seeing that some of the soldiers were on shore, they fired cannon shots at our men, which, since their force was small, obliged them to cut their cable at the hawse-holes and set sail. The Spaniards did the same and pursued them in full force the next day. And as our vessels were better sailers than theirs, they returned to the coast and landed at a river, eight leagues from Fort Caroline, and our ships returned to the River of May. Three of the Spanish vessels, however, came to the harbor and put ashore their infantry, provisions and ammunition.

Captain Ribaut, contrary to the advice of Laudonnière, who explained to him the difficulties that might be incurred, whether from the heavy winds that usually prevailed at that season, or from some other cause, though it was an obstinate act, and he always wanted to have his own way without counsel, which is a very bad thing in such matters, decided to face the Spaniard and fight him at whatever cost. With this object, he had his vessels manned and equipped with all that was necessary, and set sail on September 8. He left his men very poorly supplied and Laudonnière pretty sick. The latter did not cease to encourage his soldiers all he could and exhort them to fortify themselves to the best of their ability, so as to resist the forces of their enemy, who were getting ready to attack Laudonnière on September 20. At that time there was a very violent downpour, which continued so long that our men, who were tired out with watching, abandoned their task. They thought, too, that the enemy would not come in such a terrible storm. Some of them who went on the rampart saw the Spaniards coming, and cried: "To arms! To arms! The enemy is coming!" At this cry, Laudonnière prepared to await them, and urged his men to the fight. They wanted to protect two breaches that had not yet been repaired, but at last they were overcome and killed. Laudonnière, seeing that he could not hold out any longer, expected to be killed in getting away, and escaped into the woods with the savages, where he found a number of soldiers, whom he rallied with a great deal of trouble. Taking their way through heavy swamps and marshes, they reached the entrance of the River of May, where there was a ship commanded by a nephew of Captain Ribaut, who had not been able to get any farther than this place, on account of the great storm. The other ships were lost on the coast, as were many soldiers and sailors. Ribaut and many others were captured and cruelly and inhumanly killed; and some of them were hanged with an inscription on their backs, bearing these words: *We have not hanged these men as Frenchmen, but as Lutherans enemies of the faith.*[4]

Laudonnière, in the face of so many disasters, decided to return to France on September 25, 1565. He weighed anchor, set sail on November 11, and arrived near the coast of England. As he felt ill there, he had them put him ashore to recover his health, and from there he came to France to make his report to the King. The Spaniards, however, fortified themselves in three places to ensure themselves against every event. We shall see, in the next chapter, what punishment God gave to the Spaniards for their injustice and cruelty to the French.

CHAPTER IV

The King of France feigns to take no notice for a time of the injury that he has received from the Spaniards in the cruelty that they showed to the French. Vengeance for it was reserved for Sieur Chevalier de Gourgues. His voyage: his arrival on the coast of Florida. Is attacked by some Spaniards whom he defeats and treats as they did the French.

THE King, knowing the injustice and insults inflicted on the French, his subjects, by the Spaniards, as I have said, had reason to demand reparation and satisfaction for them of Charles V,[1] Emperor and King of Spain, on the ground of their having been committed in violation of the promise that the Spanish had made not to disturb nor molest them in the preservation of what they had gained with so much trouble in New France,[2] in accordance with the commissions of the King of France,

---

[4] This last is not well authenticated. The most recent and most careful study of this clash between the French and the Spaniards in Florida is Woodbury Lowery: *The Spanish Settlements in the United States, 1562-1574.* New York, 1905.

[1] The King of Spain at this time was Philip II.

[2] This statement is an error. The Spanish King had made no such promise. His

SAMUEL DE CHAMPLAIN

their master, of which the Spaniards were not ignorant. Nevertheless, they had put them to death ignominiously, on the specious pretence that they were Lutherans, as they said, although they were better Catholics than they were, without hypocrisy or superstition, and had been converted to the Christian faith several centuries before the Spaniards.[3]

His Majesty feigned to take no notice of this offence for a while, because the two crowns had some differences to settle first, and principally with the Emperor,[4] which prevented any satisfaction being received for such inhumanities.

But since God never deserts His own and never suffers barbarous treatment shown them to remain unpunished, these Spaniards were paid back in the same coin that they had offered the French. For in the year 1567 appeared the brave Chevalier de Gourgues, who was full of valor and courage, to avenge this insult to the French nation; and, seeing that none of the nobility with whom France abounded offered to get satisfaction for such an injury, he undertook the enterprise. And, in order not to have his purpose known beforehand, he spread abroad the rumor that an expedition was being prepared for a certain deed that he wished to accomplish on the coast of Africa. For this purpose a number of sailors and soldiers assembled at Bordeaux, where ship stores of all kinds are supplied. They provided and furnished themselves with everything that he thought would be necessary on this voyage.

He set sail on August 23 of the same year in three ships, and he had with him 250 men. Once at sea, he put into port on the coast of Africa, either to recruit, or for some other reason. But it was not for long, for he set sail at once, and made it known through some trustworthy friends of his that he had altered his first plan for another, which was more honorable than that in connection with the coast of Africa, less dangerous, and easier to carry out. And where he stopped to recruit he was told that what he said was displeasing to several of his men, who believed that the voyage was ended, and that they would have to go back with nothing accomplished. Nevertheless, they all had a great desire to try some other plan.

---

attitude was quite the contrary. Cf. Lowery, *Spanish Settlements, 1562-1574,* pp. 101-119.

[3] Champlain is in error here. The majority of the French were Calvinists, although there were some Catholics among them. See Lowery, *Spanish Settlements, 53.*

[4] This is not clear, but apparently Champlain means that the Spanish King was particularly slow to make any settlement of their difficulties.

ALGONQUIANS, HURONS AND IROQUOIS

Sieur de Gourgues, knowing the wish of his companions, who had not lost courage, and being assured in regard to his crew, found an excuse to assemble his council, whom he told the reason why he could not carry out what he had undertaken. He said that the plan must not be thought of any more, but also that there was not the slightest probability of their returning to France with nothing accomplished. He said that he knew of another undertaking not less glorious than profitable for such brave spirits as he had in his ships, of which the memory would be immortal; that it was one of the most signal exploits that could be undertaken. Each one was consumed with eagerness and desire to see the accomplishment of what he mentioned, and he told them that if he were well supported in this praiseworthy enterprise he would be proud to die in carrying it out. And as they wished Sieur de Gourgues to tell them his plan he got them all together and spoke as follows:

"My companions and faithful friends of my fortune, you are not ignorant of how much I cherish such brave spirits as you. And you have shown this courage sufficiently by the fine resolution that you have made to follow and help me in every danger and honorable risk that we shall have to undergo and face, whenever we shall be confronted by them. And you know the interest that I have in the preservation of your lives. I do not wish to involve you in the risk of an enterprise that I might know would end in ruin without honor. It would be great and reprehensible foolhardiness on my part to risk your lives in a plan as difficult as that, which I do not think this is, seeing that I have devoted a good part of my possessions and many of my friends to equip these ships and send them to sea, for I am the only undertaker of this voyage. But all that does not give me so much cause to be anxious, as I have to rejoice to see that you all are resolved upon another enterprise, which will redound to your glory: to wit, to go to revenge the injury which our nation received from the Spaniards, who inflicted such a wound upon France that she will always bleed from the sufferings and infamous treatment that they made the French endure, and the barbarous and unheard-of cruelties which they committed. The resentment that I have sometimes felt on account of it has made me shed tears of pity, and has roused my courage so much that I have resolved, with the help of God, and your help, to have just revenge for such a crime and such cruelty on the part of the Spaniards, upon these base and cowardly hearts who miserably surprised our fellow-countrymen, whom they had not dared to face with arms in their hands. They are in a bad situation, and we shall take them by surprise easily. I have men on my ships who know the country very well, and we can go there in safety. Here, dear companions, is something to inspire our courage. Show that you are as ready to carry out this good plan as to follow me. Will you not be glad to bear away triumphant laurels from the pillage of our enemies?"

He had no sooner stopped speaking than each of them cried, joyfully: "Let us go whither you will. We could not have a greater pleasure and honor than that which you propose, which is a thousand times more honorable than can be imagined. We much prefer to die in the pursuit of this just vengeance for the insult that was offered to France than to be wounded in another undertaking. The greatest desire of us all is to conquer or to die, in showing you the utmost fidelity. Command what you think best; you have soldiers who have the courage to accomplish what you command. We shall not rest until we are face to face with the enemy."

Joy increased as never before in the ships. Sieur de Gourgues had the course changed and fired several cannon shots to begin the rejoicing and to encourage all the soldiers. And then this generous chevalier set sail toward the shores of Florida, and was so favored by good weather that in a few days he arrived near Fort Caroline. At dawn the savages of the country displayed the smoke of many fires, until Sieur de Gourgues had lowered sail and dropped anchor. He sent on shore to find out from the savages what the condition of the Spaniards was. They were very glad to see Sieur de Gourgues intent upon attacking them. They stated that they were about 400 in number, very well armed, and equipped with everything necessary. When he had found out how the Spaniards were encamped he began to prepare his soldiers for the attack. Let us see if they will have the courage to stand by Sieur de Gourgues, just as they did by Laudonnière, who was ill-supplied with ammunition and with what he needed.

Then Sieur de Gourgues, having his men and some savages lead him through the heart of the woods, without being seen by the Spaniards, acquainted himself with the places and the condition in which they were. The Saturday before Low Sunday, in the month of April, 1568; he attacked the two forts violently and prepared to take them by storm, in which he encountered great resistance. And the courage of the French was shown when the battle raged, for they threw themselves headlong into the fight, at times being driven back, and then taking heart to return to the contest with more valor than before. Though severely attacked they defended better. Neither death nor wounds made them turn pale or made them lose either judgment or bravery.

Our noble chevalier, cutlass in hand, inspired them with courage, and, like a bold lion, at the head of his men, reached the top of the rampart, beat back the Spaniards and made his way among them. His soldiers followed him, fought bravely, forced an entrance into the two forts, and killed all whom they encountered; so that all except those who died, or fled, were taken prisoners by the French. Those who expected to escape into the woods were cut to pieces by the savages, who treated them as they had treated our men. Two days afterward Sieur de Gourgues took possession of the large fort, which the enemy had abandoned after some resistance, some of their number having been killed and others captured.

As he continued victorious and had come to the end of so glorious an undertaking, remembering the insult that the Spaniards had done the French, he had some of them hanged, with inscriptions on the back, bearing these words: "I have not had these men hanged as Spaniards, but as pirates, robbers, and sea rovers." After this execution he had the forts torn down and destroyed; then set sail to return to France, leaving in the hearts of the savages an everlasting regret at being deprived of so high-minded a captain. His departure was on May 30, 1568, and he reached Rochelle on June 6. From there he went to Bordeaux, where he was received with as much honor and enthusiasm as ever a captain was.

But no sooner had he arrived in France than the Emperor sent to the King to demand justice for his subjects, whom Sieur de Gourgues had hanged in the West Indies. His Majesty was so angered by this that he threatened to have Sieur de Gourgues beheaded, and he was obliged to go away for some time until the King's anger should pass off. Thus this noble Chevalier redeemed the honor of the French nation, which the Spaniards had offended, and it would have been an eternal regret to France if it had not revenged the outrage received from the Spanish nation. It was the noble undertaking of a gentleman, who carried it out at his own cost and expense, solely for honor, without other hope. He achieved it gloriously, and this glory is more to be esteemed than all the treasures of the world.[5]

---

[5] Parkman, *Pioneers of France,* 171, remarks, in regard to the account of de Gourgues' exploit: "It must be admitted that there is a strong savor of romance in the French narrative." See also Lowery, *Spanish Settlements, 1562-1574,* 316-336.

SAMUEL DE CHAMPLAIN

We have observed the great defects and failures in the voyages of Ribaut and Laudonnière. Ribaut was blamed in his for not carrying provisions for more than ten months, and not ordering land cleared and prepared for tilling, in order to be provided against the scarcity which might occur and the dangers that ships encounter at sea, or indeed their failure to arrive in time to relieve want. It at last reduced those who took part in the undertaking to the greatest extremity, even to the point of killing one another, to keep alive on human flesh, as they did on this voyage, which caused the soldiers to rebel greatly against their chief. So disorder and disobedience were rife among them. At last they were obliged, though with incredible regret and after a considerable loss of men and property, to abandon the land and possessions that they had acquired in this country; and all that for the lack of having made their plans with judgment and reason.

Experience shows that in such voyages and expeditions the kings and princes and the members of their council who have undertaken them had too little knowledge for carrying out their plans. It shows that if there have been men of experience in these matters, they have been few; for most men have tried these undertakings on the foolish reports of some tricksters, who, simply to give themselves importance, pretended to be very knowing in such matters, of which they were very ignorant. For, in order to begin and complete these enterprises with honor and profit, one must spend long years in sea voyages and be experienced in such discoveries.

The greatest mistake that Laudonnière made, when he went with the intention of spending the winter, was to provide himself with so few provisions, whereas he ought to have been governed by the example of Captain Albert's wintering at Fort Charles, whom Ribaut left so ill-supplied with everything. These omissions ordinarily occur in such undertakings, because it is supposed that those countries yield without being planted. Besides, such voyages are undertaken unreasonably, without practical knowledge or experience. It is one thing to make such plans in table talk, drawing on the imagination for the situation of places, the customs of the people who inhabit them, the profit and benefit that may be derived from them. It is a very different matter to send men across seas to distant countries, to traverse unknown shores and islands, from what it is to form such idle fancies in the mind, making ideal and imaginary voyages and navigations. That is not the way to carry out with honor the work of discovery. First, it is necessary to consider maturely the questions which arise in such matters; to communicate with those who have acquired a great deal of knowledge of them, who know the difficulties and the dangers which they offer, instead of setting out so thoughtlessly on the strength of simple report and talk. For it is of little use to discourse upon distant countries, and go to live in them, without having first explored them, and having lived in them at least a whole year, in order to understand the character of the countries, and the variety of seasons, for the sake of founding a colony there afterward. Most of the undertakers of colonies and explorers do not do this, but are satisfied merely to see the shores and hills in passing, without stopping there.

Others undertake such voyages on the strength of simple reports made to persons who, although they are very intelligent in the affairs of the world, and have had long and considerable experience, nevertheless are ignorant in these matters, believing that everything follows the rule that exists in the latitude where they are. In this they find themselves very much mistaken. For there are such strange changes in nature that it is only by seeing them that we can believe in their reality. The reasons for this are extremely varied and very numerous, and therefore I shall pass them over in silence. I have said this in passing, in order that those who come after us and who make new plans may avail themselves of these points and consider them, so that when they set sail thither, the ruin and loss of others may serve as an example and as an apprenticeship.

The third fault, and the most harmful, of Ribaut's was in not having the supplies and ammunition that he had brought for Laudonnière and his companions unloaded before exposing himself to the danger of losing everything, as he did, since he did not go there to fight the enemy, but to be always on the defensive, to assist Laudonnière with his men, to fortify himself, and to hold his own against those who should attack him. He could have seen clearly that, since it was the purpose of the enemy to take the fort, he needed to be stronger than those who guarded it, if he were not to expose himself thoughtlessly to danger and to chance. He would have done better to take account of the forces of the enemy before attacking them and being sure of victory. But, on the contrary, as a result of despising the advice of Laudonnière, who was more experienced than he in knowledge of the places, very great evil befell him.

Furthermore, in such undertakings, the ships that carry the provisions and the military stores for a colony should take as direct a course as possible, without turning aside to give chase to any other vessel, since, if

SAMUEL DE CHAMPLAIN

they found it necessary to fight and should lose, this misfortune would not be confined to themselves, but they would put the colony in danger of being lost. In that case, the men would be obliged to give up everything, and see themselves reduced to suffer a miserable death from the hunger that would attack them when the provisions were gone, on account of not being supplied and provisioned for at least two years, while waiting for the land to be cleared in order to support those who are in the country. These are great mistakes, like those of our more recent undertakers who did not have any land cleared, or find any means of doing so, in the twenty-two years during which the country has been inhabited, for they had no thought beyond getting profit from furs. The day will come when they will lose all that we possess there. This is easy to see, if the King does not establish a good system there.

These are the greatest defects that can be observed in the first voyages, and those that followed have scarcely been more fortunate.

CHAPTER V

The voyage that Sieur de Roberval despatched. Sends Alphonse of Saintonge to Labrador. His departure. His arrival. Return on account of the ice. The voyages of foreigners to the North, to go to the West (?) Indies.[1] Voyage of the Marquis de la Roche without result. His death. Noticeable defect in his undertaking.

IN the year 1541 Sieur de Roberval, who had renewed this holy undertaking, sent Alphonse, of Saintonge (one of the best navigators of his time in France) who wished, by his discoveries, to find a more northern passage toward Labrador. He had two good ships equipped with all that he needed for this discovery, and took his departure in this year, 1541.[2] And after having sailed along the northern coasts, and the lands of Labrador, in search of a passage that would facilitate commerce with the people of the East, by a shorter way than that around the Cape of Good Hope, or by the Straits of Magellan, owing to chance obstacles, and the risk that he ran from the ice, he was obliged to return; and he had no more to pride himself on than Cartier.

---

[1] It should be East Indies.
[2] Roberval despatched Cartier in 1541 and went himself with Alphonse in 1542. See Parkman, *Pioneers of France*, 216-228.

ALGONQUIANS, HURONS AND IROQUOIS

This second enterprise was only for the purpose of discovering a passage, but the other[3] was to explore the interior, and inhabit it, if possible. Thus these two voyages did not succeed. As for the passage, I shall not describe in detail the attempts of foreign nations to find a passage by the north, to go to the East Indies: how, in the years 1576, 1577 and 1578, Mr. Martin Forbichet[4] made three voyages; and, seven years afterward,[5] Humphrey Gilbert went there with five ships. He was lost on Sable Island and lived there two years.[6] Afterward John Davis, an Englishman, made three voyages;[7] got as far as latitude 72°, and passed by a strait that bears his name now. Another man, named Captain Georges, made this voyage in the year 1590, and on account of the ice was obliged to return without accomplishing anything.[8] Several others who have undertaken it have had a similar fortune.

As for the Spaniards and Portuguese, they have wasted their time there. The Dutch fared no better in searching for such a passage toward the East by way of Nova Zembla than the others who lost so much time in looking for it in the West, beyond the lands called Labrador.

All this is only to show how much honor, if this passage, which was so greatly desired, had been found, would have come to him who lighted upon it; and how much advantage to the state or realm which would have possessed it. Since, then, it is our own opinion that this enterprise is of such value, it should not be despised now, and that which cannot be done in one place can be accomplished in another, in time, provided His Majesty be pleased to assist the undertakers of so praiseworthy a project. I will leave this discourse to return to our new conquerors in the country of New France.

Sieur Marquis de la Roche, of Brittany, incited by a holy desire to raise the standard of Jesus Christ, and set up the arms of his King, took a commission, in the year 1598, from King Henry the Great (of happy memory), who felt much interest in the plan. Sieur de la Roche had several ships fitted out, with a number of men and a full equipment of

---

[3] Roberval's voyage of 1542.
[4] Frobisher.
[5] I. e., 1583.
[6] Gilbert's largest ship, the Delight, was wrecked on Sable Island, but he was lost on his return in the Squirrel.
[7] 1585, 1586, 1587.
[8] Apparently this Captain Georges should be Captain George Weymouth. If so, the voyage was in 1602. There was no Arctic voyage in 1590 that is recorded.

SAMUEL DE CHAMPLAIN

things necessary for such a voyage. But as he had no knowledge of the places, except through a pilot named Chédotel,[9] from Normandy, he landed his men on Sable Island, 25 leagues to the south of the land of Cape Breton. There the men, who stayed in this place with very few conveniences, were left for seven[10] years with no help but that of God. They were obliged to live in the earth, like foxes, for there was neither wood nor stone in this island suitable for building, except the wreckage and broken pieces of vessels that came to the coast of the island. They lived on nothing but the flesh of oxen and cows, which animals they found there in great quantity, for they had escaped from a Spanish ship which was lost on its way to inhabit the Island of Cape Breton. They dressed in the skins of seals, when they had worn out their clothes, saving the oil for their use. They also relied upon catching fish, which is plentiful about that island. They stayed there until the parliament of Rouen ordered the before-mentioned Chédotel to go to rescue these poor wretches, with the understanding that he should have half of the commodities that they had been able to collect during their sojourn in this island, such as hides, seal-skins, oil, and black foxes. This was done. Returning to France at the end of seven years, some of them went to see His Majesty in Paris, who commanded the Duke of Sully to supply their needs. He did so, to the amount of 50 crowns, to encourage them to go back. The Marquis de la Roche, meanwhile, who was trying, in court, to get the things that His Majesty had promised him for his project, was denied them at the request of certain persons who did not wish the true religion of God to grow, or to see the Catholic, Apostolic and Roman religion flourish there. This caused him so much displeasure that, on that account and for other reasons, he was attacked by a severe sickness, which carried him off. He had given all his property and labor without experiencing any result.

In this plan of his two defects may be noted: one, that this Marquis did not have some one experienced in such matters explore and reconnoitre where he was to settle, before assuming so excessive an out-lay; the other, that envious persons who were near the King in his council at this time interfered with the accomplishment of the project and the good intention that His Majesty had of conferring benefits upon him. Thus kings are often deceived by those in whom they have confidence.

---

[9] Also written Chefdostel and Chefd'hostel.
[10] Five years, 1598-1603.

ALGONQUIANS, HURONS AND IROQUOIS

The history of the past sufficiently illustrates the fact, and this instance can furnish us an example of it. This is the end of the fourth voyage. We come to the fifth.

CHAPTER VI

Voyage of Sieur de Saint Chauvin. His plan. Remonstrances made with him by Pont Gravé. Sieur de Monts goes with him. Return of St. Chauvin and Du Pont to France. Second voyage of Chauvin: his plan.

A YEAR afterward, in 1599, Sieur Chauvin of Normandy, Captain in the King's Navy, a man of great skill and experienced in navigation (who had served His Majesty in past wars, although he belonged to the religion pretending to be reformed[1]), undertook this voyage under the commission of His Majesty, at the request of Sieur du Pont Gravé, of St. Malo, a man expert in sea voyages, for he had made many of them. He was accompanied by other ships as far as Tadoussac, ninety leagues up the river; a place where they traded for fur and beaver with the savages of the country, who came there every spring. This Du Pont, desiring to find means to control this traffic, went to court, to seek some one of authority and special influence with the King, for the purpose of obtaining a commission to the effect that the trade of this river should be forbidden to all persons without the permission and consent of him who should be provided with that same commission, on condition that they should settle in the country, and make a home there. This was a good beginning and one which would not cost the King anything if what was in the commission should be carried out. It was the plan to take five hundred men there to fortify the country and defend it. The King had great confidence in this undertaker who, nevertheless, did not expect to go to any more expense than he could help; for, under the pretext of making a settlement, and of carrying out what he had promised, he wished to deprive all the subjects of the realm of trade there, and to keep the beaver for himself alone. And to give the enterprise a good start he began his preparations. The ships were equipped with such nec-

---

[1] I. e., the Protestant religion. The French Calvinists, or Huguenots, called their faith the reformed religion, and they were called the "reformed," in distinction from the followers of Luther. Catholic writers commonly prefixed "pretendue" to the word "reformée" —e. g., "la religion pretendue reformée."[9] Also written Chefdostel and Chefd'hostel.

essaries as he thought suitable for the enterprise. Many artisans set out and presented themselves at Honfleur, the place of embarkation. When his ships were out at sea he made this same Pont Gravé his lieutenant of one of them. But, since the head was of the opposing religion, this was not the way to establish the faith among those people whom they wished to subjugate. This was what was least considered. They went to the harbor of Tadoussac, the trading-place, and the affair was rather badly managed for making great progress. They decided to build a habitation there: the most disagreeable and barren place in this country, covered with nothing but pines, firs, birches, mountains and almost inaccessible cliffs, the soil very ill-fitted for any profitable cultivation, and the cold so extreme that if there is an ounce of cold forty leagues up the river there is a pound at Tadoussac. And how many times have I been astonished to see these places so frightful in the spring!

Now, when this Sieur Chauvin wished to build there, and to leave some men, and to protect them against the severe cold, although he had learned from Pont Gravé that it was not his opinion that they should build there, Pont Gravé urged Sieur Chauvin several times to go up this river, where it is better for building, for he had been on another voyage as far as the three rivers, in search of the savages, in order to trade with them.

Sieur de Monts took this same voyage for pleasure, with Sieur Chauvin, and he was of the same opinion as Gravé, and, perceiving that this place was very disagreeable, he would have been very glad to look at what was farther up the river. But whatever was the reason, whether because the time did not permit then, or because of other considerations in the mind of the undertaker, he employed several workmen to build a villa, twenty-five feet long by eighteen wide and eight feet high. It was covered with boards, with a fireplace in the middle, and was in the shape of a guard-house, and was surrounded by hurdles (which I have seen there) and a small ditch dug in the sand. For, in that country, where there are no rocks, it is all very poor sand. There was a little brook below, where they left sixteen men provided with a few necessaries, whom they could harbor in this same lodging. The little that they had was put at the disposal of all, and so it did not last long. Behold them there very warm for the winter! Having done this much, Sieur Chauvin returned, not caring to look or discover further. Pont Gravé did the same.

While they were in France our winterers consumed, in a short time, the little that they had, and when winter came upon them they were well aware of the difference between France and Tadoussac. It was the court of King Pétaud; each one wished to command. Laziness and idleness, with the diseases that attacked them, reduced them to great want, and obliged them to give themselves up to the savages, who kindly harbored them, and they left their lodging. Some died miserably; others suffered a great deal while waiting for the return of the ships.

Sieur Chauvin, seeing his men filling their lungs with the air of the Saguenay, which was very dangerous, arranged to make a second voyage, which was as fruitful as the first. He wanted to make another better planned, but he did not keep at it long before he was seized with a malady that sent him to another world.

The trouble with this undertaking was giving to a man of opposing religion a commission to establish a nursery for the Catholic, Apostolic and Roman faith, of which the heretics have such a horror and abomination. These are the defects that must be mentioned in regard to this enterprise.

CHAPTER VII

Fourth undertaking in New France by the Commander de Chaste. Sieur du Pont Gravé chosen for the voyage to Tadoussac. The author undertakes the voyage. Their arrival at the Great Sault St. Louis. Their difficulty in passing it. Their retreat. Death of this commander, which breaks up the sixth voyage.[1]

THE fourth undertaking was that of Sieur Commander de Chaste, Governor of Dieppe, who was a very honorable man, a good Catholic, and a great servant of the King. He had served His Majesty worthily and faithfully on many important occasions. And though his head bore the weight of grey hairs, as well as of years, he still wished to hand down to posterity, by this praiseworthy undertaking, his favorable opinion of the design, and even wished to go there himself, to spend his remaining years in the service of God and of his King, by making a home there; with the intention of living and dying there gloriously, as he hoped, if God had not taken him from this world sooner than he expected. One may be very sure that under his management heresy never would have

---

[1] The original has here the Arabic numeral "6." This is inconsistent with the opening line of this summary and with the conclusion of the chapter. Through some inadvertence, probably "6" was set up by the printer instead of "5."

been implanted in the Indies; for he had very Christian plans, of which I could show good proof, as he did me the honor to communicate somewhat of them to me.

After the death of Chauvin, then, he obtained a new commission from His Majesty. Inasmuch as the expense was very great, he formed a company with several gentlemen and principal merchants of Rouen, and of other places, upon certain conditions. When this was done, they had ships equipped, not only for the carrying out of this undertaking, but for discovering and peopling the country. Pont Gravé, with His Majesty's commission (as one who had already made the voyage and knew the difficulties of the passage), was chosen to go to Tadoussac, and promised to go as far as Sault St. Louis,[2] explore it, and go farther, in order to make a report on his return, and direct a second expedition. And the Sieur Commander left his position as Governor, with the permission of His Majesty, who loved him specially, to go to the country of New France.

At this time I arrived at court, having just returned from the West Indies, where I had been nearly two years and a half, after the Spaniards had left Blavet,[3] and peace was made with France. There, during the wars, I had served His Majesty under Marshal d'Aumont, de Saint Luc, and Marshal de Brissac. As I went to see Sieur Commander de Chaste from time to time, thinking that I could serve him in his purpose, he did me the favor, as I have said, to tell me something about it, and to ask me if I would like to go on the voyage to see the country, and what the undertakers were doing there. I told him that I was his servant; that as for allowing myself the liberty to go on this voyage I could not do that without the command of His Majesty, to whom I was under obligations, not only from my birth, but by reason of a pension with which he honored me, so that I might have means to support myself at court; and that if he wished to speak to him about it, and the King should command me to go, I should find it very agreeable. This he promised me, and he did so, and he received word from His Majesty for me to make this voyage, and to bring him a faithful report of it. To this end, Monsieur de Gesvre, his executive secretary, sent me with a letter addressed

---

[2] The Lachine Rapids, just above Montreal. Hereafter, in the text, it will be translated the St. Louis Rapids.

[3] Now Port Louis in the department of Morbihan. The Spaniards surrendered Blavet in June, 1598. Champlain's narrative of his voyage to the West Indies may he read in English in the edition published by the Hakluyt Society in 1859.

to Pont Gravé, telling him to receive me into his ship, and have me see and become acquainted with all I could in these places, and to aid me himself, so far as was possible in this enterprise.

Thus despatched, I left Paris, and sailed in Du Pont's ship in the year 1603. We had a good voyage as far as Tadoussac, with medium-sized barks of from 12 to 15 tons burden, and went a league up the great St. Louis Rapids. Pont Gravé and I got into a very light little boat, with five sailors, so as not to have to navigate a larger one, because of the difficulties. When we had gone a league in a sort of lake with a great deal of trouble, on account of the little water that we found in it, and had reached the foot of the rapids, which empties into this lake, we decided that it would be impossible to go farther with our skiff; for it was so raging and interspersed with rocks that we found ourselves obliged to go almost a league by land to see the upper part of the rapids, and we could not see any more of it. All that we could do was to note the difficulties; the whole country; the length of this river; the reports of savages as to what was in the land; their accounts of the people; the places; the sources of the principal rivers, especially of the great River St. Lawrence.

Then I wrote a short account,[4] and made an exact map of all that I had seen and observed, and so we returned to Tadoussac, having made but little progress. Our vessels were there trading with the savages; and when this was done we embarked, setting sail, and went back to Honfleur. There we learned the news of the death of Sieur Commander de Chaste, which was a great affliction to me, for I perceived that it would be difficult for any one else to undertake this voyage without being thwarted, unless he were a Seigneur whose authority had the power to overcome envy.

I scarcely paused at Honfleur, but went on to His Majesty, to whom I showed the map[5] of this country, with the very careful account that I had written of it. He was much pleased with it, promising not to give up the project, but to have it continued, and to favor it. Thus, the fifth voyage was broken up by the death of this Commander.

[4] Champlain's account of the voyage of 1603 was published in Paris in 1603 under the title: *Des Sauvages, ou Voyage de Samuel Champlain, de Brouage, faict en la France Nouvelle, l'an mil six cens trois.* It was translated into English by Purchas and published in *Purchas His Pilgrims.* London: 1625, vol. VI, pp. 1605-1619. This version is reprinted in the present edition, vol. II, pp. 151-229 [201-238 present edition]. This narrative was newly translated by Professor Otis for the Prince Society edition of *Champlain's Voyages.* See vol. I, pp. 231-291.

[5] This map is no longer extant.

SAMUEL DE CHAMPLAIN

I have not noted any defect in this undertaking, as far as the beginning of it was concerned. But I know that immediately several French merchants who had an interest in this business began to complain that the fur trade was closed to them for the purpose of giving it to one man.

CHAPTER VIII

Voyage of Sieur de Monts. Wishes to continue the plan of the late Commander de Chaste. Obtains a commission from the king to make discoveries farther south. Forms a company with the merchants of Rouen and Rochelle. The author goes with him. They reach Cape Héve. They discover several harbors and rivers. Sieur de Poitrincourt goes with Sieur de Monts. Complaints of this Sieur de Monts. His commission revoked.

AFTER the death of Sieur the Commander de Chaste, Sieur de Monts, of Saintonge, of the so-called reformed religion, Gentleman-in-ordinary of the King's Chamber, and Governor of Pons, who had given good service to the King in all the past wars, in whom the King had great confidence, on account of his faithfulness, which he exhibited even unto his death, was carried away by zeal and longing to people and inhabit the country of New France, and there expose his life and his property. He wished to follow in the footsteps of the late Commander in that country, where he had been, as I have said, with Sieur Chauvin, to explore, although the little that he had seen had made him lose the desire to go to the great River St. Lawrence, having seen nothing on this voyage but a rugged country. This made him wish to go farther south, to enjoy a softer and more pleasant air. And, not pausing at the accounts of it that had been given to him, he wished to look for a place of which he knew neither the situation nor the temperature, except through the imagination and the reason, which concludes that the nearer the south the warmer the climate. Desiring to carry out this noble undertaking, he got a commission from the King, in the year 1603,[1] to people and inhabit the country, on condition of implanting there the Catholic, Apostolic and Roman faith, letting each one live according to his religion.[2] That

---

[1] The text has 1623, an obvious misprint. The patent is dated Nov. 8, 1603. It is printed in Lescarbot, *Histoire de la Nouvelle France*, book IV, ch. I. It is accessible in English in Murdoch's *History of Nova Scotia*, I, 21-24.

[2] This last clause must refer to the practice of De Monts. There is nothing about religious toleration in the charter. This charter, which made De Monts the King's Lieutenant-General, or Viceroy, in 1603 over the region between the 40th and 46th paral-

being granted, he continued the company with the merchants of Rouen, Rochelle, and other places, to whom the fur trade was granted by this commission, to the exclusion of all the other subjects of His Majesty. When everything was arranged, Sieur de Monts set sail at Havre de Grace, and had several ships equipped, not only for the fur trade of Tadoussac, but for that of the shores of New France. He got together a number of gentlemen, and all sorts of artisans, soldiers and others, as many of one religion as of another, priests and ministers.

Sieur de Monts asked me if I would like to make the voyage with him. The desire that I had had on the last voyage had increased, and led me to agree to go, with the permission that the King should give me, which would allow me to go, with the understanding that I should make a faithful report to him of all that I saw and discovered. When we all were at Dieppe, we set sail. One ship went to Tadoussac; that of Pont Gravé with the commission of Sieur de Monts, to Canseau, and along the coast toward the Island of Cape Breton, to see those who were violating the regulations of His Majesty. Sieur de Monts took a lower course toward the shores of Acadie,[3] and the weather was so favorable for us that we were only a month in getting as far as Cape de la Héve.[4] When we arrived there we went on farther to look for a place to settle in, as we did not find this one pleasant. Sieur de Monts delegated me to search for some suitable place, which I did with a certain pilot whom I took with me. We discovered several harbors and rivers, when Sieur de Monts stopped at an island named St. Croix,[5] of which he thought the site strong, the soil round about very good; the temperature (in latitude 45°) mild. He had his ships come there, and employed each man, according to his station and trade, either to unload them, or to prepare a lodging promptly. When the ships were unloaded he sent them back as speedily as possible, and Sieur de Poutrincourt[6] (who had come with Sieur de Monts to see the country, with the idea of inhabiting it, and of securing

---

lels, i. e., from Philadelphia to Cape Breton, should be compared with the earlier English proprietary grants. In less than three years after Henry IV's grant to De Monts, James I granted five-sixths of this same region to the Virginia Company, April 10-20, 1606, absolutely ignoring any French claims and King Henry's patent.

[3] Acadie later meant Nova Scotia. Here it means the coast region granted to De Monts between the 40th and 46th parallels.

[4] Cape La Have on modern maps; about fifty miles southwest of Halifax.

[5] Dochet Island, in the St. Croix River.

[6] This name is spelled Poitrincourt in the text, but the accepted form, Poutrincourt, will be used.

SAMUEL DE CHAMPLAIN

the grant of some place from him, in pursuance of his commission) returned with them.

But we will let him go, while we see if we shall overcome the cold better than those who wintered at Tadoussac. When our ships had returned to France they heard an infinite number of complaints from the Bretons, the Basques, and others, of the ill-usage and bad treatment that they received on our shores, from the captains of Sieur de Monts, who seized them, prevented them from fishing and deprived them of the use of things which had always been free to them; so that if the King did not introduce some regulations there, all this navigation would be lost, and his custom-duties would, in this way, be diminished and their women and children would be made poor and miserable and be obliged to beg for their living. Petitions were sent in with regard to this, but the envy and wrangling did not cease. There was no lack in court of persons who promised that, for a sum of money, Sieur de Monts' commission should be annulled. The affair was so conducted that Sieur de Monts did not know how to prevent the estrangement of the King toward him, by certain personages in favor, who had promised the King to support three hundred men in this country. So, in a short time, His Majesty's commission was revoked at the price of a certain sum that a certain personage received, without His Majesty's knowing anything about it.[7] Such was the recompense for the three years that Sieur de Monts had spent, with an outlay of more than 100,000 livres.[8] In the first of these three years he suffered a great deal and endured great distress on account of the severe cold and the long duration of snow three feet deep, for five months; although at any time one could reach the shores, where the sea does not freeze, except at the mouth of rivers, which are clogged with ice making its way to the sea. Besides, almost half of his men died from the disease of the country,[9] and he was obliged to send the remainder of his men back with Sieur de Poutrincourt, who was his lieutenant that year, Pont Gravé having been it the year before.

These are the plans of Sieur de Monts which were broken up. He promised to go farther south to make a settlement that should be healthier

---

[7] The King's minister, Sully, revoked the patent in July, 1607. For fuller details see H. F. Biggar, *The Early Trading Companies of New France,* 63-64.

[8] The livre, at this time, contained about as much silver as two francs, and its purchasing value was equal, approximately, to about six francs to-day, or $1.20. Perkins, *France Under Richelieu and Mazarin,* II, 371.

[9] Scurvy.

and milder than the Island of St. Croix, where he had spent the winter. Since that time some people have been at Port Royal,[10] where they liked it better, because they did not find the winter so harsh in latitude 45°. To recompense these losses, 6000 livres were ordered given him by the Council of His Majesty, to be taken from the ships that were going to trade for furs.

But to what expense would he have had to be put in all the ports and harbors to collect this sum, to find out who had traded, and the right proportion to be levied on over eighty ships which frequent these shores? It was giving him an endless task, necessitating an expense in excess of the receipts, as he well perceived. For Sieur de Monts got almost nothing out of it, and was obliged to let this decree go as he could. This was how these matters were managed by His Majesty's Council. God pardon those whom He has called, and improve those who are living! Heavens! what further enterprise could any one risk, when everything is revoked in this way, without judging maturely of things, before any results can he forthcoming? Those who have the least knowledge make the most complaint and wish to be thought to know more than those who have full experience; and they speak only from envy, or for their own interest, on false reports and appearances, without informing themselves further.

There is something to find fault with in this undertaking: namely, two opposing religions never produce great results for the glory of God among the infidels, whom one wishes to convert. I have seen the minister and our curé come to blows in a religious quarrel. I do not know which was the more courageous, or which gave the better blow, but I know very well that the minister complained sometimes to Sieur de Monts of having been beaten, and they ended the controversy in this way. I will leave you to judge if it was a pleasant sight; the savages were sometimes on one side, sometimes on the other, and the French mixed in according to their respective beliefs, and reviled first one and then the other religion, although Sieur de Monts made peace as much as he could. These insults were really a means to the infidel of making him still more hardened in his infidelity.

Now, since Sieur de Monts did not wish to go to live on the St. Lawrence River, he ought to have sent some one to explore a place suitable for the foundation of a colony, which would not be liable to be abandoned like that of St. Croix, and Port Royal, where no one knew

---

[10] Annapolis Basin, Nova Scotia.

the place; and he ought to have expended from four to five thousand livres, so as to be sure of the place, and even to have had some one pass a winter there, in order to get acquainted with the climate. If that had been done, there is no doubt at all that the soil, and the warmth such as would have been found in a good climate, would have induced the settlers to stay there. And even if Sieur de Monts's commission had been revoked they would not have given up living in the country within three years and a half, as was done in Acadie, but enough ground would have been cleared to enable them to send commodities to France. If these matters had been well managed, little by little we should have adapted ourselves to the situation, and the English and the Flemish would not have got the benefit of places that they took from us, where they have settled to our loss.[11]

It will not be out of place to gratify the curious reader, and especially those who make sea voyages, with a description of the discoveries of these coasts during three years and a half while I was in Acadie, both at the settlement at St. Croix, and at Port Royal, when I had opportunity to see and discover everything, as will be seen in the following book.

---

[11] Champlain refers to the English settlements in New England and to the Dutch occupation of New Netherland.

BOOK II

CHAPTER 1

Description of la Héve. Of Port Mouton. Of Cape Negro. Of the Cape Sable and Sable Bay. Of Cormorant Island. Of Cape Fourchu. Of Long Island. Of Bay Saint Mary. Of Port Saint Margaret, and of all the remarkable things that there are along the coast of Acadie.

CAPE LA HÉVE[1] is a place where there is a bay containing several islands covered with firs, and a great tract of oaks, young elms and birches. It is on the coast of Acadie, in latitude 44° 5', and the declination of the compass was 16° 15',[2] 75 leagues northeast of Cape Breton.

Seven leagues from this cape is another called Port Mouton[3], where are two little rivers in latitude 44 degrees and some minutes, where the soil is very stony and filled with undergrowth and heather. There are a great many rabbits there, and there is a good deal of game, because of the ponds which are there.

Going along the coast one sees a very good harbor for vessels, and in the interior a little river, which goes pretty far into the land. I named it the harbor of Cape Negro,[4] because of a rock which, from a distance, resembles one. It rises above the water near a cape where we went the same day, which is four leagues from it, and ten leagues from Port Mou-

---

[1] Cape La Have, some twenty miles west of Lunenburg, Nova Scotia.
[2] Before the invention of the chronometer the exact determination of longitude was impossible. Champlain adopted the method of determining location by giving the latitude and indicating the declination of the needle from the true north. It was supposed that in this way the longitude could be determined approximately. Champlain's explanation of his system and his method of drawing his maps will be found in *Voyages of Champlain*, Prince Society edition, III, 219-224, and in Laverdière, *Voyages, 1613,* p. 270, ff.
[3] The name is still in use.
[4] Negro Harbour.

ton. This cape is very dangerous, on account of the rocks which project into the sea. The coasts that I saw up to that point are all low, covered with the same wood as that at Cape la Héve, and the islands are all full of game. Going along farther we passed the night at Sable Bay, where the ships can anchor, without any fear of danger.

Cape Sable, two good leagues from Sable Bay, is also very dangerous, on account of certain rocks and reefs that extend almost a league into the sea. From there one goes to Cormorant Island, which is a league from it, so named because of the infinite number of these birds that are on it; and we filled a large barrel with their eggs. From this island, going west about six miles, crossing a bay which runs up two or three leagues to the north, one comes upon several islands that project two or three leagues into the sea, of which the area of some is perhaps two, of others three leagues, and of others less, as far as I could judge. Most of them are very dangerous to approach in large vessels, on account of the high tides and the rocks which are on a level with the water. These islands are covered with pine trees, firs, birches and aspens. A little farther on there are four more. On one of them there are so many of the birds called penguins that one can easily kill them with a stick. On another there are sea wolves.[5] On two others there is such a quantity of birds of different varieties that one who had not seen them could not imagine them, such as cormorants, ducks of three kinds, geese, *marmettes*,[6] bustards, sea parrots, snipe, vultures, and other birds of prey; sea gulls, dunlins of two or three species; herons, large sea gulls, curlews, sea pyes, divers, ospreys, *appoils*, crows, cranes, and other kinds, which make their nests there. I named them Seal Islands.[7] They are in latitude 43½°, distant from the mainland, or Cape Sable, four or five leagues. From there we went to a cape that I called Forked Harbor,[8] since such was its shape, distant from the Seal Islands from five to six leagues. This harbor is very good for ships at the entrance, but inside it is almost entirely dry at low tide, except the channel of a little river, all surrounded by meadows which make this place rather pleasant. Cod fishing is good there near the har-

---

[5] Seals. Commonly called sea wolves by the early navigators. Slafter. *Loup marin* will, after this, be rendered "seals" in this translation.

[6] This word is not given in the dictionaries. In many cases the identification of animals and birds and plants mentioned by the early explorers is very difficult and requires the expert knowledge of the naturalist. American fauna and flora were generally given the names of those European fauna and flora which they most resembled.

[7] The name is still in use.

[8] Port Fourchu. The name survives in Cape Fourchu. It is just west of Yarmouth.

SAMUEL DE CHAMPLAIN

bor. We went north ten or twelve leagues without finding any harbor for our ships, only a number of coves, or very fine beaches, where the land seemed suitable for cultivation. The woods there are very beautiful, but they contain very few pines and firs. This coast is very safe, without islands, rocks, or shallows; so that, in my judgment, ships can go there with confidence. A quarter of a league from the coast I came to an island, which is called Long Island, lying north northeast and south southwest, which makes a passage to the Great French Bay,[9] so named by De Monts.

This island is six leagues long, and in some places nearly one league wide, and in other places only a quarter of a league. It is covered with a quantity of wood, such as pines and birches. The whole coast is bordered with very dangerous rocks, and there is no place suitable for ships, except that at the end of the island there are several refuges for shallops, and two or three rocky islands, where the savages hunt seals. The tides run very high there, particularly at the little passage of the island, which is very dangerous for vessels, if they venture going through it.

Going northeast two leagues from the passage of Long Island, one finds a cove where ships can anchor in safety. It is a quarter of a league in circumference. Its bottom is nothing but mud, and the land surrounding it is all bordered with rather high rocks. In this place, according to the report of a miner, called Master Simon, who was with me, there is a very good silver mine.[10] Some leagues farther there is a little river, called the Boulay,[11] where the tide comes half a league inland, at the entrance of which one can easily anchor ships of a hundred tons burden. A quarter of a league from this place there is a good harbor for vessels where we found an iron mine, which the miner thought yielded fifty per cent. Sailing three leagues farther to the northeast, one comes upon another rather good iron mine, near which there is a river surrounded by fine, pleasant meadows. The soil round about is as red as blood. Some leagues farther along there is another river which is dry at low tide, except its channel, which is very small.[12] This runs near Port Royal. At the upper end of this bay there is a channel which is also dry at low tide. About it are a number of fields and good lands to cultivate, although covered

[9] The Bay of Fundy.
[10] Little River on Digby Neck. Slafter.
[11] Sandy Cove.
[12] "South Creek, or Smelt River, which rises near Annapolis Basin, or the Port Royal Basin of the French." Slafter.

ALGONQUIANS, HURONS AND IROQUOIS

with a quantity of beautiful trees of all kinds, as I have said above. This bay, from Long Island to the upper end, may extend about six leagues. All the coast of the mines is rather high ground, intersected by capes, which appear round and project a little into the sea. On the other side of the bay, to the southeast, the land is low and good, and there is a very good harbor, and at its entrance a bar over which one must go, where, at low tide, the water is a fathom and a half deep. When one has passed this he finds three fathoms and a good bottom. Between the two points of the harbor there is a pebbly island which is covered at high tide. This place extends half a league into the land. The tide there goes down three fathoms, and there are quantities of shellfish there, such as mussels, snails and cockles. The soil is the best that I have seen. I called this harbor the harbor of Saint Margaret.[13] All this southeast coast is much lower land than that of the mines, which are only a league and a half from the coast of Port Saint Margaret, the width of the bay, which is three leagues at its entrance. I measured the altitude at this place, and I found it was in latitude 45½° and a little more, and the declination of the needle was 17° 16'. This bay was named Saint Mary Bay.

CHAPTER II

Description of Port Royal, and its peculiarities. Of High Island. Of the Harbor of Mines. Of the Great French Bay. Of the River Saint John, and what we have noticed between the Harbor of Mines and this place. Of the Island called by the savages Manthane. Of the Etechemins River, and several beautiful islands in it. Of Saint Croix Island, and other conspicuous things on this shore.

PASSING[1] Long Island, with the cape six leagues to the northeast, one comes to a cove where ships can drop anchor in 4, 5, 6 and 7 fathoms of water. The bottom is sand. This place serves only as a roadstead. Continuing two leagues in the same direction we enter one of the most beautiful harbors in this whole coast, where a great number of ships could go in safety. The mouth is 800 paces wide and 25 fathoms deep; it is two leagues long and one league wide. I named it Port Royal.[2] Three

---

[13] Weymouth Harbour.

[1] This chapter begins another exploring trip, and the narrative is taken up at the farthest point reached in the earlier exploration. For the intermediate events see *Voyages of Champlain,* Prince Society edition, II, 18-21.

[2] Annapolis Basin.

rivers empty into it, one of which is rather large. It comes from the east, and is called the River *Esquille,* the name of a little fish the size of a smelt which it yields in great quantity. Herring are also caught there, and other kinds of fish of which there is an abundance in their season. This river is almost a quarter of a league wide at the mouth, where there is an island, perhaps half a league in circumference, covered with wood, like all the rest of the land, such as pines, firs, spruces, birches, aspens, and some oaks, though comparatively few. This river has two mouths, one on the north shore, the other on the south of the island. That on the north is the better. There ships can drop anchor in the shelter of the island in 5, 6, 7 and 8 fathoms of water. But one must guard against certain shallows near the island and the mainland, which are very dangerous if one does not know the channel.

I went 14 or 15 leagues up the river, where the tide rises, and it is not navigable much farther inland. At this place it is 60 paces wide and about 1½ fathoms deep. The land about this river is covered with a great number of oak, ash and other trees. Between the mouth of the river and the place where we were, there are many meadows, but they are flooded by the high tides. They are crossed by many little brooks, on which shallops and boats can go in high water. Within the harbor there is another island, nearly two leagues away from the first, where there is another little river which runs a good way inland. I named this one the River St. Anthony.[3] Its mouth is about four leagues across the woods from the end of Saint Mary Bay. As for the other river, it is only a brook filled with rocks, which one could not ascend in any way whatever, for lack of water.[4] This place is in latitude 45°, and the declination of the needle is 17° 8'.

Leaving Port Royal and going 8 or 10 leagues to the northeast of the cape, along the coast of Port Royal, I crossed a part of the bay, some 5 or 6 leagues, to a place that I named the Cape of Two Bays,[5] and passed by an island which is one league from it and is also one league in circumference. It rises some 40 or 45 fathoms in height and is all surrounded by great rocks; except in one place, where there is a slope, with a saltwater pond at the foot. The water comes in below a pebbly point in the form of a spur. The top of the island is flat, covered with trees, and it has a very beautiful spring. In this place there is a copper mine. From there

---

[3] Bear River.
[4] Sometimes called Moose River and sometimes Deep Brook. Slafter.
[5] Cape Chignecto.

ALGONQUIANS, HURONS AND IROQUOIS

I went to a harbor a league and a half from it, where there is also a copper mine. This harbor is in latitude 45⅔ degrees. It is dry at low tide. To enter, it is necessary to place buoys and to mark the sand bar at the mouth, which extends along a channel parallel with the mainland on the other side. Then one enters a bay, which is almost a league long and half a league wide. In some places the bottom is muddy and sandy, and vessels can run aground there. The sea there rises and falls from four to five fathoms. This Cape of Two Bays, where the harbor of mines is situated, is so called because to the north and the south of the cape there are two bays which run up east northeast and northeast some 12 to 15 leagues;[6] and there is a strait at the opening of each bay not more than half a league wide. Beyond the strait it suddenly widens to about 3, 4 or 5 leagues.[7] There are also several islands in this bay, where there are ponds, and two or three little rivers which flow into it, by which the savages go in their canoes to Tregaté, and to Misamichy in the Gulf of Saint Lawrence, partly by water, partly by land.

All the country that I saw after the little passage on Long Island, sailing along the coast, is nothing but rocks, with no place where ships could go in safety, except Port Royal. The country is covered with a quantity of pines and birches, and, in my opinion, it is not especially fertile.

We went west two leagues to the Cape of Two Bays, then north five or six leagues and crossed the other bay.[8] Going west some six leagues one finds a little river,[9] at the mouth of which is a rather low cape, which projects into the sea; and somewhat inland a mountain the shape of a Cardinal's hat.[10] In this place there is an iron mine, and there is no anchorage, except for shallops. Four leagues west southwest there is a rocky point,[11] which projects a little seaward, where there are very great tides which are very dangerous. Near this point there is a cove about half a league in circumference, in which there is a very good iron mine. Four leagues farther along there is a beautiful bay, which cuts into the land and has within it three islands and a rock. Two of the islands are one

---

[6] Chignecto Bay and Basin of Mines.
[7] That is, Chignecto Bay.
[8] Chignecto Bay.
[9] Quaco River.
[10] Porcupine Mountain. Ganong. Notes from Ganong will, henceforth, be marked G.
[11] McCoy's Head, G.

league west of the cape,[12] and the other is at the mouth of one of the largest, deepest rivers that I had yet seen, which I called the River Saint John, because it was on that day that I arrived there,[13] and which is called by the Savages Ouygoudy.[14] This river is dangerous, if one is not familiar with certain points and rocks on both banks. It is narrow at its mouth, then begins to widen and, having doubled its swiftness, narrows once more and makes a sort of fall between two big rocks, where the water flows with such rapidity that if one throw a piece of wood into it, it is sucked to the bottom and one sees it no more; but, by waiting for high tide[15] one can go through this strait easily, and then it widens to about a league in some places, and contains three islands, on which there are a great many meadows and beautiful trees, such as oaks, beeches, walnuts,[16] and wild grapevines. The inhabitants of the country go by this river as far as Tadoussac, which is on the great River Saint Lawrence, and cross but little land to get there. It is 65 leagues from the River St. John to Tadoussac. At its mouth, which is in latitude 45⅔ degrees, there is an iron mine. Shallops cannot go more than fifteen leagues in this river, because of the rapids, which can be navigated only by using the canoes of the savages.

From the River St. John I went to four islands, on one of which was a great quantity of birds called magpies. Their young are as good as young pigeons. This island is three leagues from the mainland. Farther west there are other islands: among them one having an area of six leagues, which is called by the savages Menane.[17] At the south of this there are, among the islands, several harbors suitable for ships. From the Magpie Islands I went to a river in the mainland called the River of the Etechemins, from a tribe of savages so called in their country, and we passed by such a number of beautiful islands that I could not count them. Some had an area of two leagues, some three, others more or less. They are all in a bay,[18] in my judgment of more than fifteen leagues in

---

[12] Negro Head, G.

[13] June 24, St. John's Day.

[14] In all probability a mistake. Ouygoudy was the name the Indians gave to their camping-ground on Navy Island, G.

[15] It is passable only at half tide, G.

[16] Professor Ganong believes that *noyers* means butternuts here.

[17] Grand Manan. Champlain used the form Manthane in his first account (1613), and that name is given in the heading to this chapter. Laverdière says that Menane is the true name.

[18] Passamaquoddy Bay.

circumference, with several good places for as many ships as one would wish. Round about there is good fishing: cod, salmon, bass, herring, halibut and other fishes in great number. Going west northwest, three leagues past the islands, one enters a river, almost half a league wide at its mouth,[19] in which there are two islands one or two leagues further up: one very small,[20] near the mainland on the west; and the other in the middle.[21] The latter has a circumference of eight or nine hundred paces and rises out of the water three or four fathoms high, with rocky sides, except in one small place where there is a little point of sand and clayey soil, useful for making bricks and other necessary things. There is another sheltered place for ships of from eighty to a hundred tons, but it is dry at low tide. The island is covered with firs, birches, maples and oaks. It is in itself a very good site, and there is but one stretch of about forty paces where its sides are lower, and that is easy to fortify. The shores of the mainland being distant from each other on both sides from about nine hundred to a thousand paces, ships could not pass up the river without being at the mercy of the cannon from the island, which is the place that we believed to be the best, whether for situation, the excellence of the soil, or for such intercourse as it is proposed to have with the savages of these shores and inland. For it is in the midst of those whom we hope to pacify in time, abolishing the wars that they have with one another, in order both to obtain service from them and to convert them to the Christian faith. This place was named, by De Monts, St. Croix Island.[22] Going farther up, one sees a large bay[23] in which there are two islands—one high, the other flat—and three rivers, two of medium size, of which one flows in from the east and the other from the north, and the third, a large one, flowing in from the west:[24] that is the River of the Etechemins. Two leagues up this there is a rapid, where the savages carry their canoes on the land about 500 paces. Then they enter the river again. From there, after crossing a bit of land, one comes to the River

[19] St. Croix, G.

[20] Little Dochet (pronounced "Doshay"), G.

[21] Dochet, G.

[22] For a most complete study of St. Croix Island and the part it played in diplomatic controversy see W. F. Ganong, *Dochet (St. Croix) Island,* Transactions of the Royal Society of Canada, 2d Series, vol. VIII, sect. 4, 127-231. This monograph is fully illustrated with maps, plans and photographs.

[23] Oak Bay, G.

[24] The St. Croix.

SAMUEL DE CHAMPLAIN

Norembegue,[25] and the St. John. The place where the rapid is ships cannot get through, on account of its being nothing but rocks, and of there being only four or five feet of water. In May and June there are such big catches of herring and bass that one could load boats there with them. The soil is of the finest, and there are 15 or 20 acres of cleared land. The savages sometimes go there five or six weeks during the fishing season. All the rest of the country is covered with very thick forests. If the land were cleared, grain would grow very well. This place is in latitude 45⅓ degrees, and the variation of the needle is 17° 32'. A settlement was made in this place in the year 1604.[26]

CHAPTER III

Of the coast, peoples, and river of Norembegue.

Continuing[1] from the St. Croix River along the coast about 25 leagues, we passed a great quantity of islands, banks, reefs and rocks, which project more than four leagues into the sea in some places. I called them the Ranges. Most of them are covered with pines and firs, and other poor kinds of wood. Among these islands there are a great many good, fine harbors, but they are not attractive. I went near an island about four or five leagues long. The distance from this island to the mainland on the north is not a hundred paces. It is very high with notches here and there, so that it appears, when one is at sea, like seven or eight mountains rising close together. The tops of most of them are without trees, because they are nothing but rock. The only trees are pines, firs and birches. I called it the Island of the Desert Mountains.[2] It is in latitude 44½°.

The savages of this place, having made an alliance with us, guided us on the Pemetegoit River,[3] so called by them, and told us that their captain, named Bessabez, was the chief of the river. I think that this river is the one which several pilots and historians call Norembegue, and which

---

[25] Norumbega, The Penobscot.
[26] Champlain, in this narrative, omits the story of the establishment of this settlement. For it see *Voyages of Champlain,* Prince Society Ed., II, 34-38.
[1] This exploring trip was begun Sept. 2, 1604, *Voyages of Champlain* II, 38.
[2] Isle des Monts Déserts. Mount Desert Island. It was discovered Sept. 5, 1604.
[3] The Penobscot, Sept. 7. The name Penobscot is a corruption of one of the Indian names, for which see Slafter in *Voyages of Champlain*, II, 40, and Laverdière, *Oeuvres de Champlain, Voyage de 1613*, 31.

most of them have described as large and spacious, with a great number of islands, and having its mouth in latitude 43° and 43½°, and others in latitude 44°, more or less.[4] As for the variation of the needle I never have read anything about it, or heard any one speak of it. It has been said also that there is a large city, well populated with savages who are skillful and expert making use of cotton thread. I am confident that most of those who mention them did not see them, and speak from what they heard from those who knew no more about them than they did.[5] I know very well that there are some people who may have seen the mouth of it, because, as a matter of fact, there are a quantity of islands, and it is in latitude 44°, at its mouth, as they say. But there is nothing to show that any one ever entered it, for they would have described it in a different way, so that so many people would not doubt it. I shall state, then, what I discovered and saw from the beginning, as far as I went.

In the first place, at its mouth, 10 or 12 leagues from the mainland, there are several islands, which are in latitude 44°, and in 18° 40' of the declination of the needle. The Island of Mount Desert makes one of the points at its mouth, and lies toward the east; and the other is low land, and is called by the savages Bedabedec.[6] It is west of this, and they are nine or ten leagues apart; and nearly in the middle of the sea there is another island which is so high and striking that I named it Isle Haute.[7] All about there is an infinite number of them, of varying sizes, but the largest is that of Mount Desert. The fishing for different kinds of fish is very good there, as is also the hunting for game. Three or four leagues from the point of Bedabedec,[8] following the mainland to the north, through which this river flows, are some very high hills which, in fine weather, can be seen 12 or 15 leagues out at sea.[9] Proceeding on the south side of Isle Haute, sailing along it about a quarter of a league, where there are some reefs which are out of the water, heading to the west until all the mountains that are north of this island are opened up, you can feel sure that when you see the eight or nine summits of Mount

---

[4] Actually a little over 44°. The text follows here the reading of the 1613 text.

[5] Champlain probably refers to the account of the city of Norumbega, which was contained in *Histoire Universelle des Indes Occidentales*, Douay, 1607, and to that of Jean Alfonse. Both these are quoted and refuted by Lescarbot, *Histoire de la Nouvelle France*, ed. Tross, II, 470-473.

[6] The region about Rockland and Camden, Slafter.

[7] The name is still used.

[8] Owl's Head.

[9] The Camden Hills.

SAMUEL DE CHAMPLAIN

Desert Island, and that of Bedabedec, you will be opposite the River of Norembegue. In order to go into it, it is necessary to head the ship to the north, which is over the highest mountains of this Bedabedec, and you will not see any islands in front of you; and you can enter safely, with plenty of water, although you see a quantity of breakers, islands and rocks east and west of you. You must avoid them with the lead in hand; and I think, from what I have been able to judge, that one cannot enter this river at any other place, except with small vessels or shallops; for (as I have said above) the quantity of islands, rocks, shallows, banks and breakers is such everywhere that it is strange to see.

Now, to return to our route, at the entrance of the river there are some beautiful islands which are very pleasant like meadows. I went as far as a place to which the savages guided us, where it is not more than an eighth of a league wide, and some two hundred paces from the land, on the west, there is a rock, level with the water, which is dangerous.[10] From there to Isle Haute it is fifteen leagues: and from this narrow place (which was the narrowest that we had found), after making about seven or eight leagues, we came upon a little river, near which we had to anchor, inasmuch as in front of us we saw a quantity of rocks visible at low water; and also because, if we had wished to go farther, it would have been impossible to make half a league, on account of a waterfall there, which came down a slope seven or eight feet. I saw it from a canoe with the savages that we had with us, and found only enough water there for a canoe. But beyond the falls, which are about two hundred paces wide, the river is beautiful and delightful as far as the place where we anchored. I went ashore to see the country, and, as far as I went, going hunting, I found it pleasant and agreeable. The oaks there seemed to have been planted for pleasure. I saw few firs, but a good many pines on one bank of the river; on the other it was all oaks, and a little brushwood which spread a good way inland; and I will say that from the entrance to where I went, which was about 25 leagues,[11] I did not see any city, or village, or appearance of there having been any, although there were one or two cabins of the savages, with no one in them, which were made in the same way as those of the Souriquois,[12] covered with the bark of trees; and, as far as I could judge, there are not many savages on this river,

---

[10] Fort Point Ledge, near Castine.
[11] Champlain went up to the present site of Bangor.
[12] The Micmacs of Nova Scotia.

which is called Pemetegoit. They do not come there any more than to the islands except some months in summer, during the season for fishing and hunting, which are very good there. They are a people who have no fixed habitation, as far as I have found out and learned from them: for they winter sometimes in one place, sometimes in another, where they see that the hunting for wild beasts is better; for they live from it as necessity compels, without having anything in reserve for times of scarcity, which is sometimes very great.

Now, this river must necessarily be the Norembegue; for, going past it as far as latitude 41°, to which I coasted along, one sees no other in the latitudes above mentioned, except that of the Quinibequy,[13] which is almost as high up, but not of so great length. On the other hand, there cannot be any other which rises far inland, inasmuch as the great River Saint Lawrence runs along the coast of Acadie and of Norembegue, and there is not more than 45 leagues of land between them, or 60 at the widest place in a straight line.

Now I will leave this discourse, to return to the savages who took me to the falls of the Norembegue River. They went to inform Bessabez, their chief, and other savages, who went on another little river to inform theirs, named Cabahis, and tell him of our arrival.

On the sixteenth of the month,[14] about thirty savages came to us, on the assurance of those who had served us as guide. This Bessabez came also to find us that same day, with six canoes. As soon as the savages who were on land saw him coming, they all fell to singing, dancing and jumping until he was ashore; then afterward they all sat down on the ground in a circle, according to their custom when they wish to make a speech, or have a feast. Soon after Cabahis, the other chief, arrived also with twenty or thirty of his companions, who withdrew to one side and greatly enjoyed looking at us, for it was the first time that they had seen Christians. Some time afterward I went ashore with two of my companions and two of our savages, who served us as interpreters, and ordered those on our boat to approach the savages and have their arms ready for use if they noticed any movement among these people against us. Bessabez, seeing us ashore, had us sit down, and began to smoke with his companions, as they usually do before making their speeches, and made us pre-

[13] The Kennebec.
[14] September, 1604.

sents of venison and game.[15] All the rest of the day and the night following, they did nothing but sing, dance and make good cheer, until the dawn. Then each one returned, Bessabez with his companions on his side, and we on ours, well satisfied at having made the acquaintance of these people.

On the seventeenth of the month I took the altitude and found the latitude was 45° 25'.[16] This done I departed, to go to another river called Quinibequy,[17] 35 leagues away from this place and almost 15 from Bedabedec. This tribe of savages of Quinibequy is called Etechemins as well as those of Norembegue.

The eighteenth of the month I went near a little river where Cabahis was. He came with us in our boat about 12 leagues. I asked him where the River Norembegue came from, and he told me that it comes from beyond the fall which I have mentioned above, and that after going some distance on it one enters a lake, by way of which they go to the St. Croix River, a small part of the way by land; then they enter the Etechemins River.[18] Besides, another river flows into the lake, and on it they go several days, and then enter another lake, and they go through the middle of this, and, when they reach the end, they go some distance by land, and afterward enter a little river which flows into the great St. Lawrence River.[19] All these people of Norembegue are very tawny, dressed in beaver skins and other furs, like the Canadian and Souriquois[20] savages, and they have the same way of living.

This is an exact statement of all that I observed, whether of the coasts, the people, or the River Norembegue, and not of the marvels that any one has written about them. I believe that this place is as agreeable in winter as St. Croix.

---

[15] In preparing this narrative Champlain omitted the account of the negotiations given in the narrative of 1613. *Voyage de 1613*, 36-37; *Voyages of Champlain*, II, 46.

[16] The correct latitude should have been 44° 46'. S.

[17] The Kennebec.

[18] By the east branch of the Penobscot, the Matawamkeag River.

[19] By the Penobscot to the northwest through Lake Pemadumcook, and next through Lake Chesuncook, etc., till the upper waters of the Chaudière were reached. Champlain failed to understand that the lake entered by way of the Matawamkeag, going toward the St. Croix, was different from the one passed through going toward Quebec.

[20] The Micmacs.

ALGONQUIANS, HURONS AND IROQUOIS

CHAPTER IV

Discovery of the Quinibeguy River, which is on the coast of the Almouchiquois, as far as latitude 42°, and the particulars of the voyage. How the men and women pass the time during the winter.

SKIRTING the coast westward[1] one passes the mountains of Bedabedec, and we saw the mouth of the river, where one may approach with large ships, but where there are some shallows that one must avoid, lead in hand. Going about eight leagues, running westward along the coast, we passed a number of islands and rocks jutting out a league into the sea, and went as far as an island ten leagues from Quinibequy. At the entrance of this river there is a rather high island, which we named the Tortoise,[2] and between this and the mainland there are some scattering rocks, which are covered at high tide; nevertheless, one always sees the water break above them. Tortoise Island and the river lie south southeast, and north northwest. At the entrance there are two medium-sized islands—one on one side, and the other on the other; and some 300 paces inward there are two rocks, where there are no woods, but there is a little grass. We anchored 300 paces from the mouth, in five or six fathoms of water. I decided to go inland, to see the upper part of the river and the savages who live there. When we had gone some leagues our boat came near being lost on a rock that we grazed in passing. Farther along we met two canoes which had come for hunting birds which, for the most part, are moulting at that season and cannot fly. We accosted these savages, and they guided us. Going on farther to see their captain, called Manthoumermer, when we had made from seven to eight leagues, we passed by certain islands, straits and brooks, which flow into the river, where I saw some beautiful meadows. And when we had coasted along an island about four leagues in length, they led us to where their chief was with twenty-five or thirty savages.[3] As soon as we had anchored he came to us in a canoe a little apart from ten others which accompanied it. Drawing near to our boat he made a speech, in which

[1] Champlain here omits the incidents of the first winter of the colony, 1604-05. For them see *Voyages of Champlain*, II, 49-55; Laverdiere, Voyage de 1613, 40-45. The narrative now takes up the explorations of the summer of 1605, where the exploration of 1604 stopped.

[2] Seguin Island, reached July 1.

[3] At Wiscasset Harbor. For Champlain's route after entering the mouth of the Kennebec see Slafter in *Voyages of Champlain*, II, 58.

he made it clear that he was glad to see us, and that he wished to have our alliance, and make peace with their enemies with our help, saying that the next day he would send to us two other savage captains who were in the interior—one called Marchim and the other Sasinou, chief of the Quinibequy River.

The next day they guided us down the river by another way than that by which we came, to go to a lake; and passing some islands each of them left an arrow near a cape[4] by which all the savages pass. They think that, if they do not do that, some misfortune will befall them, so the devil makes them believe; and they live in this superstition, as they do in many others.

Beyond this cape we passed a very narrow rapid, but not without great difficulty; for, although we had a good, fresh wind and filled our sails with it as much as possible, we could not get through in that way, and were obliged to fasten a hawser to some trees and to pull on it. Thus we managed to get through by the strength of our arms, aided by the favorable wind. The savages who were with us carried their canoes on the land, as they could not get them through with paddles. After having cleared this rapid we saw some beautiful meadows. I was very much astonished with regard to this rapid, because when we went along with the tide ebbing we had it in our favor, but when we were at the rapid we found it against us, and after we had passed the rapid the tide was ebbing, as before, for which we were very glad.[5]

Following our route we came to the lake,[6] from three to four leagues long, where there are some islands. Two rivers flow into it—the Quinibequy, which comes from the north northeast,[7] and the other from the northwest, by which Marchim and Sasinou were expected. When we had waited for them all that day and saw that they were not coming, we decided to make some use of the time. We weighed anchor, and two savages came with us from this lake to guide us, and this day we anchored at the mouth of the river, where we caught a quantity of various kinds of good fish. Meantime our savages went hunting, but failed to return. The way by which we descended that river is much safer and better than that by which we had come. Tortoise Island, which is at the

---

[4] Hockomock Point.
[5] For an explanation of this curious phenomenon see Slafter's note in *Voyages of Champlain*, II, 59.
[6] Merrymeeting Bay.
[7] The Androscoggin.

mouth of that river, is in latitude 44°, and the declination of the needle is 19° 12'. About four leagues from there, in the sea, toward the southwest, are three little islands where the English fish for cod. One can go from this river[8] across the land as far as Quebec, some 50 leagues, without passing more than one portage of two leagues. Then one enters another little river[9] which empties into the great River St. Lawrence. This Quinibequy river is very dangerous for ships for half a league, because there is so little water, and there are big tides, rocks and shallows as much outside as within it. There would be a good channel if it were well explored. The little that I saw of the country along the banks of this river is very poor, for there is nothing but rocks on all sides. There is a quantity of small oaks and very little tillable ground. There is an abundance of fish here, as in the other rivers mentioned above. The people live like those of our settlement, and tell us that the savages who plant Indian corn are very far inland, and that they have given up doing so on the shores, on account of the war that they had with the others, who took it from them. This is what I have been able to learn of this place, which I do not believe is any better than the others.

The savages that live on all these shores are very few in number. During the winter, if there is a great deal of snow, they hunt the moose,[10] and other animals, upon which they live most of the time; and if there is not much snow it is not to their advantage, inasmuch as they cannot get anything without excessive labor, which causes them to endure and suffer a great deal. When they do not hunt they live on a shellfish which is called the clam. They dress themselves in winter in good furs of the beaver and the moose. The women make all the clothes, but not so neatly but that one sees the flesh under the arms, for they are not skillful enough to make them fit better. When they go hunting they take a kind of racket, twice as big as those on our side of the water, which they attach to their feet, and they can go on the snow in this way without sinking in; the women and children, as well as the men, looking for the tracks of animals. Then, when they have found them, they follow them until they see the beast, and then they shoot at it with their bows, or kill it with stabs of swords fastened to the end of a short pike staff, which is easily done, since these animals cannot walk on the snow without sink-

---

[8] The Kennebec.
[9] The Chaudière.
[10] *Eslans*, elk, here means moose; usually called by its Indian name, *orignac*.

ing into it. Then the women and children come to the place and make a hut there, and give themselves a feast. Afterward they return to see if they can find others.

Coasting along by the shore we anchored behind a little island near the mainland,[11] where we observed more than eight savages running along the shore to see us; dancing and signifying the pleasure that they felt. I visited an island, which is very beautiful on account of what grows on it, for there are beautiful oaks and walnuts, the land is cleared, and there are many vines, which bear beautiful grapes in their season—they were the first that I had seen on all these shores since I was at Cape la Héve. We called it the Isle of Bacchus.[12] When the tide was high we weighed anchor and entered a little river, where we could not go before, inasmuch as it is a bar harbor and has only half a fathom of water at low tide, a fathom and a half when the sea is at half tide, and two fathoms when it is high. When one is within it one finds 3, 4, 5 and 6 fathoms. When we had anchored, a lot of savages came to the bank of the river and began to dance.[13] Their captain at the time, whom they called Honemechin, was not with them. He arrived about two or three hours afterward with two canoes. Then he went off, circling all about our boat. These people shave the hair on the top of their heads rather high up and wear the rest very long, combing and twisting it in the back in various ways very neatly with feathers that they fasten to the head. They paint their faces black and red, like other savages that I have seen. They are an active people, with well-formed bodies. Their weapons are pikes, clubs, bows and arrows, on the end of which some put the tail of a fish called the *signoc*;[14] others use bone, and still others have them all of wood. They till and cultivate the ground, which we had not seen done before. Instead of ploughs they have an instrument of wood, very strong, made like a spade. The inhabitants of the country call this river the Choüacoet.[15]

I went ashore to see their tillage on the bank of the river, and I saw their corn, which is Indian corn. They make gardens of it, planting three

[11] Stratton Island. A short passage occurs just before this in the 1613 narrative which records the sight of some mountains to the west, which are identified as the White Mountains. Cf. Slafter's note in *Voyages of Champlain*, II, 61.

[12] Richmond Island. S.

[13] These Indians Champlain calls Almouchiquois in his earlier narrative, *Voyages*, II, 63. They are the same as the Massachusetts of the early English settlers.

[14] The horseshoe crab. Champlain gives a picture of this shellfish in his map of 1612.

[15] The Saco. Champlain reached this point July 9, 1605.

or four grains in a place, then heaping up a quantity of earth with the shells of that same fish, the signoc,[16] on them, then planting again as much as three feet off, and so on. Among the corn in each hill they plant three or four Brazilian beans,[17] which are of various colors. When they are grown they intertwine among this corn, which grows five or six feet high, and keep the field very free from weeds. We saw there many squashes[18] and pumpkins and some tobacco, which they also cultivate. The Indian corn that I saw there was two feet high, and some of it was three. They sow it in May and harvest it in September. As for the beans, they were beginning to blossom, as were also the squashes and pumpkins. I saw there a great quantity of nuts, which are small, and have several divisions. There were not any yet on the trees, but we found enough of them underneath that had fallen the year before. There are also a great many vines, which bear a very beautiful berry, from which we made a very good verjuice, something that we had not seen before, except in the Isle of Bacchus, nearly two leagues distant from this river. Their settled habitation, the tillage and the beautiful trees, gave me the impression that the air there is milder and better than that where we passed the winter, and than that of other places on the coast. The forests in the interior are very light, but, nevertheless, consist of oaks, beeches, ashes and young elms. In wet places there are a great many willows. The savages stay in this place all the time, and have a big cabin surrounded by palisades made of rather large trees placed side by side, whither they retire when their enemies come to war against them; and they cover their cabins with oak bark. This place is very pleasant and as agreeable as any one could see. The river is full of fish and is surrounded with meadows. At its mouth there is an island which would make a good fortress, where one would be safe.

[16] The shell of the horseshoe crab used as a shovel.

[17] The kidney bean, commonly used as string beans. *Phaseolus vulgaris*. This bean is indigenous in America, and probably came to be called the Brazilian bean because it was supposed to have been introduced into France from Brazil.

[18] The familiar summer squash, indigenous in America.

SAMUEL DE CHAMPLAIN

CHAPTER V

The Choüacoet River. Places that the author discovered there. Cape of Islands. Canoes of the people made of birch bark. How the savages of that country revive those who faint away. Use stones instead of knives. Their chief honorably received by us.

ON Sunday, the twelfth of the month,[1] we left the river called Choüacoet. Coasting along the shore, after having made six or seven leagues, we were obliged by a contrary wind to anchor and go ashore, where we saw two meadows, each a league long and half a league wide. From Choüacoet to this place (where we saw some little birds, which have a song like blackbirds, and are black, except the end of the wings, which are orange)[2] there are a great many grapevines and nut trees. This coast is sandy in most places from Quinibequy. This day we turned back two or three leagues toward Choüacoet, as far as a cape that we named Island Harbor,[3] good for ships of a hundred tons. It is among three islands.

Heading northeast a quarter north,[4] near this place, one enters another harbor[5] where there is no passage (although there are islands), except that by which one enters. At the entrance there are some dangerous rocks, with the sea breaking over them. On these islands there are so many red currants that one sees nothing else in most places, and there are an infinite number of pigeons, of which we caught a good many. The Island Harbor is in latitude 43° 25'.

Sailing along the coast we noticed smoke on the shore of the sea. We approached as near as possible, and saw no savages, which made us think that they had fled from the place. The sun was sinking, and we could not find any place to pass that night, because the coast was flat and sandy. Heading south, in order to keep off shore, so that we might anchor, when we had made about two leagues, we observed a cape on the mainland, south a quarter southeast[6] of us, perhaps six leagues away. Two leagues to the east we saw three or four rather high islands,[7] and to the west a large bay. The shores of this bay, as far as the cape, run inland

[1] July 12, 1605, fell on Tuesday. L.
[2] The Redwing blackbird. S.
[3] Cape Porpoise Harbor. S.
[4] I. e., northeast by north.
[5] Goose Fair Harbor. S.
[6] I. e., south by east. This was Cape Anne.
[7] The Isles of Shoals.

from where we were about four leagues. It is two leagues wide from north to south, and three at its entrance.[8] And not discovering any place suitable to put up in, we decided to go to that cape under short sail a part of the night, and approached it as far as where the water was 16 fathoms deep. There we anchored to await the dawn.

The next day we went to this cape, where there are three islands near the mainland full of trees of different kinds, as at Choüacoet, and on the whole coast; and to another flat one, where the sea breaks, which juts out into the sea a little farther than the others, where there is not any wood at all. We named this place Island Cape.[9] Near it we perceived a canoe with five or six savages in it who were coming to us, who, when they were near our boat, went away to dance on the shore. I landed to see them, and gave each one a knife and some biscuit, which caused them to dance again better than before. When this was over, I made them understand, as best I could, that they should show me how the coast lay. After having depicted for them, with a piece of charcoal, the bay and the Island Cape, where we were, they represented for me, with the same crayon, another bay, which they showed as very large.[10] They put six pebbles at equal distances, thus giving me to understand that each of these stood for as many chiefs and tribes. Then they represented within this bay a river[11] which we had passed, which extends very far, and has shoals. We found a great many vines in this place, with green grapes on them a little larger than peas, and many nut trees, on which the nuts were no larger than musket balls. These savages told us that all who lived in this country cultivated and planted the soil, like the others that we had seen before. This place is in latitude 43 degrees and some minutes.

Doubling the cape[12] we entered a cove, where there are quantities of vines, Brazilian peas,[13] pumpkins, squashes, and some roots that are good, which the savages cultivate, and which taste somewhat like chards.[14]

[8] The broad water at the mouth of the Merrimac.
[9] Cape Anne.
[10] Massachusetts Bay.
[11] The Merrimac.
[12] This paragraph and the two short ones following are taken from the description of the voyage of 1606 and are inserted here to make the record of the exploration of this coast a continuous narrative. See *Voyages of Champlain*, II, 111-112. See Laverdière's note, *Voyage de 1632*, I, 86.
[13] Probably for beans by a slip of the pen.
[14] This plant was the Jerusalem artichoke. S.

SAMUEL DE CHAMPLAIN

This place, which is rather pleasant, is fertile in walnut[15] trees, cypresses,[16] oaks, ashes and beeches, which are very beautiful.

We saw there a savage who hurt his foot so badly, and lost so much blood, that he fell in a faint. A number of others surrounded him and sang some time before they touched him. Then, making certain signs with the feet and hands, they moved his head, and, with a sigh, he came to himself. Our surgeon dressed the wound and he was not prevented, on that account, from going off gaily.

When we had sailed half a league[17] we noticed several savages on the point of a rock. They ran dancing along the shore toward their companions to warn them of our coming. When they had shown us the direction in which they lived they made a sign with smoke, to show us their dwellings. We anchored near a little island,[18] from which we sent our canoe to carry them knives and cakes. We perceived, from the number of them, that these places were more inhabited than the others that we had seen. After we had spent two hours studying these people, whose canoes are made of birch bark, like those of the Canadians, Souriquois and Etechemins, we weighed anchor, and, with the prospect of good weather, we set sail. Continuing our route west southwest, we saw many islands on both sides. Having made seven or eight leagues, we anchored near an island,[19] where we saw a great deal of smoke all along the shore and many savages running to see us. We sent two or three men in a canoe toward them, to whom we gave some knives and beads to present to them. They were much pleased with these things, and danced several times in acknowledgment. We could not find out the name of their chief, because we did not understand their language. All along the shore there is a great deal of land cleared, and planted with Indian corn. The country is very pleasant and agreeable, with a great many beautiful trees. Those who inhabit it have canoes made all in one piece, very easy to upset if one is not skillful in managing them. We had not seen any of that kind before. This is how they make them: after having taken much trouble and spent a long time in felling the largest and tallest tree that they can find, with stone hatchets (for at that time they had no other

---

[15] I.e., hickory trees.
[16] The red cedar. S.
[17] The exploration of July, 1605, is here resumed.
[18] Thatcher's Island. S.
[19] Probably in Boston Harbor, near the western end of Noddle's Island, now East Boston. S.

kind, unless some of them got some from the savages on the coast of Acadie, who got them in the fur trade), they take off the bark, and round it all but one side, where they set fires every little way all along the log. Sometimes they take red-hot pebbles, which they also put on it, and when the fire is too fierce they extinguish it with a little water; not entirely, but only enough to prevent the edge of the canoe from being burned. When it is as much hollowed out as they wish, they scrape it all over with these stones. The pebbles with which they do the cutting are like our musket flints.

The next day, the 17th of the month, we weighed anchor to go to the cape, which we had seen the day before, and which was south southwest[20] of us. This day we could make only five leagues, and we passed some islands covered with wood.[21] I recognized in the bay everything that the savages of Island Cape had described to me. As we continued our course, a great many people came to us from the islands and the mainland in canoes. We anchored a league from the cape, which I named Saint Louis,[22] where we saw smoke in several places. When we were trying to go there our boat ran on a rock, where we were in great danger; for, if we had not got it off promptly, it would have overturned into the sea, which was ebbing, where there were about five or six fathoms of water. But God preserved us, and we anchored near this cape, whither came fifteen or sixteen canoes of savages, some of them containing fifteen or sixteen, who began to show signs of great joy, and made a variety of speeches, which we did not understand at all. We sent three or four men ashore in our canoe, to get some water, and to see their chief, named Honabetha. He was given some knives, and other trinkets, which I thought it proper to give them. He came alongside to see us, with a number of his companions, of whom there were as many on the bank as in their canoes. We received the chief very kindly, and gave him good cheer; and when he had been there some time he returned. The men whom we had sent to them brought us some little squashes the size of one's fist, which we ate as a salad, like cucumbers. They are very good. They brought, also, some purslane, which grows freely amongst the Indian corn, and of which they take no more account than of weeds. We saw, in this place, a great many little houses scattered about the fields where they plant their Indian corn.

[20] Southeast?
[21] In Boston Bay.
[22] Brant Point. S.

SAMUEL DE CHAMPLAIN

There is, besides, in this bay a very large river,[23] which I named River du Gas. I think it rises in the direction of the Iroquois, a tribe[24] that has open war with the Montagnais of the great Saint Lawrence River.

CHAPTER VI

Continuation of the discoveries along the coast of the Almouchiquois, and what we specially noticed there.

THE next day we rounded Cape St. Louis, so named by us, a rather flat country, in latitude 42¾°, and this day made two leagues along a sandy shore. In going by we saw there a great many cabins and gardens, and entered a little bay. Two or three canoes came toward us, on their way from catching cod and other fish, which abound there. They catch them with hooks made of a piece of wood, into which they drive a bone shaped like a harpoon, which they fasten very carefully so that it shall not come out, the whole being in the form of a hook. The line which is attached to it is of hemp, I think, like that in France; and they told me that they gathered the plant for it in their land without cultivating it, indicating to us that it was four or five feet high.[1] This canoe went back to the land to warn those of this settlement, who made fires in our honor; and we saw eighteen or twenty savages come to the edge of the water and dance. Our canoe went ashore to give them some trinkets, with which they were very much pleased. Some of them came to us and asked us to come to their river. We weighed anchor to do so, but we could not enter it because of the little water that we found there, as it was low tide. And so we were obliged to anchor at the mouth. I went ashore, where I saw a great many more savages, who received us very graciously. I explored the river, where I observed nothing but an arm of water which extended a little inland. This land is, in part, cleared. In it there is only a brook which cannot carry boats, except at high tide. This place is about a league in circumference. At one side of the entrance to it there is a sort of island

---

[23] Probably the Charles River. Apparently added at the end of the chapter to make complete the description of Boston Bay, although it would naturally have been mentioned earlier. The river was named after De Monts, whose family name was Du Guast (also spelled Gua, or Gas).

[24] Champlain's maps greatly contract the width of the land between the coast and Lake Champlain.

[1] The swamp milkweed, or Indian hemp. S.

covered with wood, principally pines, which is connected at one end with some pretty long sand dunes; on the other side there is rather high ground. There are two islets in this bay, that one does not see unless one is within it. And in this bay the sea is almost dry at low tide. This place is very noticeable from the sea, inasmuch as the shore is very flat, except the cape at the entrance of the bay. We named it Cape St. Louis Harbor[2] it being distant two leagues from this cape, and ten from the Island Cape. It is in about the same latitude as Cape St. Louis.

We left this place,[3] and, coasting along the shore southward, we made four or five leagues and passed near a rock level with the water. Continuing our course we perceived land which we thought was islands; but, getting near it, we discovered that it was the mainland, north northwest of us, and that it was the cape of a large bay[4] more than 18 or 19 leagues in circumference, where we were so engulfed that we had to turn completely about to round the cape that we had seen. We named it Cape Blanc[5] because it was sand and dunes which looked white. A favorable wind served us well in this place, for without it we should have been in danger of being cast on the shore. This bay is very safe, provided one does not go nearer the shore than a good league, for it has no islands or rocks, except the one of which I have spoken, which is near a river that runs some distance inland.[6] We named this river Ste. Suzanne du Cap Blanc. From it to Cape St. Louis is ten leagues across. Cape Blanc is a sandy point which bends around to the south six leagues. This coast consists of lofty sand dunes, which are conspicuous as one comes from the sea. Sounding at about 15 or 18 leagues from the land one finds 30, 40 and 50 fathoms of water all the way until one comes to 10 fathoms, near the shore, which is very safe. There is a great stretch of open country on the shore before one enters the woods, which are very agreeable and pleasant to see. We anchored off the shore and noticed several savages, toward whom four of our men went. Walking on a sand dune they saw a sort of bay and some cabins bordering it all around. When they were about a league and a half from us there came dancing toward them

[2] This was the harbor of Plymouth. See *Voyages of Champlain*, II, 78, for his plan and the identification of the places on it. This harbor had been visited by Martin Pring in 1603, and Capt. John Smith explored it in 1614 and named it Plymouth.
[3] On July 19, 1605.
[4] Cape Cod Bay.
[5] Cape Cod.
[6] Wellfleet Harbor.

SAMUEL DE CHAMPLAIN

(as they told us) a savage who had come down from the high part of the coast and who returned there shortly afterward to warn those of his settlement of our coming.

The next day[7] we went to the place that our men had discovered, which we found to be a very dangerous port, because of shallows and bars, and where we saw breakers in every direction. It was almost low tide when we entered it, and there were only four feet of water in the northern passage; at high tide there are two fathoms. When we were in it we found this place rather large, perhaps three or four leagues in circumference, all surrounded by little houses, about which each occupant had as much land as was necessary for his support. A rather pretty little river empties into it. At low tide it is about three and a half feet deep. There are also two or three brooks bordered by meadows. This place would be very fine, if only the harbor were good. I took the altitude and found the latitude 42°, and the variation of the needle 18° 40'. A great many savages came to us, both men and women, who ran up from every direction dancing. We named this place Port de Mallebarre.[8]

The next day we went, with our arms, to see their settlement, going a league along the coast. Before arriving at their cabins, we entered a field planted with Indian corn in the way that we have already described. It was in flower and was five and a half feet high. There was some less advanced, planted later. We also saw a great many Brazilian beans, and squashes of various sizes, good to eat; some tobacco and some roots that they cultivated, which have the taste of the artichoke. The woods are filled with oaks, walnuts[9] and very beautiful cypresses,[10] which are reddish and have a very good odor. There were also several fields that were not cultivated at all, because they were letting the soil lie fallow; when they wish to plant it they burn the grass and then till it with their wooden spades. Their cabins are round, covered with great mats made of reeds, and on the top, in the middle, there is about a foot and a half open, where the smoke of the fires that they make escapes. We asked them if that was their settled home, and if it snowed there much; which we could not very well ascertain, as we did not know their language, although they tried as hard as they could to tell us by signs, taking some

[7] July 20.
[8] Nauset Harbor.
[9] Here probably hickories.
[10] Red cedars.

sand in their hands, then spreading it on the ground and showing that it was the color of our neck-bands and that it came upon the earth to the depth of a foot. Others of them showed us that it was less; giving us also to understand that the harbor never freezes. But we could not find out whether the snow lasted long or not. Nevertheless, I think that the region is temperate, and that the winter is not severe.[11]

None of the savages this side of the Island Cape wear either gowns or furs, except very rarely, and what gowns they do wear are made of grass and of hemp, and scarcely cover their bodies, reaching only to the thighs. They have only the private parts concealed with a small piece of skin. And the women, too, except that with them it comes down a little lower in the back than with the men. All the rest of the body is naked. When the women came to see us they wore gowns open in the front. The men cut off their hair on the top of the head, like those at the Choüacoet River. I saw, among other things, a girl with her hair dressed quite neatly, with a skin dyed red, embroidered on the upper part with little beads of shell. A part of her hair hung down her back, and the rest was braided in different ways. These people paint their faces red, black and yellow. They have almost no beard, and pull it out as fast as it grows, and their bodies are well proportioned. I do not know what government they have, and I think that in that they resemble their neighbors, who have not any, and do not know how to worship or to pray. For arms they have only pikes, clubs, bows and arrows. They appear, to look at them, good-natured and better than those in the north; but, to tell the truth, they are bad, and even the little we saw of them enabled us easily to discern their character. They are great thieves, and if they cannot secure a thing with their hands they try to do so with their feet, as we have often experienced. One should be on one's guard with these people and constantly distrust them, without ever letting them be aware of it. They bartered their bows, arrows and quivers with us for pins and buttons; and if they had had anything better they would have done the same thing. They gave us a great deal of tobacco, which they dry, then powder. When they eat Indian corn they boil it in earthen pots, which they make differently

---

[11] At this point Champlain omits the account given in his earlier narrative of the fray with the Indians, which resulted in the death of a sailor. This was the first recorded clash between the French and the Massachusetts Indians. See *Voyages of Champlain*, II, 83-84. Laverdière, *Voyages, 1613*; pp. 67-68.

SAMUEL DE CHAMPLAIN

from our method. They also bray it in wooden mortars and reduce it to flour, then make cakes and biscuits of it, like the Indians of Peru.[12]

There is some cleared land, and they are clearing some every day. This is how they do it: they cut the trees three feet from the ground, then burn the branches on the trunk, and plant their corn between these cut trees, and in the course of time take up the roots. There are also some beautiful meadows which would feed a goodly number of cattle. This harbor is very beautiful and good. There is enough water in it for ships, and one can be sheltered there behind the islands. It is in latitude 43°, and we named it Beauport.[13]

The last day of September[14] we departed from Beauport, passed by Cape St. Louis,[15] and sailed all night toward Cape Blanc.[16] In the morning, one hour before dawn, we found ourselves to the leeward of Cape Blanc, in Baye Blanche,[17] in eight feet of water, a league from the land. We anchored there, in order not to go any nearer before daylight and to see how the tide was. Meanwhile, we sent our shallop to make soundings. Not more than eight feet of water was found, so that it was necessary to decide, while we waited for daylight, what we should do. The water lowered to five feet, and sometimes our bark went aground on the sand, always without any shock or any damage, for the sea was fine and we had not less than three feet of water under us. Then the sea bean to rise, which gave us great hope.

When it was day we observed a very low, sandy shore, off which we were, only more to the leeward. Thither we sent the shallop to make soundings in the direction of some rather high land, where we thought that there was a great deal of water, and, in fact, we found there seven fathoms. We anchored there, and at the same time prepared the shallop, with nine or ten men, to go ashore to look at a place where we thought

---

[12] Nauset Harbor, on the southeast bend of Cape Cod, was the end of the exploration of 1605. The earlier narrative records a few more observations about the Indians, etc., and then tells of the return and the removal of the settlement from St. Croix to Port Royal and its history down to Sept. 5, 1606, when Poutrincourt set out to make further exploration of the coast to the south. Champlain roughly fitted the narrative of the voyage of 1606 on to that of the 1605 voyage with some overlapping. It begins in the following paragraph with some further observations about Cape Anne.

[13] Gloucester Harbor.
[14] Sept. 30, 1606.
[15] Brant Point.
[16] Cape Cod.
[17] Cape Cod Bay.

there was an excellent harbor, to which we could go if the wind should rise higher than it then was. Having explored we entered it in 2, 3 and 4 fathoms of water. When we were within we found 5 or 6 fathoms. There were a great many oysters there, which were very good. We had not seen them before, and we called the place Oyster Harbor.[18] It is in latitude 42°. Three canoes of savages came to us. This day the wind was favorable for us, and so we weighed anchor to go to Cape Blanc, distant from this place five leagues north a quarter northeast, and we doubled it.

The next day, October 2, we arrived off Mallebarre,[19] where we sojourned some time, on account of an adverse wind. During this time we went with the shallop, with a dozen or fifteen men, to visit the harbor. There a hundred and fifty savages came to meet us, singing and dancing, according to their custom. When we had seen this place we returned to our ship and, as the wind was favorable, we sailed along the coast toward the south.

CHAPTER VII

Continuation of these explorations as far as Port Fortuné, some twenty leagues from there.

WHEN we were about six leagues from Mallebarre we anchored near the shore, as the wind was unfavorable. Along the shore we perceived some smoke made by the savages, which decided us to go to see them, and, with this object, the shallop was equipped. But when we were near the beach, which is sandy, we could not reach it for the swell was too great. When the savages saw this they launched a canoe and eight or nine of them came toward us singing and making signs of the joy that they felt at seeing us. Then they showed us that lower down there was a harbor, where we could put our bark in a safe place. As the shallop could not get to the shore it came back to the bark, and the savages returned to the shore after we had treated them kindly.

The next day, the wind being favorable, we continued our course five leagues to the north,[1] and had no sooner gone thus far than we found three or four fathoms of water a league and a half from the shore. When

---

[18] Probably Barnstable Harbor. S.
[19] Nauset.
[1] A mistake for the south.

SAMUEL DE CHAMPLAIN

we had gone a little farther the bottom rose to a fathom and a half, and two fathoms, which gave us some apprehension, as we saw the sea breaking on all sides, and did not see any passage by which we could return on our course, for the wind was directly contrary.

Being thus entangled among the breakers and sand-bars it was necessary to take our chances on a passage where we could judge that there was the most water for our bark, which drew at least four feet, and we went among the breakers to where it was four and a half feet deep. At last we succeeded, by the grace of God, in getting by a sandy point which juts almost three leagues into the sea, south southeast, a very dangerous place. Doubling this cape, which we named Cap Batturier,[2] a dozen or thirteen leagues from Mallebarre, we anchored in two and a half fathoms of water, for we perceived that we were surrounded on all sides by breakers and shoals, except in some places where the sea was not so rough. We sent the shallop to find a channel, so that we might go to a place which we judged to be the one that the savages had told us about; and we thought, too, that there was a river there, where we could be safe.

When our shallop arrived there, our men went ashore and looked over the place. Then they came back, bringing a savage with them, and told us that we could enter there at high tide, which we decided to do. Immediately we weighed anchor and, under the guidance of the savage, who piloted us, we anchored at a roadstead[3] in front of the harbor, where there were six fathoms of water and a good bottom. We could not enter the harbor, for night had overtaken us.

The next day some one was sent to place beacons on the end of a sand bank at the mouth of the harbor; then, as it was high tide, we entered in two fathoms of water. When we got there we praised God that we were in a place of safety.[4] Our rudder, which had broken, had been repaired with ropes, and we feared lest, among these shallows and strong tides, it would break again, which would have caused us to be lost.

Within this harbor there is only one fathom of water, and at high tide two. On the east there is a bay which runs northward about three leagues. In it there are an island and two other little coves, which make the landscape beautiful. There is a good deal of cleared land, and there are many little hills, where they raise corn and other grains upon which they live.

---

[2] Monomoy Point. The distances are overestimated, S. Cap Batturier means Cape of Shoals.

[3] Chatham Roads, or Old Stage Harbor. S.

[4] Stage Harbor, Chatham. S.

ALGONQUIANS, HURONS AND IROQUOIS

There are also very beautiful vines there, a great many walnuts, oaks, cypresses[5] and a few pines. All the people here are very fond of tilling the soil, and store Indian corn for the winter, which they preserve in the following way: they make trenches on the hillsides in the sand, five or six feet, more or less, deep; put their corn and other grains in big sacks made of grass, and throw them into these trenches and cover them with sand three or four feet above the surface of the earth. They take from their store at need, and it is as well preserved as it could be done in our granaries.[6]

In this place we saw some five or six hundred savages who were all naked, except their private parts, which they cover with a little piece of doe-skin or seal-skin. The women also cover theirs with skins, or white leaves, and all have the hair well combed, and braided in various ways, like the Choüacoet[7] women, and are well proportioned in their bodies, which are olive-colored. They deck themselves with feathers, shell beads and other gew-gaws, which they arrange very neatly in a sort of embroidery. Their arms are bows, arrows and clubs; and they are not so much great hunters as good fishermen and husbandmen.

As to what their regulations, government and belief may be, I have only been able to conjecture, and I think that they are not different, in these respects, from our Souriquois and Canadian savages who worship neither the sun, nor the moon, nor anything else, and pray no more than the beasts. Still, they have among them some persons who, they say, have an understanding with the devil, in whom they have great faith, who tell them everything that is to befall them, although lying most of the time. They hold them as prophets, although they deceive them, as the Egyptians and Bohemians[8] do the simple villagers. They have chiefs whom they obey in questions of war, but not otherwise. They work and do not have any higher rank than their companions.

---

[5] Cedars.

[6] The Pilgrim Fathers found such stores. Bradford writes: "And heaps of sand newly padled with their hands, which they digging up, found in them diverce faire Indian baskets filled with corne, and some in eares, faire and good, of diverce collours." *History of Plymouth Plantation*, ed. 1898, p. 99. See also the other quotations in *Voyages of Champlain*, II, 121.

[7] I. e., the Maine Indians.

[8] The Gypsies. Egyptians, in the popular form, "Gypsies" came to be the common English name for these wandering fortune-tellers, while in French it came to be "Bohemians"; hence the origin of "Bohemian" in the sense of unconventional.

SAMUEL DE CHAMPLAIN

Their habitations are separated from one another according to the land that each can occupy, and are large, made circular, covered with matting, or the leaf of the Indian corn. They are furnished only with a bed or two, raised a foot from the ground, made of a number of pieces of wood piled one upon another, on top of which they put a reed mat, in the Spanish fashion (a sort of matting two or three fingers thick), on which they sleep.[9] They have a great many fleas in summer, even in the fields. When we went walking we were so covered with them that we had to change our clothes.

All the harbors, bays and shores from Choüacoet are filled with every kind of fish, like those on the coasts of Acadie, and in such abundance that I can assure you that there was not a day or a night when we did not see and hear pass by our boat more than a thousand porpoises, which were chasing the small fish. There is also a quantity of various kinds of shellfish, and especially oysters. Game birds are very abundant there.

It would be a very suitable place for building and laying the foundations of a commonwealth, if the harbor were a little deeper and the entrance to it safer than it is. It was named Port Fortuné,[10] on account of an accident that happened there. It is in latitude $41^1\!/\!_3$ degrees and is 13 leagues from Mallebarre. We saw all the surrounding country, which is very beautiful, as I have said above, and we saw a great many little houses here and there.

Having left Port Fortuné, and gone six or seven leagues, we sighted an island, which we named La Soupçonneuse,[11] because from a distance we had several times thought that it was something besides an island. Coasting along to the southwest nearly twelve leagues we passed near a river which is very small and difficult to approach, because of shallows and rocks at its mouth. I gave it my name.[12] All that we saw of this coast consists of low and sandy lands, which are not lacking in beauty and

---

[9] Cf. the quotations, from Gookin and Mourt's Relation, in *Voyages of Champlain*, II, 125.

[10] Chatham. Five men who stayed on shore overnight, contrary to Poutrincourt's orders, were surprised by the Indians and several of them killed. See *Voyages of Champlain*, II, 126-130. Laverdière, *Voyages, 1613*, 105-107.

[11] The Doubtful, Martha's Vineyard. S.

[12] This was the tidal passage commonly called Wood's Hole. It is to be regretted that those who wished to get rid of this homely name should have tried to transform Hole into a supposed Norse "Holl," an imaginary relic of the Norsemen, instead of trying to revive this earliest authentic name, Champlain River.

fertility, although hard to reach. There are no shelters, very many reefs, and there is little water for nearly two leagues from the land. The most that we found was seven or eight fathoms in some channels, though it did not extend more than the length of a cable; then one suddenly returned to two or three fathoms. No one should trust himself to it without having become very familiar with it by taking soundings.

These are all the coasts that we explored, whether in Acadie or among the Etechemins and Almouchiquois,[13] I made a very exact map of what I saw of them, which I had engraved in the year 1604,[14] and it has since been published with the accounts of my first voyages.[15]

CHAPTER VIII

Discovery from Cape la Héve to Canseau, very much in detail.

GOING from Cape de la Héve[1] to Sesambre,[2] which is an island so called by some people from St. Malo, 15 leagues from La Héve, one finds a great many islands, which we named Les Martyres, because formerly some Frenchmen were killed there by the savages. These islands are in several inlets and bays. In one of them there is a river called Ste. Marguerite,[3] seven leagues from Sesambre, in latitude 44° 25'. The coasts and islands are covered with a great many pines, firs, birches and other poor kinds of trees. Fishing is abundant and also bird-hunting.

From Sesambre we passed a very safe bay of about seven or eight leagues in extent, with no islands in it, except at the bottom, where there is the mouth of a little river with not much water in it.[4] Then, heading northeast by east, we came to a harbor eight leagues from Sesambre,

[13] I. e., whether in Nova Scotia or New England.

[14] Evidently copyist's error. No doubt the map of 1612 is meant, which is reproduced in *Voyages of Champlain*, III, 228. Slafter calls it the map of 1613, but the date on the map is 1612.

[15] Champlain omits here the account of the return voyage, of the winter of 1606-07 at Port Royal, of which Lescarbot has given such an entertaining account, and of the following spring and summer until about the middle of August, 1607. See *Voyages of Champlain*, II, 132-150. Laverdière, Voyages, 1613, 108-126.

[1] Champlain left Port Royal August 11, 1607, but he does not begin his description in this narrative until he strikes new ground, going east on the coast of Nova Scotia.

[2] Now Sambro. S.

[3] The name still survives.

[4] Halifax Harbor.

which is quite good for ships of 100 to 120 tons. At its mouth there is an island, from which, at low tide, one can go to the mainland. We named this place Port Ste. Heleine.[5] It is in latitude 44° 40', a little more or less.

From this place we went to a bay called The Bay of All Islands, which has an area of perhaps 14 or 15 leagues,[6] dangerous places on account of the sand-bars, shallows and reefs that are there. The country looks very poor, being filled with the same kinds of wood that I have mentioned above.

From there we went along to near a river six leagues distant, which is called Green Island River, because it has one at its mouth.[7] This short stretch that we went was filled with a great many rocks jutting almost a league into the sea, where the water breaks a great deal. It is in latitude 45¼°.

From there we went to a place where there is a bay and two or three islands, and a rather fine harbor,[8] three leagues from Green Island. We also passed several islands that are in a row, and named them Les Isles Rangées. They are six or seven leagues from Green Island. After this we passed by another bay,[9] where there are several islands, and went as far as a place where we found a ship which was fishing among some islands that are somewhat distant from the shore, four leagues from Les Isles Rangées. We called this place Savalette Harbor,[10] from the captain of the boat that was fishing. He was a Basque.

Leaving this place we arrived at Canseau[11] on the 27th of the month.[12] It is distant from Savalette Harbor six leagues, in which space we passed a great many islands before we reached Canseau. The raspberries on them were plentiful beyond description.

All the shores that we coasted along, from Cape Sable to this place, consist of moderately high land and cliffs; for the most part places bordered by a number of islands and reefs which jut out into the sea sometimes nearly two leagues. They are very bad for ships to approach; nev-

[5] Perpisawick Inlet. S.
[6] Nicomtau Bay and the islands in and near it.
[7] The River St. Mary and Wedge Island. L.
[8] Country Harbor.
[9] Tor Bay.
[10] White Haven.
[11] Spelled Canseau by Champlain in 1632 and Campseau in 1613. The modern English form is Canso.
[12] August. Champlain omits here the meeting with Champdoré and Lescarbot at Canseau. *Voyages of Champlain*, II, 154.

ertheless, there is no lack of good harbors and roadsteads along these coasts and islands. As for the land, it is worse and more disagreeable than in other places that we had seen, except about some rivers and brooks where the country is rather pleasant. In these places the winter must be cold, and it lasts almost six months.

This port of Canseau is among islands, and it is very hard of approach, if the weather is not good, on account of the rocks and reefs all about.

From this place to the Island of Cape Breton, which is in latitude 45¾°, and 14° 50' of the variation of the needle, it is eight leagues; and to Cape Breton 25 leagues. Between the two there is a large bay entering about nine or ten leagues into the land. It makes a passage between the Island of Cape Breton and the mainland, which extends to the great Bay of Saint Lawrence, by which one goes to Gaspé and Isle Percée, where there is fishing. This passage by the Island of Cape Breton is very narrow. Large ships do not go through it at all, although there is enough water there, because of the great currents and the violence of the tides. We named this place Running Passage.[13] It is in latitude 45¾°.

This Cape Breton Island is triangular in form, 80 leagues in circumference, and is, for the most part, mountainous land, yet in some places pleasant. In the middle of it there is a sort of lake,[14] where the sea enters from the north a quarter northeast and from the south a quarter southeast,[15] and there are many islands filled with a great deal of game, and shellfish of several kinds; among others, oysters which have not much flavor. In this place there are several harbors and places for fishing, namely, English Harbor,[16] two or three leagues from Cape Breton; and the other, Niganis, 18 or 20 leagues farther north. The Portuguese formerly wished to inhabit this island, and passed a winter there, but the severity of the weather and the cold made them abandon their settlement.[17] When I had seen all these things I returned to France, having spent four years equally divided between the settlement at St. Croix and Port Royal.[18]

[13] Le Passage Courante: the Gut or Strait of Canso.

[14] Great Bras d'or Lake.

[15] That is, the northern entrance lies north by east and the southern south by east. There is no natural entrance at the south, but one has been made by digging a canal through the narrow Isthmus of St. Peter's.

[16] Later named Louisbourg.

[17] Possibly at the time of the exploration of Fagundes, 1521. See Harrisse, *Discovery of North America*, 182, ff.

[18] More exactly three years and four months from May, 1604 to September, 1607.

BOOK III

CHAPTER I

Voyages of Sieur de Poutrincourt in New France, where he left his son, Sieur de Biencourt. The Jesuit fathers who were sent there, and their progress in making the Christian faith flourish.[1]

THE late Sieur de Poutrincourt, the elder, having obtained a grant from Sieur de Monts, in virtue of his commission, of some lands adjacent to Port Royal, which he had abandoned, the settlement remaining in his right, this Sieur de Poutrincourt made every endeavor to settle it and left there his son, Sieur de Biencourt, whom, while he was considering how to establish himself there, the people of Rochelle and the Basques assisted in most of his expeditions, in the hope of getting furs by this means. But his plan did not succeed as he wished, for the very charitable Madame de Guercheville interfered in this matter, in kindness and consideration toward the Jesuit fathers. This is the account of it.

This Sieur Jean de Poutrincourt, before Sieur de Monts left New France, asked him for Port Royal as a grant. This he bestowed upon him, on condition that within the following two years this Sieur de Poutrincourt should go there himself with several other families, to cultivate and settle the country; which he promised to do in the year 1607. The late King Henry the Great ratified and confirmed this grant and told the late Reverend Father Coton that he wished to make use of their company for the conversion of savages, promising two thousand livres for their maintenance. Father Coton obeyed the commandment of His Majesty; and among others of their fathers Father Biard presented himself to be employed in so holy a voyage; and in the year 1608 he was sent

[1] In his account of these events Champlain followed very closely Father Biard's *Relation de la Nouvelle France*, etc., Lyons, 1616, for which see Thwaites's *Jesuit Relations*, vols. III and IV.

to Bordeaux, where he remained a long time without hearing anything further of the expedition to Canada.

In the year 1609 Sieur de Poutrincourt arrived at Paris. The King having been informed of it, and knowing that contrary to His Majesty's expectations, he had not stirred from France, was very much vexed with him. In order to please His Majesty, he equipped himself for the voyage. Upon this resolution Father Coton offered to give him some monks. Then Sieur de Poutrincourt told him that it would be better to wait until the next year, promising that as soon as he should arrive at Port Royal he would send back his son, with whom the Jesuit fathers could come.

In fact, in the year 1610, this Sieur de Poutrincourt set out at the end of February and reached Port Royal in the month of June following, where, having assembled as many savages as he could, he had about twenty-five of them baptized on Saint John the Baptist's Day [June 24] by a priest called Messire Josué Fleche, surnamed The Patriarch.

A little while afterward he sent Sieur de Biencourt, his son, aged 19, back to France to carry the good news of the baptism of the savages, and to arrange that he should soon be assisted with provisions, with which he was ill-supplied, to pass the winter there.[2]

The Reverend Father Christofle Balthazar, Provincial, commissioned the fathers Pierre Biard and Remond Masse to go with Sieur de Biencourt. The King—Louis the Just—caused to be delivered to them five hundred crowns promised by the King, his father, and several rich ornaments given by Madame de Guercheville and Madame de Sourdis. When they arrived at Dieppe there was some discussion among the Jesuit fathers and the merchants, which caused the fathers to retire to their College of Eu.

When Madame de Guercheville knew this, she was very indignant that the tradesmen had been so presumptuous as to have offended and thwarted these fathers, and said that they ought to be punished; but their only chastisement lay in their not being admitted to the expedition. And, knowing that the equipment would not go above four thousand livres, she took up a collection in the court, and by this kind action she got that sum, with which she paid the merchants who had troubled these fathers, and cut them off from all association with them; and, with

---

[2] To see how closely Champlain followed Biard's *Relation*, cf. *Jesuit Relations*, III, 615.

the rest of this sum and other large property, she established a fund for the maintenance of these fathers, not wishing them to be a charge to Sieur de Poutrincourt. She also arranged that the profits that came from furs and fish, which the ship should bring back, should not revert to the benefit of the associates and other merchants, but should go back to Canada, in the possession of Sieur Robin and Sieur de Biencourt, who should use it for the support of Port Royal and the French who were living there.

In reference to this it was decided and ordained that since this money of Madame de Guercheville had been designed for the benefit of Canada, the Jesuits should take part in the profits of the association of Sieur Robin and Sieur de Biencourt, and share them with them.

It was this contract of partnership that spread about so many rumors, complaints and outcries against the Jesuit fathers, who, in that and everything else, are justly governed according to God and to reason, to the shame and confusion of those who envy and malign them.

On January 26, 1611, the same fathers embarked with this Sieur de Biencourt, whom they helped with money to get the ship off, and to alleviate the great want that they experienced in this voyage; since, in coasting along the shores, they stopped and sojourned in several places before arriving at Port Royal, which was on June 12, 1611,[3] Whitsunday; and during this voyage these fathers had a great scarcity of provisions, and of other things, according to the accounts of the pilot, David de Bruges, and the captain, Jean Daune—both of them of the so-called reformed religion—who confessed that they found these good fathers quite different from what they had been described.

Sieur de Poutrincourt, desiring to return to France, to order his affairs better, left his son, Sieur de Biencourt, and the Jesuit fathers behind him. Altogether, they numbered about twenty persons. He left there in the middle of July of the same year, 1611, and arrived in France at the end of the month of August.

During the winter this Sieur de Biencourt caused annoyances to the people of the son of Pontgravé, whose name was Robert Gravé, whom he treated pretty badly; but, at last, through the efforts of the Jesuit fathers, everything was pacified, and they remained good friends.

As Sieur de Poutrincourt was seeking in France every means of aiding his son, Madame de Guercheville, who was pious, virtuous and very

---

[3] The correct date is May 22. L.

much devoted to the conversion of the savages, having already collected some funds, communicated with him in regard to the matter, and said that she would very gladly join the company, and that she would send some Jesuit fathers with him for the aid of Canada.

The contract of partnership was approved, this lady being empowered by her husband, Monsieur de Liencour, first Equerry of the King and Governor of Paris. By the contract it was fixed that she should, at this time, give a thousand crowns for the cargo of a ship, provided that she should share the profit that this voyage should yield, and of the lands that the King had given to Sieur de Poutrincourt, as set down in the original of the contract. This Sieur de Poutrincourt reserved for himself Port Royal, and its lands; not intending that they should be included in the common stock of the other lordships, capes, harbors and provinces that he said he had in this country near Port Royal. This lady requested him to produce titles to show that these lordships and lands belonged to him and how he possessed so large a domain. But he excused himself by saying that his titles and papers were in New France.

When this lady heard this, as she was suspicious of Sieur de Poutrincourt, and wished to guard herself against being taken by surprise, she made a contract with Sieur de Monts that he should cede back to her all the rights, deeds and claims that he had, or ever had had, in New France, derived from the gift made him by the late Henry the Great. Madame de Guercheville obtained letters from His Majesty, now reigning, in which the gift was made anew to her of all the lands of New France from the great river as far as Florida, excepting only Port Royal, which was what Sieur de Poutrincourt possessed then, and nothing else.

This lady gave money to the Jesuit fathers to put into the hands of some merchant at Dieppe, but this Sieur de Poutrincourt inveigled these same fathers into giving him four hundred of this thousand crowns.

He sent, in charge of this expedition, an employee of his called Simon Imbert Sandrier, who acquitted himself rather badly in the management of this equipped and freighted ship. He left Dieppe December 31, in the height of winter, and reached Port Royal January 23, the next year, 1612.

Sieur de Biencourt was very glad, on the one hand, to see fresh aid coming; and, on the other hand, he was annoyed that Madame de Guercheville was out of the company,[4] according to what this Imbert

---

[4] Madame de Guercheville through acquiring De Monts's titles and through the king's grant had become the proprietary of all the northeastern coast with the exception of Port Royal, an accession of power which superseded the partnership with Poutrincourt.

SAMUEL DE CHAMPLAIN

told him. He was also disturbed by complaints that the Jesuit fathers made to him of the bad management of this expedition by this Imbert, who wrongfully and without cause accused the fathers. Nevertheless, they obliged him to confess that he was fooling when he spoke to this Sieur de Biencourt.[5]

At last, all these matters having quieted down and been pardoned, Father Masse, who was with the savages to learn their language, became ill in a place where he was in great want, for everything was in disorder in this settlement. Father Biard lived at Port Royal, where he suffered great fatigue and great want during several days, being compelled to collect some acorns and roots for his sustenance.

Meanwhile, they were fitting out a vessel in France to withdraw the Jesuits from Port Royal, and found a new settlement in another place. The captain of this vessel was La Saussaye, who had with him thirty persons who were to winter there, including two Jesuits and their servants, who were to land at Port Royal. He already had with him two other Jesuit fathers, namely: Father Quentin and Father Gilbert du Thet, but they were to go back to France with the crew, which numbered 38. The Queen had contributed to the expense for arms, powder and ammunition. The ship was 100 tons burden. It left Honfleur March 12, in the year 1613, and reached La Héve, in Acadie, May 16, where they set up the arms of Madame de Guercheville as a sign of possession. They came to Port Royal, where they found only five persons—two Jesuit fathers, Hébert, an apothecary (who took the place of Sieur de Biencourt while he went to a long distance to look for provisions), and two other persons. It was to him that they presented the letters from the Queen to release the fathers and permit them to go wherever it seemed good to them; which was done, and these fathers withdrew their goods from the country and left some provisions to this Hébert, so that he should not be in need.

They went from this place, and settled the desert mountains at the mouth of the Pemetegoet,[6] River. The pilot reached the coast on the east of the Island of Mount Desert,[7] where the fathers stayed, and they gave thanks to God, erecting a cross, and had the holy sacrifice of the Mass; and this place was named St. Sauveur.[8] It is in latitude 44⅓ degrees.

---

[5] Cf. Biard in *Jesuit Relations*, III, 239-243.
[6] Penobscot.
[7] L'isle des Monts Deserts.
[8] Frenchman's Bay. Parkman, *Pioneers of France*, 302. Cf. Biard's *Relation, Jesuit Relations*, III, 265.

ALGONQUIANS, HURONS AND IROQUOIS

They had scarcely begun to settle themselves there, and to clear the land, when the English appeared and gave them something quite different to be concerned about.

Ever since the English had established themselves in Virginia, in order to provide themselves with codfish they had been accustomed to come to fish sixteen leagues from the Island of Mount Desert; and, arriving there for this purpose in the year 1613, they were caught by the fogs and cast up on the shores of the savages of Pemetegoet, who, supposing them to be French, told them that there were others of them at St. Sauveur. The English being in need of provisions, and all the men in poor condition, ragged and half-naked, found out all they could about the strength of these Frenchmen; and having got a response in accordance with their desire, they went straight to them and made ready to fight them. The Frenchmen, seeing a single ship at full sail approaching, without knowing that ten others were near by, recognized that it was English. Immediately Sieur de la Motte le Vilin, Lieutenant Saussaye and some others rushed on board their ship to defend it. La Saussaye remained on shore with most of his men; but, in the end, the English, being stronger than the French, after some fighting took our men. The English numbered 60 soldiers and had 14 pieces of cannon. In this fight Gilbert du Thet was killed by a musket shot; some others were wounded and the rest were captured, except Lamets and four others who ran away. Afterward they went aboard the French ship, took possession of it, pillaged what they found there and took away the commission of the King which La Saussaye had in his chest. The captain who commanded this ship was named Samuel Argall.

The enemy went ashore and hunted for La Saussaye, who had fled to the woods. The next day he came to find the Englishman, who received him kindly. Being asked for his commission he went to his chest to get it, believing that it had not been opened. He found there all his clothes and conveniences, except the commission, which greatly astonished him. And then the Englishman, feigning indignation, said to him: "What? You gave us to understand that you had a commission from the King, your master, and cannot produce it? Then you are outlaws and pirates who deserve death." Thereupon the English divided the plunder among themselves.

The Jesuit fathers, seeing the danger to which the French were exposed, labored with Argall until they succeeded in pacifying the English, and Father Biard, by strong arguments, proved to him that all their men were people of substance, and recommended by His Most Christian Majesty. The Englishman made believe that he agreed with him, and accepted the arguments of the fathers, and they said to Sieur de la Saussaye: "It is altogether your fault to let your letters get lost in that way." And afterward they had these same fathers to dine at their table.

There was talk of sending the Frenchmen back to France, but they did not wish to give them anything but a shallop for the thirty of them, to go in search of a passage along the coast. The fathers explained to them that it was impossible for a shallop to suffice to carry them without danger. And then Argall said: "I have found another device to take them to Virginia." The workmen were promised that they should not be forced in point of religion, and that after one year of service they should be sent back to France, and three of them accepted this offer. Sieur de la Motte, also, had consented, from the beginning, to go to Virginia with this English captain, who honored him because he had found him doing his duty; and he allowed him to take some of his men with him and Father Biard; that they should be four, namely, two fathers and two others, and that they should be taken to the islands where the English fish for cod, and that he should give orders to them that by their means he[9] could pass over to France. This the English captain granted him very willingly.

In this way it was possible for the shallop to carry the men divided into three companies. Fifteen were with the pilot who had got away, fifteen with the Englishman, and fifteen in the shallop that had been given, in which Father Masse was; and it was delivered into the hands of La Saussaye, and this same Father Masse, with some provisions; but there were no sailors. By good fortune the pilot met it, which was a great benefit to them, and they went as far as Sesambre, beyond La Héve, where Robert Gravé's ship and another ship were. They divided the Frenchmen into two companies, to take them over to France, and arrived at St. Malo without having run any risk from storms.

Captain Argall took the fifteen Frenchmen and the Jesuit fathers to Virginia. When they got there the head man of the place, called the Marshal, the military commander of the country, threatened to put the fathers and all the Frenchmen to death, but Argall opposed him with all his power, saying that he had given them his word. And, seeing that he

---

[9] It should be "they." Cf. the passage in Biard's *Relation, Jesuit Relations*, IV, 22, 23.

ALGONQUIANS, HURONS AND IROQUOIS

was too weak to sustain and defend them, he resolved to show the commissions that he had taken; and when the Marshal saw them he was appeased, and promised that the word that had been given them should be kept to them.

This Marshal assembled his council and resolved to go to the coast of Acadie, and there to raze all the habitations and fortresses as far as latitude 46°, with the pretence that all that country belonged to him.[10]

Upon this resolution of the Marshal, Argall resumed his course with three vessels, divided the Frenchmen among them and returned to St. Sauveur. He thought he should find La Saussaye there, and a ship recently arrived, but he learned that he had returned to France. They set up a cross there, in place of that which the fathers had placed there, which they broke down, and on theirs they inscribed the name of the King of Great Britain, for whom they took possession of this place.

Then they went to St. Croix, which he burned. He also took away all the landmarks that were there, and carried off a supply of salt that they found in it.[11]

Afterward he went to Port Royal, guided by a savage whom he took by force, the Frenchmen being unwilling to direct him. He went ashore, made an entrance, saw the dwelling and, not finding any one in it, took what there was of plunder, had it burned, and in two hours the whole was in ashes. And he took all the landmarks that the French had put there, so that those who were there were forced to abandon this abode and go with the savages.

A wicked and unnatural Frenchman, who was with those who escaped into the woods, approaching the edge of the water, shouted loudly and demanded that they should parley. This was granted him, and then he said: "I was surprised that, since there is with you a Spanish Jesuit, named Father Biard, you do not put him to death for a bad man who will do you harm if he can, if you let him." Is it possible that the French nation produces such monsters of men, so detestable as sowers of calumnious falsehoods, in order to make these good fathers lose their lives?

---

[10] Biard adds that Argall was instructed to hang La Saussaye and his men. *Jesuit Relations*, IV, 34, 35. This order of Dale's may be compared with the destruction of the French in Florida by Menendez, except that Menendez acted under instructions from the King, while it is hard to see any basis, whatever, of authority for Dale's action. Cf. Parkman's strong expressions, *Pioneers of France*, 312-13.

[11] Cf. Biard, *Jesuit Relations*, IV, 37.

SAMUEL DE CHAMPLAIN

The English left Port Royal November 9, 1613. In this voyage the winds and storms were such that the three ships got separated from one another. The bark in which there were six Englishmen could not be recovered afterward, but Captain Argall's ship reached Virginia. He informed him[12] who Father Biard was and he[13] took him to be a Spaniard, and was waiting for him to put him to death.[14] He[15] was then in the third vessel, which was under the command of a captain named Turnel, a mortal enemy of the Jesuits; and this vessel was so beaten about by the southwest wind that, bearing off to the east, he was obliged to stand for the Azores, 500 leagues from Virginia. They now killed all the horses that had been taken from Port Royal, which they ate in lieu of other provisions. At last they reached an island of the Azores, and then he said to the father: "God is provoked with us, and not with you,[16] for the evil that we have made you suffer unjustly. But I am surprised that Frenchmen off there in the woods, in the midst of so much misery and apprehension, should have spread the rumor that you are Spanish; and they not only said it and assured us of it, but they signed the statement."

"Monsieur," said the father, "you know that, in spite of all the calumnies and slanders, I never spoke ill of those who accused me; you are witness of the patience that I have had in the face of such adversity, but God knows the truth. Not only have I never been in Spain, nor has any of my relatives, but I am a good and loyal Frenchman in the service of God, and of my King, and I shall always show, at the peril of my life, that they are wrong who slander me, and who call me Spanish. God forgive them, and may He be pleased to deliver us from their hands, and you particularly, for our good, and let us forget the past."

Then they went to anchor in the roadstead of the island of Fayal, which is one of the Azores; but they were obliged to anchor in this harbor[17] and to hide the fathers in some place in the hold of the ship,

---

[12] I. e, Argall told Dale, the Governor of Virginia. See Biard's *Relation, Jesuit Relations*, IV, 52, 53.

[13] I. e., Governor Dale.

[14] This sentence is very blind in the French. It has been interpreted in the light of Biard's *Relation*, from which the story was hastily compiled.

[15] I. e., Father Biard.

[16] The French here "et nous contre vous" (and we with you). Biard's text has "mais non pas contre vous." It is evident that the copyist, or compositor, substituted "nous" for "non pas." Cf. *Jesuit Relations*, IV, 56, 57.

[17] I. e., they finally had to enter the harbor, instead of anchoring outside in the roadstead.

ALGONQUIANS, HURONS AND IROQUOIS

and make them give their word that they would not reveal themselves, which they promised.

The ship was inspected by the Portuguese, who went down where the fathers were. The latter saw them without making any sign; and, nevertheless, if they had made themselves known to the Portuguese, they would have been delivered at once, and all the English would have been hanged; but these inspectors, as a result of not looking carefully, did not see the Jesuit fathers at all, and went back to land; and thus the English were delivered from the danger in which they were of being hanged. They went to fetch all that they needed, then weighed anchor, put to sea, and expressed many thanks to the fathers, whom they caressed; and, no longer thinking them Spanish, they treated them as kindly as possible; they admired their great constancy and virtue in enduring the things that they had said to them, and were nothing but kindness and witnesses of good friendship until they reached England; the fathers having shown them in this way what was contrary to the opinion of a good many enemies of the Catholic church and to the prejudice of the truth, namely: that their doctrine teaches that it is not necessary to keep the faith with heretics.

At last Argall[18] reached the harbor of Milfier,[19] in the year 1614, in the province of Wales, where the captain was imprisoned for having neither passport nor commission. His General had it and had become separated from him, as his Vice-Admiral had done.[20] The Jesuit fathers told how it all took place, and afterward Captain Argall[21] was released, and returned to his ship, and the fathers were kept on land, loved and cherished by many people. And, in consequence of the account that the captain of their ship gave of what took place in the Azores, the news came to London, to the Court of the King of Great Britain, where the ambassador of His Most Christian Majesty hastened on the release of the fathers. They were conducted to Dover, and from there went to France, and withdrew to their College in Amiens, after having been nine months and a half in the hands of the English.

---

[18] Champlain here, in hurried compilation, forgot that Argall got back safely to Virginia, and that it was Turnel who was driven to the Azores and then went to England. See above, p. 151 [p. 73].

[19] Milford.

[20] Argall probably had the commission, but whether he is referred to by the "General" or "Vice-Admiral" is not clear. Only one superior to Turnel is mentioned by Biard. *Jesuit Relations*, IV, 68-69.

[21] Turnel.

SAMUEL DE CHAMPLAIN

Sieur de la Motte also arrived in England at the same time, in a vessel which came from the Bermudas, having been to Virginia. He was captured in his ship and arrested, but released through the mediation of Monsieur du Biseau, at that time ambassador of the King in England.

Madame de Guercheville, having been informed of all this, sent La Saussaye to London to ask for the restoration of the ship, and that was all that one could obtain at that time. Three Frenchmen died in Virginia and four remained there while a great effort was being made for their release.

The fathers baptized there thirty little children, except three who were baptized at the approach of death.[22]

It must be admitted that this enterprise was thwarted by many misfortunes that one could well have avoided at the beginning, if Madame de Guercheville had given three thousand six hundred livres to Sieur de Monts, who wished to have a settlement at Quebec, and everything quite different. I spoke of it two or three times to the Reverend Father Coton, who managed this affair. He would have liked to have the treaty made with few conditions, or by other means, which could not be to the advantage of this Sieur de Monts, which was the reason why nothing was done; although I was able to explain to this father what advantages he could have in the conversion of the infidels, as well as for the commerce and traffic that could be carried on by means of the great River Saint Lawrence much better than in Acadie, which is difficult to secure, on account of the infinite number of its harbors, which cannot be guarded without large forces. Acadie, furthermore, is little peopled with savages; and, in addition, one cannot get through these regions into the interior where there are a number of inhabitants of sedentary character. This can be done by the River Saint Lawrence much more easily than by the shores of Acadie.

Still further [I told him] that the Englishman[23] who was fishing at that time near some islands 13 to 14 leagues from the Island of Mount Desert, which is at the mouth of the River Pemetegoet, would do what he could to injure our men, as he was near Port Royal and other places. This could not then be expected at Quebec, where the English are not

---

[22] Too hastily condensed. Biard says the Jesuits baptized "about twenty, and these were little children, except three," etc. *Jesuit Relations*, IV, 87.

[23] The singular number here should probably be a plural. Perhaps the text was dictated to a copyist who, in the phrase, faisait alors ses pesches, may have written "faisait" for "fasaient."

ALGONQUIANS, HURONS AND IROQUOIS

acquainted at all. If this Madame de Guercheville had taken possession of Quebec at that time, one could have had assurance that by the watchfulness of the Jesuit fathers, and the instructions that I could have given them, the country would have been much better supplied; and that the Englishman would not have found it stripped of provisions and of arms, and would not have taken possession of it, as he has done in these last wars.[24] He has done this as a result of the acts of some bad Frenchmen, added to the fact that then these fathers did not have with them any man to conduct their affairs, except La Saussaye, who was little experienced in knowledge of places. But it is in vain that men talk and act; one cannot avoid what it pleases God to arrange.

All this shows how enterprises planned in haste, and without any solid foundation, and carried out without regard for the real substance of the affair, always come out badly.

CHAPTER II

Second undertaking of Sieur de Monts. Advice that the author gave him. Obtains commission from the King. His departure. Buildings that the author makes in Quebec. Outcries against Sieur de Monts.

LET us return and follow the second undertaking of Sieur de Monts, who did not lose courage at all, and did not wish to dally in so good a course. The Reverend Father Coton having refused to come to an agreement with him about the 3,600 livres, he spoke especially with me of his plans. I gave him counsel, and advised him to go to settle on the great River Saint Lawrence, with which I was familiar through the voyage that I had made to it;[1] and I gave him a taste of the reasons why it was more appropriate and convenient to inhabit that place than any other. He resolved upon it; and with this end he spoke of it to His Majesty, who agreed with him, and gave him a commission to go to settle in the country. And to enable him to sustain the expense more easily, he interdicted the traffic of furs to all his subjects for one year only.[2]

---

[24] Champlain refers to the capture of Quebec by the Kirkes in 1629. The story is told in Parkman, *Pioneers of France*, 435-445.

[1] In 1603. See below, vol. II, pp. 151-229 [201-238].

[2] The commission is given in *Voyages of Champlain*, II, 160-163; and in the original in Laverdière, *Voyages, 1613*, 136-137.

SAMUEL DE CHAMPLAIN

For this purpose he had two ships equipped at Honfleur and made me his lieutenant in the country of New France in the year 1608. Pont Gravé started first to go to Tadoussac, and I went after him in a ship loaded with things necessary and suitable for a settlement. God favored us so fortunately that we arrived at the harbor of Tadoussac,[3] on that river, at which place I had all the goods unloaded, with the men, laborers and artisans, to go up the river to find a place convenient and suitable for a settlement. When I had found the narrowest place in the river, which the natives call Quebec,[4] I had a settlement built and established there, and had the ground cleared, and had some garden plots made. But while we were working with so much labor, let us see what was going on in France with regard to the carrying out of this undertaking.

Sieur de Monts had stayed in Paris, on account of some affairs of his son; and, while hoping that His Majesty would continue to allow him this commission, he had not been long in peace when it was insisted more than ever that he ought to go to the Council. The Bretons, Basques, Rochelois and Normans renewed the complaints;[5] and, gaining the ears of those who wished to befriend them, said that it was a people that was concerned, that it was a public interest. But it was not perceived that these were envious people, who did not ask for their own good, but rather for their ruin, as will become evident in the sequel of this narrative.

However that may have been, the commission was revoked for the second time, without any power to stop it. It would be necessary, on this account, to return from Quebec the next spring; so that he who should put the most into it would lose the most; and this would, no doubt, be Sieur de Monts, who wrote me what had taken place. This gave me occasion to return to France to view these commotions. The building remained in the hands of Sieur de Monts, who came to an agreement in regard to it with his partners some time later. He, meanwhile, put it into the hands of a certain merchant of La Rochelle, under stated conditions, to serve them as a shelter where they could deposit their merchandise and trade with the savages. It was at that time that I made the overture to

---

[3] June 3, 1608.

[4] Champlain omits here the incidents of the stay at Tadoussac, of his exploration of the Saguenay and of the voyage to Quebec. Cf. *Voyages of Champlain*, II, 164-175. Some of the details are inserted below, p. 168, ff. [p. 82, ff.]

[5] I.e., against De Monts's monopoly privileges.

ALGONQUIANS, HURONS AND IROQUOIS

the Reverend Father Coton, for Madame de Guercheville,[6] to see if she wished to have it; which could not be, as I have said above, since the trade was open until another commission should be issued which should afford a better regulation than in the past.

I went to find Sieur de Monts, to whom I explained all that had taken place in our winter quarters, and what I had been able to discover and learn of the conveniences that one might hope for on the great River St. Lawrence; which was the occasion of my seeing His Majesty, in order to give him a special account, in which he took great pleasure. Sieur de Monts, in the meantime, carried away by a desire to keep his hold on this matter at whatever cost, at once did all that he could to have a new commission. But those who envied him, by means of favor at court, had so shaped matters that his labor was in vain. Observing this, on account of the desire that he had to see his lands peopled, he did not give up wishing to continue the settlement, even without a commission, and to have the interior of the country up this river explored more in detail. And for the execution of this enterprise he united with the Company to have some vessels equipped, as did several others, to whom the traffic was not interdicted, who followed in our footsteps and carried off the gain derived from the pains of our labor, without having been willing to contribute to the undertakings.

When the ships were ready, Pont Gravé and I set sail[7] to make this voyage in the year 1610, with artisans and other laborers, and hindered by bad weather. Arriving at the harbor of Tadoussac,[8] and at that of Quebec, we found each one there in good spirit.

Before going farther I have thought that it would not be out of place to write a description of the great river, and of some discoveries that I made up this St. Lawrence River; of its beauty and the fertility of the country, and of what took place in the wars against the Iroquois.[9]

[6] See above, p. 158 [p. 77].
[7] March 7.
[8] April 26.
[9] Champlain now goes back to the events of 1608 in Canada.

SAMUEL DE CHAMPLAIN

CHAPTER III

Departure of the author, to go to settle the great River St. Lawrence. Description of the harbor of Tadoussac; of the River Saguenay; of the Isle of Orleans.

AFTER having recounted to the late King all that I had seen and discovered, I set sail to go to settle the great River St. Lawrence at Quebec, as the lieutenant, at that time, of Sieur de Monts. I left Honfleur April 13, 1608, and the third of June arrived at Tadoussac,[1] 80 or 90 leagues from Gaspé, and anchored in the roadstead of Tadoussac, which is one league from the harbor. This is like a cove at the mouth of the River Saguenay, where there is a tide that is very strange on account of its swiftness. Here sometimes violent winds rise and bring on great cold. It is said that it is 45 or 50 leagues from the harbor of Tadoussac to the first fall of this river,[2] which comes from the north northwest. This harbor is small, and it could not hold more than twenty ships. There is enough water, and it lies in the shelter of the River Saguenay and of a little rocky island which is almost intersected by the sea. The rest is high mountains, where there is little land, unless it be rocks and sand covered with trees, such as firs and birches. There is a little pond near the harbor enclosed by mountains covered with trees. At the entrance of the harbor there are two points, one on the southwest side running out nearly a league into the sea, which is called the Point aux Allouettes;[3] the other on the northwest side running out an eighth of a league and called Rocky Point.[4] The winds from the south southeast strike the harbor, but are not to be feared, but the wind from the Saguenay certainly is. The two points just mentioned are dry at low tide.

In this place there were a number of savages who came there to trade in furs. Many of them came to our ship with their canoes, which are eight or nine feet long and about a foot or a foot and a half wide in the middle, and diminish at both ends. They are very apt to upset if one does not know well how to manage them. They are made of birch bark, strengthened inside with little hoops of white cedar, very neatly arranged, and they are so light that a man can easily carry one of them. Each one can carry the weight of a hogshead. When they wish to cross the land, to

---

[1] See above, p. 162 [p. 79].
[2] The Saguenay.
[3] Lark Point.
[4] Now called Pointe aux Vaches.

go to some river where they have business, they carry them with them. From Choüacoet[5] all along the coast as far as Tadoussac they are all alike.

I visited some places on the River Saguenay, which is a beautiful river and very deep, say from 80 to 100 fathoms. Fifty leagues from the mouth of the harbor, it is said, there is a great waterfall,[6] which comes from a very high place and with great impetuosity. There are some very barren islands in this river, being nothing but rocks covered with small firs and heather. The river is half a league wide in some places and a quarter at its mouth, where the current is so strong that it still flows out when the tide is three-quarters flood in the St. Lawrence. All the land that I saw consisted of nothing but mountains and promontories of rock, for the most part covered with firs and birches—a country very disagreeable from whatever point of view; in short, it is a real desert without inhabitants. When I went hunting in the places that seemed to me the most pleasant I found nothing but little birds like swallows, and some river birds that come there in summer. Except those there are none at all, on account of the excessive cold of that region. This river comes from the northwest.[7]

The savages informed me that after passing the first rapid they pass eight others, then go a day without finding any; and then again they pass ten others and come to a lake[8] which takes them three days. In each day they can easily make ten leagues going up stream. At the end of the lake there are people who are nomads. There are three rivers that empty into this lake. One comes from the north, very near the sea,[9] where they said it was a great deal colder than in their country; the other two come from other regions of the interior, where there are tribes of savages who are nomads and live by hunting only. This is the region where our savages go to carry the merchandise that we give them in exchange for the furs that they have, such as beaver, marten, lynx and others, which are there in great quantity and which they then bring to our ships. These northern people said to our men that they see the salt water; and if that is true, as I think is certainly so, it cannot be anything but a gulf which cuts into the land on the north.[10] The savages said that it might be forty

---

[5] The Saco River, Maine.

[6] Probably the falls of the Chicoutimi, 45 feet high. The Chicoutimi empties into the Saguenay about 95 miles above Tadoussac.

[7] Cf. the narrative of the voyage of 1603, vol. II, p. 175, below. [p. 212]

[8] Lake St. John.

[9] The Mistassini, by which the Indians went to Hudson Bay. L.

[10] Hudson Bay.

or fifty days' journey from this sea on the north to the harbor of Tadoussac, because of the difficulty of the roads and rivers, and because the country is very mountainous and is covered with snow the greater part of the year. This is a true statement of what I learned of this stream. I have often wished to make this discovery, but I have not been able to do it without the savages, who have been unwilling to have me or any other of our men go with them. Nevertheless, they have promised me that I shall go.[11]

CHAPTER IV

Discovery of the Hare Island; of the Island of Coudres, and of the Falls of Montmorency

I left Tadoussac[1] to go to Quebec, and passed near an island which is called Hare Island, about six leagues from this port. It is two leagues from the land on the north and nearly four leagues from the land on the south. From Hare Island we went to a little river which is dry at low tide, where at some 700 to 800 paces inland there are two waterfalls. We named it Salmon River,[2] on account of catching some there. Running along the northern shore we came to a point that projects into the sea, which we named Cape Dauphin,[3] three leagues from Salmon River. From there we went to a cape that we named Eagle Cape,[4] eight leagues from Cape Dauphin. Between the two there is a large bay, at the head of which is a little river that dries up at low tide, and we named it Flat River or Malle Baye.[5] From Eagle Cape we went to the Isle aux Coudres,[6] a league distant and about a league and a half long.[7] It is somewhat level and grows narrower at the ends. At the western end there are some meadows and rocky points, which project somewhat into the river; and on

---

[11] Champlain never had this opportunity. Hudson Bay was first approached from the land side in 1662 by Radisson and Chouart, more commonly called Grosseilliers, his landed title. Cf. S. E. Dawson, *The St. Lawrence*, 323-325.

[1] June 30, 1608.

[2] It is now Black River. S.

[3] Cape Salmon.

[4] Goose Cape. S.

[5] The modern spelling is Malbaie; part of it is now named Murray Bay.

[6] The name is still in use. It means Hazel Island.

[7] The translation here follows Laverdière's reconstruction of the text. *Voyages, 1632*; part I, p. 134.

the southwest side there are many reefs; yet it is attractive, on account of the woods that surround it. It is distant about half a league from the land on the north, where there is a little river that comes from some distance in the interior, which we named Rivière du Gouffre,[8] since abreast of it the tide runs with extraordinary swiftness; and, although it looks calm, it is always much in motion, its depth being very great; but the river itself is shallow, and there are a great many rocks at its mouth and all about it. From the Isle aux Coudres we coasted along the shore and reached a cape that we named the Cap de Tourmente,[9] which is seven leagues from it, and we called it that because, with ever so little wind, the water rises as if it were high tide. In this place the water begins to be fresh. From there we went to the Island of Orleans, two leagues, on the south side of which there are a number of islands—low, covered with trees and very pleasant, full of large meadows and a great deal of game. Some of these islands are, as far as I could judge, two leagues long, and others a little more or less. All about them there are a great many rocks and shallows that are very dangerous to cross. These are about two leagues distant from the mainland on the south. All this shore, both on the north and on the south, from Tadoussac to the Island of Orleans, is mountainous and the soil is very poor, with nothing but pines, firs and birches, and some very bad rocks; and in the greater part of these places one would not know how to go.

Then we skirted the Island of Orleans on the south side, which is a league and a half from the mainland, and on the north side it is half a league. It is six leagues long and one league wide, or a league and a half in some places. It is very pleasant on the north side, owing to the great extent of woods and meadows; but the passage on that side is very dangerous, because of the great number of points and rocks between the mainland and the island. There are a great many beautiful oaks on the island, and in some places nut trees, and on the edges of the woods vines and other trees such as we have in France.

This place is the beginning of the beautiful and fertile country of the great river and is 120 leagues from its mouth. At the end of the island there is a torrent of water from the north side, which I named the Falls of Montmorency. It comes from a lake which is about ten leagues in the

[8] The name is still in use. It means River of the Whirlpool. S.
[9] Cape Tourmente, 1920 feet high. The name means Tempest Cape.

interior and it falls from a height of nearly 25 fathoms,[10] above which the land is level and pleasant to look at, although inland there are seen high mountains, which seem to be from 15 to 20 leagues distant.

CHAPTER V

Arrival of the author at Quebec, where he made his place of abode. Habits of the savages of that Country.

FROM the Island of Orleans to Quebec it is one league. When I arrived there on July 3[1] I looked for a suitable place for our buildings, but I could not find any more convenient or better situated than the point of Quebec, so called by the savages, which is filled with nut trees and vines. I immediately employed some of our workmen in cutting them down, in order to put our buildings there.[2] Some I set to sawing boards, some to digging a cellar and making ditches, and others I sent to Tadoussac with the boat to get our supplies. The first thing that we made was the storehouse in which to put our provisions under cover, which was promptly finished through the diligence of each one and the care that I had of it. Near this place is a pleasant river, where formerly Jacques Cartier passed the winter.[3]

While the ship-carpenters, the wood-sawers and other workmen, worked on our lodging I set all the others at clearing the land about the building, in order to make the garden-plots in which to sow grain and seeds, to see how they would all turn out, for the soil appeared very good.

Meanwhile a great many savages were in cabins near us, fishing for eels, which begin to come about September 15 and go away on October 15. At this time all the savages live on this manna and dry enough of it to last through the winter to the month of February, when the snow is

---

[10] The height of the falls is given as 265 feet in Baedeker's *Canada*, p. 53.

[1] 1608.

[2] The spot was near "where the Champlain Market now stands in the lower town of the present city, and partly on the site now occupied by the Church of Notre Dame des Victoires." S. E. Dawson, *The St. Lawrence*, 254.

[3] Champlain here omits the story of the conspiracy of the locksmith; the description of the buildings and a discussion of the site of Cartier's winter quarters in 1535, which he gave in his narrative of 1613. Cf. *Voyages of Champlain*, II, 176-188; Laverdière, *Voyages, 1613*, 148-161.

about two and a half feet deep, or three at the most. And when the eels and other things that they collect have been prepared they go to hunt the beaver, which they do until the beginning of January. They were not very successful in the beaver hunt, for the water was too high and the rivers had overflowed, as they told us. When their eels give out they have recourse to hunting the elk[4] and other wild beasts, which they can find, while waiting for the spring. At that time I was able to supply them with several things. I made a special study of their customs.

All these people are so much in want that sometimes they are driven to live on certain kinds of shellfish and to eat their dogs and the skins with which they protect themselves against the cold. If some one should show them how to live and teach them how to till the soil, and other things, they would learn very easily, for there are a good many of them who have good judgment and reply intelligently to what is asked of them. There is an evil tendency among them to be revengeful, and to be great liars, and one cannot rely upon them, except with caution and when one is armed. They make promises enough, but keep few of them, most of them being without law, as far as I could see, and, besides, full of false beliefs. I asked them what ceremonies they employed in praying to their god; they told me that they made use of none, except that each prayed in his heart as he wished. This is why they have no law, and do not know what it is to worship God and pray to Him, but live like brute beasts; but I think that they would soon be converted to Christianity if some people would settle among them and cultivate their soil, which is what most of them wish. They have among them some savages whom they call Pilotois, who, they believe, talk with the devil face to face, who tells them what they must do, whether in case of war or in regard to other matters; and if he should command them to carry out a certain enterprise they would obey his command at once. They believe, also, that all the dreams that they have are true; and, in fact, there are a great many of them who say that they have seen and dreamed things which have come to pass or will take place. But, to tell the truth about the matter, these are diabolical visions, which deceive them and lead them astray. This is all that I have been able to learn about their brutish belief.

All these people are well-built, without deformity, and are active. The women are equally well-formed, plump, and of a tawny complexion, because of certain pigments which they put on which make them look olive-colored. They are dressed in skins; a part of the body is covered,

[4] I. e., the moose.

the rest is naked; but in winter they make up for it, for they are dressed in good furs, like elk, otter, beaver, bear, seal, deer and roe, which they have in great quantity. In winter, when there is a great deal of snow, they make a sort of racquets, which are three or four times as large as those in France,[5] which they attach to their feet, and in this way they can go in the snow without sinking in; without them they could not hunt or go in many places. They have an odd sort of marriage, namely: when a girl is fourteen or fifteen years old, and she has several suitors, she may associate with all of them that she likes. Then at the end of five or six years she makes her own choice from them of a husband, and they live together to the end of their lives. But if, after living some time together, there are no children, then the man may unmarry himself and take another wife, saying that his own is good for nothing. Thus the girls are freer than the women.

After marriage they are chaste, and the husbands are, for the most part, jealous. They give presents to the fathers or relatives of the girls whom they have married. These are the ceremonies and ways that they employ in their marriages.

As for their burials, when a man or a woman dies, they dig a big grave, where they put all the possessions that they had, such as kettles, furs, axes, bows, arrows, robes and other things; then they put the body in the grave and cover it with earth, and put a great many large pieces of wood on top, and one piece erect. This they paint red on the upper part. They believe in the immortality of the soul, and say that they will be happy in other lands with their relatives and friends who are dead. In the case of captains and others in positions of authority, they come, after the death, three times a year for a celebration and dance, and sing on the grave.

They are very timid and constantly fear their enemies, and scarcely sleep at all wherever they are, although I reassured them every day as much as I could and advised them to do as we do, namely: let some watch while others sleep, and let each one have his arms ready, like him who was on guard; and that they should not take dreams for the truth, on which to rely. But these teachings were of little use, and they said that we understood better than they how to protect ourselves against these things, and that in time, if we should come to live in their country, they would learn.

[5] I. e., the racquets used for tennis.

ALGONQUIANS, HURONS AND IROQUOIS

CHAPTER VI

Planting of vines at Quebec by the author. His kindness to the poor savages.

ON the first of October I had wheat planted, and on the fifteenth rye.

On the third of the month there was white frost in some places, and the leaves began to fall from the trees on the fifteenth.

On the twenty-fourth of the month I had some native vines planted, which came on very finely. But after I had left the settlement, to come to France, they were all spoiled from neglect, which was a great grief to me on my return.

On November 18 there was a great snowfall, but it stayed only two days on the ground.

On February 5[1] it snowed hard.

On the twentieth of the month we saw some savages on the other side of the river, begging us to come to their aid, but it was beyond our power to do so, on account of the great amount of drifting ice in the river. Hunger pressed these poor, miserable creatures so hard that, not knowing what to do, they resolved to die—men, women and children—in the attempt to cross the river, in the hope that they cherished that I would come to their rescue in their extreme want. Having then taken this resolution, the men and women took their children and got into their canoes, thinking to reach our side through an opening in the ice that the wind had made; but they were scarcely in the middle of the river before their canoes were caught and broken into a thousand pieces by the ice. They had the presence of mind to throw themselves, with their children, whom the women carried on their backs, upon a large cake of ice. While they were on it one could hear them crying out in such a way as to excite great pity; and they expected nothing but death. But fortune so favored these poor wretches that a big piece of ice struck so hard against the side of the one upon which they were that it threw them on the shore. When they saw this favorable turn, they reached the shore with as much joy as they had ever had in doing so, in spite of the great hunger from which they had suffered. They came to our settlement looking so thin and worn that they seemed like skeletons, most of them not able to stand up. I was astonished to see them and at the way in which they had crossed, when I thought of how feeble and weak they were. I

[1] 1609.

had bread and beans given to them, but they could not wait for them to be cooked to eat them; and I loaned them some bark of trees to cover their cabins. As they were making their cabins they discovered a piece of carrion that I had thrown out nearly two months before to attract foxes, of which we caught black and red ones, like those in France but having much more fur. This carrion was a sow and a dog, which had been exposed to the warm weather and the cold. When the weather was growing mild it smelled so strong that one could not stay near it. Nevertheless, they lost no time in seizing it and taking it to their cabin, where they devoured it at once half cooked, and never did meat seem to taste better to them. I sent two or three men to warn them that they should not eat it, if they did not wish to die. As they approached their cabin they smelled such a stench of this half-warmed-up carrion, of which each savage had a piece in his hand, that they thought they should vomit, and so they scarcely stopped there at all. However, I did not fail to help them as much as I could; but it was little, considering their numbers, and in one month they would have eaten up all our provisions, if they could have got hold of them, they are such gluttons. For when they have food they do not keep anything in reserve, but make good cheer with it continually, day and night; then afterward they die of hunger.

They did another thing, besides, as distressful as the first. I had had a dog placed in the top of a tree, to allure martens and birds of prey. I took pleasure in this, inasmuch as, ordinarily, this carrion was set upon by them. These savages went to the tree, and, since they were too weak to climb it, cut it down and at once took away the dog, which was nothing but skin and bones, with the head tainted and smelling bad; and it was at once devoured.

This is the pleasure that they have the most often in winter. In summer they are able to support themselves, and to get provisions, so as not to be attacked by such extreme need, from the rivers, which are full of fish, and from hunting birds and wild animals. The soil is very fine and good for cultivation, if only they would take the trouble to sow Indian corn, as all their neighbors do—the Algonquins, Hurons and Iroquois—who are not assailed with so cruel famines, because they know how to provide against them by the care and foresight that they exercise; with the result that they live happily, compared with these Montagnais, Canadians[2] and Souriquois who live along the seacoast. The snow and ice

---

[2] The name applied in Champlain's time to the Indians along the St. Lawrence, below the Saguenay. L.

stay on the ground five months; that is, from the month of December until toward the end of April, when it is almost all melted. From Tadoussac to Gaspé, Cape Breton, Newfoundland and the Great Bay[3] the snow and ice continue in most places until the end of May, at which date sometimes the mouth of the great river is sealed with ice; but at Quebec there is not any, which shows a strange difference for 120 leagues of distance in longitude, for the mouth of the river is at latitude 49°, 50° and 51°, and our settlement is in latitude 46½°. As for the country, it is beautiful and pleasant, and brings all sorts of grain and seeds to maturity. There are all the kinds of trees there that we have in our forests on this side of the sea, and a great many fruits, although they are wild, because they are not cultivated; such as walnuts, cherries, plum trees, vines, raspberries, strawberries, green and red gooseberries and a good many other little fruits which are rather good there. There are also several kinds of good herbs and roots. There are plenty of fish to catch in the rivers, and there are a great many meadows and an enormous quantity of game.

On the eighth of April at this season[4] the snow was all melted and, nevertheless, the air was still pretty cold until into May, when the trees began to put forth their leaves.[5]

CHAPTER VII

Journey from Quebec to the Island of St. EIoi, and the meeting that I had with some Algonquin and Ochtaiguin savages.

WITH this purpose[1] I departed on the eighteenth of the month. The river begins to widen here, sometimes to a league and even a league and a half in some places. The country becomes more and more beautiful. The banks of the river are partly hills and partly level land without rocks, except a very few. As for the river, it is dangerous in many places, because

[3] The part of the Gulf of St. Lawrence between Labrador and Newfoundland.
[4] 1609.
[5] Champlain omits here the account of the scurvy which he gave in the narrative of 1613. Cf. *Voyages of Champlain*, II, 197-200; Laverdière, *Voyages, 1613*, 170-172.
[1] That is, to explore the country of the Iroquois. June 7 Champlain had left Quebec, to go to Tadoussac on business; he now returned and is starting from Quebec, June 18. See references in preceding note.

of sandbars and rocks, and is not good to sail in without the lead in hand. The river is very abundantly supplied with several sorts of fish, not only such as we have on this side of the sea, but others that we have not. The country is all covered with large, high forests of the same kinds of trees that we have about our settlement. There are also many vines and nut trees on the bank of the river and a great many little brooks and rivers which are navigable only with canoes. We passed near Point St. Croix.[2] This point is sandy. It projects a little into the river, and is exposed to the northwest wind, which beats upon it. There are some meadows, but they are submerged every time the tide is high. The tide falls nearly two and a half fathoms. This passage is very dangerous to go through, on account of the quantity of rocks that lie across the river, although there is a good channel which is very crooked, where the river runs like a mill-race, and one must take plenty of time for the passage. This place has deceived a great many people, who thought that they could not go through it except at high tide for lack of a channel, but we have found the contrary. As for going down, one can do it at low tide; but to go up would be very difficult, unless there should be a high wind, because of the great current; and so it is necessary to wait until the tide is one-third flood to pass, when the current in the channel is 6, 8, 10, 12 and 15 fathoms deep.

Continuing our course we came to a river which is very pleasant. It is nine leagues from St. Croix and twenty-four from Quebec. We named it St. Mary's River.[3] The whole length of this river from St. Croix is very beautiful.

Continuing our route I met two or three hundred savages, who were in cabins near a little island called St. Eloi, a league and a half from St. Mary. We investigated and found that they were some tribes of savages called Ochateguins[4] and Algonquins, who were going to Quebec, to assist us in exploration of the countries of the Iroquois, against whom they carry on mortal combat, sparing nothing that belongs to them.

After having recognized them I went ashore to see them and asked who their chief was. They told me that they had two of them—one named Iroquet and the other Ochasteguin, whom they pointed out to me---and I went to their cabin, where they received me well, according to their custom. I began to explain to them the purpose of my journey,

---

[2] Point Platon. Dawson, *St. Lawrence*, 236.
[3] Now the Ste. Anne. L.
[4] The Hurons.

with which they were very much pleased; and, after talking of several things, I withdrew. Some time afterward they came to my shallop, where they made me accept some skins, showing a good many signs of pleasure, and then they returned to land.

The next day the two chiefs came to find me. Then they remained some time without saying a word, meditating and smoking constantly. After having thought it all over, they began to harangue in a loud voice all their companions who were on the river bank, their arms in their hands, listening very attentively to what their chiefs said to them, namely: that nearly ten moons ago, as they reckoned, Iroquet's son had seen me, and that I had given him a kind reception, and that we desired to assist them against their enemies, with whom they had been at war for a long time, because of a great deal of cruelty that the enemy had shown toward their tribe, on the pretext of friendship; and that, having always desired vengeance since that time, they had asked all the savages on the bank of the river to come to us, to form an alliance with us, and that they never had seen Christians, which had also induced them to come to see us, and that I might do as I wished with them and their companions; that they had no children with them, but men who knew how to fight and were full of courage, and who were familiar with the country and the rivers in the country of the Iroquois; and that now they begged me to return to our settlement, that they might see our houses; that after three days we should return all together to the war, and that for a sign of great friendship and joy I should have muskets and arquebuses fired, and that they would be very much pleased; which I did. They gave great cries of astonishment, and especially those who never had heard nor seen them before.

After I had heard them I replied to them that to please them I should be very glad to go back to our settlement, to give them more pleasure, and that they might infer that I had no other intention than to engage in war, since I carried with me nothing but arms, and not merchandise for barter, as they had been led to understand; that my desire was only to accomplish that which I had promised them; and that if I had known of any one who had made evil reports to them, I should regard such as enemies more than they themselves did. They told me that they did not believe any of it, and that they had heard nothing said; but the contrary was true, for there were some savages who told ours. I contented myself in waiting for an opportunity to be able to show them in reality something different from what they could have expected of me.

SAMUEL DE CHAMPLAIN

CHAPTER VIII

Return to Quebec, and then continuation with the savages to the Rapids of the River of the Iroquois.

THE next day we all set out together to go to our settlement, where they enjoyed themselves five or six days, which passed in dances and festivities, because of the desire that they felt that we should be in the war.

Pont Gravé came at once from Tadoussac with two little barks full of men, in response to a letter in which I begged him to come as promptly as he could.

When the savages saw him coming they rejoiced more than before, especially as I told them that he had given me some men to assist them, and that perhaps we should go together.

On the twenty-eighth of the month I left Quebec, to assist the savages. On the first of June[1] we reached St. Croix, 15 leagues from Quebec, with a shallop equipped with all I needed.

I left St. Croix on June [July] 3, with all the savages, and we passed the Trois Rivières,[2] which is a very beautiful country, covered with a great many beautiful trees. From this place to St. Croix it is 15 leagues. At the mouth of this river there are six islands, of which three are very small and the others from 1500 to 1600 paces long, very pleasant to look at; and near Lake St. Peter, about two leagues up the river, there is a small rapid, which is not very difficult to pass. This place is in latitude 46 degrees, less some minutes. The savages of the country gave us to understand that some days' journey off there is a lake through which the river passes. The lake is ten days' journey long,[3] and then one passes some falls, and afterward three or four more lakes five or six days' journey long; and at the end there are four or five leagues by land and then one enters directly into another lake, where the Saguenay has its principal source.[4] The savages come from this place to Tadoussac. The Trois Rivières is twenty days' journey for the savages; and they say that at the end of this river there are some people who are great hunters, without a

---

[1] This should be July.
[2] The river is now the St. Maurice. The town is Three Rivers. It is at the head of tidewater.
[3] Lake Ontario.
[4] Champlain here fell into a misunderstanding of what the Indians meant.

fixed abode, and that they can see the Northern Sea[5] in less than six days' journey. What little land I have seen is sandy, rather high, with hills crowded with pines and firs on the river banks; but about a quarter of a league inland the woods are very beautiful and open, and the country is level.

Continuing our route as far as the entrance to Lake St. Peter, which is a very pleasant and level country, we crossed the lake in 2, 3 and 4 fathoms of water. It may be eight leagues long and four wide. On the north side we saw a very pleasant river extending some fifty leagues into the interior; and I named it St. Suzanne;[6] and on the south side there are two of them, one called Rivière du Pont[7] and the other Rivière de Gennes[8]—which are very beautiful and in a fine, fertile country. The water is almost still in the lake, which is very full of fish. On the north side land can be seen some 12 or 15 leagues from the lake, which is rather mountainous. Having crossed the lake we passed by a great number of islands of different sizes, where there are a great many nut trees and vines, and beautiful meadows, with quantities of game and wild animals, which come from the mainland to these islands. The fish there are more plentiful than in any other place in the river that we have seen. From these islands we went to the mouth of the River of the Iroquois,[9] where we stayed two days and refreshed ourselves with good venison, birds and fish, which the savages gave us. Here there was some controversy among them on the subject of the war, with the result that there were only a certain number of them who decided to go with me, and the others returned to their country with their wives and the merchandise that they had got in trade.

Starting from the mouth of this river, which is about 400 or 500 paces wide and is very beautiful, running southward,[10] we reached a place which is in latitude 45°, about 22 or 23 leagues from Trois Rivières. The whole river, from its mouth to the first rapid,[11] which is 15 leagues,

[5] Hudson Bay.
[6] The River du Loup. L.
[7] The Nicolet. L.
[8] The Yamaska. L.
[9] The Richelieu.
[10] The Richelieu runs north. Champlain, however, often speaks of the course of a river in this way, saying that the course of a certain river goes north when he means that one following up the course would go north.
[11] The word "sault" is usually rendered "rapid" or "rapids" in this translation when these words would ordinarily be used by an English writer.

is very smooth and bordered with woods, as are all the other places named above, and of the same varieties. There are nine or ten beautiful islands before one reaches the first rapid of the Iroquois, which are about a league or a league and a half long, covered with a quantity of oaks and nut trees. The river is nearly half a league wide in some places, and is very full of fish. We did not find less than four feet of water. The entrance to the rapid is a sort of lake,[12] into which the water descends, which is about three leagues in circumference, and there are some meadows there where no savages are settled, on account of the wars. There is very little water at the rapid, which flows with great swiftness, and there are a great many rocks and stones, which prevent the savages from going up by water; but in returning they descend very well. All this country is very level, full of forests, vines and nut trees. Up to this time no Christians had been as far as this place except us, and we had a good deal of trouble getting up the river with oars.

As soon as I had reached the rapids I took five men and we went ashore to see if we could get by this place, and we went about a league and a half without seeing any chance of it, unless we should venture in water running with great rapidity, where on both sides there were a great many stones which are very dangerous, and where the water was very shallow. The rapids may be 600 feet wide. And when we saw that it was impossible to cut the trees and make a way, with the few men that I had, I decided, by the advice of each of them, to do something different from what we had promised, inasmuch as the savages had assured me that the roads were easy; but we found the contrary true, which I have already said, which was why we returned from them to our shallop, where I had left some men to guard it, and to tell the savages, when they should arrive, that we had gone to explore along this rapid.

When we had seen what we wished to of this place, as we were returning we met some savages who had come to explore as we had done. They told us that all their companions had reached our shallop. There we found them much pleased and satisfied that we had gone in this way without a guide, except for the reports that they had several times given us.

Having come back, and having seen what little chance there was of passing the rapids with our shallop, I was troubled; and I was much disappointed to return without having seen a large lake filled with beautiful islands and a great deal of beautiful country bordering the lakes,

---

[12] Chambly Basin.

where their enemies live, as they had represented it to me. After thinking things over by myself, I resolved to go there to fulfill my promise and the desire that I felt, and I set out with the savages in their canoes and took with me two men who volunteered. For when our men saw, in good earnest, that I intended to go with their canoes, their hearts failed them, which resulted in my sending them back to Tadoussac.

I went directly to speak to the captains of the savages, and gave them to understand that they had told us the contrary to what I had seen at the rapids, namely, that it was beyond our power to go up it with the shallop; nevertheless, that this would not hinder me from aiding them as I had promised. This news saddened them very much, and they wished to make another decision; but I told them and urged upon them that they ought to hold to their first plan; and that I, with two others, would go to the war with them in their canoes, to show them that, as for myself, I would not fail to keep my word to them, although I should be alone; and that, at that time, I did not wish to force any one of my companions to embark except those who volunteered, of whom I had found two, that I would take with me.

They were very much pleased at what I told them, and at hearing the decision that I had made, and they kept promising to show me beautiful things.

CHAPTER IX

Departure from the rapids of the Iroquois River. Description of a large lake. Of the encounter with the enemy that we had at this lake, and of the manner in which they attacked the Iroquois.

I left these rapids of the Iroquois River on July 2.[1] All the savages began to carry their canoes, arms and baggage by land about half a league, in order to get by the swiftness and force of the rapids. This was quickly accomplished.

Then they put them all in the water, and two men in each boat, with their baggage; and they made one of the men from each canoe go by land about a league and a half, the length of the rapid, which is not so violent as at its mouth, except in certain places where rocks obstruct the river, which is not more than 300 or 400 paces wide. After we had passed

[1] This date in all probability should be the 12th. L.

SAMUEL DE CHAMPLAIN

the rapid, which was not without difficulty, all the savages who had gone by land by a pretty good path and level country, although there were a great many trees, re-embarked in their canoes. My men went by land, too, and I by water, in a canoe. They had a review of all their men and found that they had twenty-four canoes, with sixty men in them. When they had had their review, we continued on our way as far as an island three leagues long,[2] covered with the most beautiful pines that I had ever seen. They hunted, and caught some wild animals there. Going on farther, about three leagues from there, we encamped, to rest that night.

Immediately they all began, some to cut wood, others to strip off the bark of trees to cover their cabins, to provide shelter for themselves; others began to fell big trees for a barricade on the bank of the river about their cabins. They know so well how to do this that in less than two hours five hundred of their enemy would have had a good deal of trouble to attack them without losing a great many of their number. They do not barricade the side toward the river, where their canoes are drawn up, so as to be able to embark, if occasion requires.

When they were lodged they sent three canoes with nine good men, as is their custom in all their encampments, to reconnoitre for two or three leagues, to see if they can discover anything. Later these come back. They sleep all night, relying upon the exploration of these scouts, which is a very bad custom among them; for sometimes they are surprised while asleep by their enemies, who knock them in the head before they have a chance to get up to defend themselves.

Being aware of that, I explained to them the mistake that they were making, and told them that they ought to watch, as they had seen us do every night, and have men on the lookout, to listen and see if they saw anything; and that they should not live like beasts. They told me that they could not keep watch, and that they worked enough by day in hunting; and, above all, when they go to war, they divide their bands into three parts, viz., one part to hunt, distributed in various places; one to constitute the main body, who are always under arms; and the other part as scouts, to explore along the rivers, to see if there is any mark or sign to indicate that their enemies have passed, or their friends. This they recognize by certain marks that the chiefs of different tribes exchange. These are not always alike, and they inform themselves from

[2] Sainte-Thérèse. L.

time to time when they are changed. In this way they recognize whether those who have passed are friends or enemies. The hunters never hunt in advance of the main body, or of the scouts, in order not to cause alarm or disorder, but in the rear, and in the direction where they do not expect their enemies; and they continue thus until they are two or three days' journey from their enemies, when they go at night by stealth, all in a body, except the scouts. And by day they retire within the thickest part of the woods, where they rest, without wandering off, or making any noise, or lighting any fire, even when necessary for food, during this time, in order not to be noticed if, by chance, their enemies should pass. They do not make any fire, except for smoking; and they eat Indian meal cooked, which they soak in water, like porridge. They preserve this meal for times of need, and when they are near their enemies, or when they are retreating after an attack, they do not care to hunt, but retreat at once.

In all their encampments they have their Pilotois, or Ostemoy, a kind of persons who act as soothsayers, in whom these people believe. The soothsayer builds a cabin surrounded by sticks of wood, and covers it with his robe. When it is done he ensconces himself inside in such a way that he cannot be seen at all; then he takes hold of one of the posts of his cabin and shakes it, muttering some words between his teeth, by which he says he invokes the devil, who appears to him in the form of a stone and tells him whether they will find their enemies and kill many of them. This Pilotois lies flat on the ground, motionless, only making believe to speak to the devil; then suddenly he rises to his feet, talking and writhing in such a way that, although he is naked, he is all in a perspiration. All the people are about the cabin, seated on their buttocks like monkeys. They told me often that the shaking of the cabin that I saw was caused by the devil and not by the man who was inside, although I observed the contrary; for it was (as I have already said) the Pilotois who seized one of the props of the cabin and made it move so. They also told me that I should see fire come out of the top, which I did not see at all. These rogues also disguise their voices and make them sound big and clear and speak in a language that is unfamiliar to the other savages; and when they make it sound broken the savages believe that it is the devil who speaks, and that he is saying what is to happen in their war, and what they must do. Nevertheless, all these rascals who play soothsayer do not speak two true words out of a hundred and impose upon these poor folk, like plenty of others in the world, in order to get their living from the people. I often admonished them that all that they did was sheer folly, and that they ought not to put faith in it.[3]

Now, after they have learned from their soothsayers what is to happen to them, they take as many sticks, a foot long, as they themselves number, and represent their chiefs by others a little longer. Then they go into the woods and clear a place five or six feet square, where the chief, as field sergeant, arranges all the sticks in the order that seems good to him; then he calls all his companions, who all come armed, and shows them the rank and order that they are to keep when they fight with their enemies. All the savages watch this attentively, noticing the figure which their chief has made with these sticks, and afterward they retire and begin to arrange themselves as they have seen these sticks, and then mingle with one another, and return directly to their order; continuing this two or three times, and doing it at all their encampments, without needing a sergeant to make them keep in their ranks, which they know well how to keep, without getting into confusion. This is the rule that they abide by in their warfare.

We left the next day, continuing our course in the river as far as the entrance to the lake. In this there are many pretty islands, which are low, covered with very beautiful woods and meadows, where there is a quantity of game, and animals for hunting, such as stags, fallow-deer, fawns, roebucks, bears and other animals which come from the mainland to these islands. We caught a great many of them. There are also many beavers, not only in this river, but in many other little ones which empty into it. These places, although they are pleasant, are not inhabited by any savages, on account of their wars. They withdraw as far as possible from the river into the interior, in order not to be suddenly surprised.

The next day we entered the lake, which is of great extent, perhaps 50 or 60 leagues long.[4] There I saw four beautiful islands 10, 12 and 15 leagues long,[5] which formerly had been inhabited by savages, like the River of the Iroquois; but they had been abandoned since they had been at war with one another. There are also several rivers which flow into the lake that are bordered by many fine trees, of the same sorts that we have

---

[3] "This mode of divination was universal among the Algonquin tribes, and is not extinct to this day among their roving Northern bands." Parkman, *Pioneers of France*, 344.

[4] Lake Champlain is about 90 miles long.

[5] These dimensions are overstated three-fold, S. The islands were Isle la Motte, Long Island, Grand Isle, and Valcour. L.

ALGONQUIANS, HURONS AND IROQUOIS

in France, with a quantity of vines more beautiful than any I had seen in any other place; many chestnut trees, and I have not seen any at all before, except on the shores of the lake, where there is a great abundance of fish of a good many varieties. Among other kinds there is one called by the savages Chaousarou,[6] which is of various lengths; but the longest, as these people told me, is eight or ten feet. I saw some of them five feet long, as big as a man's thigh, with a head as large as two fists, a snout two and a half feet long, and a double row of very sharp and dangerous teeth. Its body is, in all respects, like that of the pike, but it is armed with scales so strong that a dagger could not pierce them, and it is silver grey in color. And the end of its snout is like that of a pig. This fish fights all the others in the lakes and rivers, and is wonderfully cunning, to judge from what the people have assured me, which is, that when it wishes to catch certain birds, it goes into the rushes or weeds which border the lake in several places, and puts its snout out of the water without moving at all, so that when the birds come to light on its snout, thinking that it is the trunk of a tree, the fish is so skillful in closing its snout, which had been half open, that it draws the birds under the water by the feet. The savages gave me a head of one of them. They set great store by them, saying that when they have a headache they bleed themselves with the teeth of this fish where the pain is, and it passes off at once.

Continuing our course in this lake on the west side I saw, as I was observing the country, some very high mountains on the east side, with snow on the top of them.[7] I inquired of the savages if these places were inhabited. They told me that they were---by the Iroquois---and that in these places there were beautiful valleys and open stretches fertile in grain, such as I had eaten in this country, with a great many other fruits; and that the lake went near some mountains, which were perhaps, as it seemed to me, about fifteen leagues from us. I saw on the south others not less high than the first, but they had no snow at all.[8] The savages told me that it was there that we were to go to find their enemies, and that these mountains were thickly peopled. They also said it was necessary to pass a rapid,[9] which I saw afterward, and from there to enter another

---

[6] The gar pike, or bony-scaled pike. See the note in *Voyages of Champlain*, II, 216.

[7] The Green Mountains. Mr. Slafter thinks Champlain took outcroppings of white limestone for snow. The Green Mountains would not have snow on them in July, as they are only about 4000 feet high.

[8] The Adirondacks.

[9] The outlet of Lake George.

SAMUEL DE CHAMPLAIN

lake, three or four leagues long;[10] and that when we had reached the end of that it would be necessary to follow a trail for four leagues, and to pass over a river[11] which empties on the coast of the Almouchiquois,[12] near the coast of Norumbegue;[13] and that it was only two days' journey by their canoes, as I have [also] learned since from some prisoners that we took, who described to me very much in detail all that they had found out themselves about the matter through some Algonquin interpreters who knew the Iroquois language.

Now, as we began to approach within two or three days' journey of the home of their enemies, we did not advance more, except at night, and by day we rested. Nevertheless, they did not omit, at any time, the practice of their customary superstitions, to find out how much of their undertakings would succeed, and they often came to me to ask if I had dreamed, and if I had seen their enemies. I answered them "no," and told them to be of good courage and to keep up hope. When night came we pursued our journey until daylight, when we withdrew into the thickest part of the woods and passed the rest of the day there. About ten or eleven o'clock, after having taken a little walk around our encampment, I went to rest; and I dreamed that I saw the Iroquois, our enemies, in the lake, near a mountain, drowning within our sight; and when I wished to help them our savage allies told me that we must let them all die, and that they were worthless. When I woke up they did not fail to ask me, as is their custom, if I had dreamed anything. I told them the substance of what I had dreamed. This gave them so much faith that they no longer doubted that good was to befall them.

When evening came we embarked in our canoes to continue on our way; and, as we were going along very quietly, and without making any noise, on the twenty-ninth of the month,[14] we met the Iroquois at ten o'clock at night at the end of a cape that projects into the lake on the west side,[15] and they were coming to war. We both began to make loud cries, each getting his arms ready. We withdrew toward the water and the Iroquois went ashore and arranged their canoes in line, and began to

---

[10] Lake George.
[11] The Hudson.
[12] The Massachusetts coast.
[13] Adopting Laverdière's emendation founded on the text of the 1613 narrative. The text of the 1632 narrative merely repeats Almouchiquois twice.
[14] July 29, 1609.
[15] At Ticonderoga.

cut down trees with poor axes, which they get in war sometimes, and also with others of stone; and they barricaded themselves very well.

Our men also passed the whole night with their canoes drawn up close together, fastened to poles, so that they might not get scattered, and might fight all together, if there were need of it; we were on the water within arrow range of the side where their barricades were.

When they were armed and in array, they sent two canoes set apart from the others to learn from their enemies if they wanted to fight. They replied that they desired nothing else; but that, at the moment, there was not much light and that they must wait for the daylight to recognize each other, and that as soon as the sun rose they would open the battle. This was accepted by our men; and while we waited, the whole night was passed in dances and songs, as much on one side as on the other, with endless insults, and other talk, such as the little courage they had, their feebleness and inability to make resistance against their arms, and that when day came they should feel it to their ruin. Our men also were not lacking in retort, telling them that they should see such power of arms as never before; and much other talk, as is customary in the siege of a city. After plenty of singing, dancing, and parleying with one another, daylight came. My companions and I remained concealed for fear that the enemy should see us, preparing our arms the best that we could, separated, however, each in one of the canoes of the Montagnais savages. After arming ourselves with light armor, each of us took an arquebuse and went ashore. I saw the enemy come out of their barricade, nearly 200 men, strong and robust to look at, coming slowly toward us with a dignity and assurance that pleased me very much. At their head there were three chiefs. Our men also went forth in the same order, and they told me that those who wore three large plumes were the chiefs; and that there were only three of them; and that they were recognizable by these plumes, which were a great deal larger than those of their companions; and that I should do all I could to kill them. I promised them to do all in my power, and said that I was very sorry that they could not understand me well, so that I might give order and system to their attack of the enemy, in which case we should undoubtedly destroy them all; but that this could not be remedied; that I was very glad to encourage them and to show them the good-will that I felt, when we should engage in battle.

As soon as we were ashore they began to run about 200 paces toward their enemy, who were standing firmly and had not yet noticed my companions, who went into the woods with some savages. Our men began to call me with loud cries; and, to give me a passageway, they divided into two parts and put me at their head, where I marched about twenty paces in front of them until I was thirty paces from the enemy. They at once saw me and halted, looking at me, and I at them. When I saw them making a move to shoot at us, I rested my arquebuse against my cheek and aimed directly at one of the three chiefs. With the same shot two of them fell to the ground, and one of their companions, who was wounded and afterward died. I put four balls into my arquebuse. When our men saw this shot so favorable for them, they began to make cries so loud that one could not have heard it thunder. Meanwhile the arrows did not fail to fly from both sides. The Iroquois were much astonished that two men had been so quickly killed, although they were provided with armor woven from cotton thread and from wood, proof against their arrows. This alarmed them greatly. As I was loading again, one of my companions fired a shot from the woods, which astonished them again to such a degree that, seeing their chiefs dead, they lost courage, took to flight and abandoned the field and their fort, fleeing into the depths of the woods. Pursuing them thither I killed some more of them. Our savages also killed several of them and took ten or twelve of them prisoners. The rest escaped with the wounded. There were fifteen or sixteen of our men wounded by arrow shots, who were soon healed.

After we had gained the victory they amused themselves by taking a great quantity of Indian corn and meal from their enemies, and also their arms, which they had left in order to run better. And having made good cheer, danced and sung, we returned three hours afterward with the prisoners.

This place, where this charge was made, is in latitude 43 degrees and some minutes, and I named the lake Lake Champlain.

CHAPTER X

Return from the battle, and what happened on the way.

AFTER going eight leagues, toward evening they took one of the prisoners and harangued him about the cruelties that he and his people had inflicted on them, without having any consideration for them; and said that similarly he ought to make up his mind to receive as much.

ALGONQUIANS, HURONS AND IROQUOIS

They commanded him to sing, if he had any courage; which he did, but it was a song very sad to hear.

Meanwhile our men lighted a fire, and when it was blazing well, each one took a brand and burned this poor wretch little by little, to make him suffer greater torment. Sometimes they stopped and threw water on his back. Then they tore out his nails and put the fire on the ends of his fingers and on his privy member. Afterward they flayed the top of his head and dripped on top of it a kind of gum all hot; then they pierced his arms near the wrists, and with sticks pulled the sinews, and tore them out by force; and when they saw that they could not get them, they cut them. This poor wretch uttered strange cries, and I pitied him when I saw him treated in this way; and yet he showed such endurance that one would have said that, at times, he did not feel any pain.

They strongly urged me to take some fire and do as they were doing, but I explained to them that we did not use such cruelties at all, and that we killed them at once, and that if they wished me to fire a musket shot at him I would do it gladly. They said "no," and that he would not feel any pain. I went away from them, distressed to see so much cruelty as they were practising upon this body. When they saw that I was not pleased at it, they called me and told me to fire a musket shot at him; which I did without his seeing it at all. After he was dead they were not satisfied, for they opened his belly and threw his entrails into the lake; then they cut off his head, his arms, and his legs, which they scattered in different directions, and kept the scalp, which they had skinned off, as they had done with all the others that they had killed in the battle.

They committed also another wickedness, which was to take the heart, which they cut into several pieces and gave to a brother of his and others of his companions, who were prisoners, to eat. They put it into their mouths, but would not swallow it. Some Algonquin savages, who were guarding them, made some of them spit it out and threw it into the water. This is how these people treat those whom they capture in war; and it would be better for them to die in fighting, or to kill themselves on the spur of the moment, as there are many who do, rather than fall into the hands of their enemies. After this execution we resumed our march to return with the rest of the prisoners, who always went along singing, without any hope of being better treated than the other. When we arrived at the rapids of the River of the Iroquois,[1] the Algonquins

---

[1] The Richelieu.

SAMUEL DE CHAMPLAIN

returned to their country, and also the Ochateguins[2] with some of the prisoners. They were well pleased with what had taken place in the war, and that I had gone with them readily. So we separated with great protestations of friendship, and they asked me if I did not wish to go into their country to aid them always as a brother. I promised that I would do so, and I returned with the Montagnais.

After informing myself, through the prisoners, about their country, and about how large it might be, we packed up the baggage to return; which we did with such speed that every day we made 25 or 30 leagues in their canoes, which is the ordinary rate.[3] When we were at the mouth of the River Iroquois, there were some of the savages who dreamed that their enemies were pursuing them. This dream at once led them to move the camp, although the night was very bad on account of winds and rain; and they went to pass the night among some high reeds, which are in Lake St. Peter, until the next day. Two days afterward we reached our settlement, where I had them given bread, peas and beads, which they asked me for to ornament the heads[4] of their enemies, in order to make merry on their arrival. The next day I went with them in their canoes to Tadoussac, to see their ceremonies. As they approached the shore each one took a stick with the heads of their enemies hung on the ends, with these beads on them, singing one and all. When they were near the shore the women undressed entirely naked and threw themselves into the water, going in front of the canoes, to take the heads to hang afterward to their necks, like a precious chain. Some days afterward they made me a present of one of these heads and of two sets of their enemies' weapons,

---

[2] Hurons.

[3] This is an overstatement, unless it means with a rapid current.

[4] Here, apparently in the sense of scalps. Champlain uses "teste," "head," where we should expect "chevelure," which was used for "scalp" by the later writers.

It is possible that he used the word (or form) "test" which is recorded in Cotgrave's *French and English Dictionary*, 1673, as meaning "the scalp or skull of the head," and that the printer set it up "teste." In Robert Sherwood's *Dictionary English and French*, 1672, the definition of the hairy scalp is: "Perecraine; tais, test, tests." In James Howell's *Lexicon Tetraglotton: An English-French-Italian-Spanish Dictionary*, London, 1660, the definition is the same, except that the second word is spelled "teste." There would be no need of discussing this point except for the fact that Champlain's words might be taken as evidence that the Canadian Indians beheaded their captives, as was true of the New England Indians.

On this question see "*The Scalp Trophy*," by Francis C. Clark, The Magazine of History, January, 1906, 29-39 and February, 1906, 105-114. That the Canadian Indians practiced scalping in Cartier's time (1535) is proved by his remark "et nous fut par

ALGONQUIANS, HURONS AND IROQUOIS

to preserve, in order to show them to the King; which I promised to do, to give them pleasure.

CHAPTER XI

Defeat of the Iroquois near the mouth of this River Iroquois.

IN the year 1610,[1] when I had gone with a bark and some men from Quebec to the mouth of the River Iroquois, to wait for 400 savages, who were to join me, so that I might aid them in another war, which turned out to be more imminent than we thought, an Algonquin savage in a canoe came swiftly to warn me that the Algonquins had encountered the Iroquois, who numbered one hundred, and that they were well barricaded, and that it would be hard to get the upper hand of them if the Misthigosches (as they call us) did not come promptly.

At once the alarm began among some of the savages, and each one jumped into his canoe with his arms. They were promptly ready, but in confusion; for they hurried so, that, instead of advancing, they delayed themselves. They came to our bark, begging me to go with them in their canoes, and my companions also, and urged me so hard that I embarked in one with four others. I asked La Routte, who was our pilot, to stay in the bark and send me four or five more of my companions.

When we had gone about half a league across the river, all the savages went ashore and, abandoning their canoes, took their shields, bows, arrows, clubs and swords, which they fasten to the end of big sticks, and began to run into the woods in such a way that we soon lost them from view, and they left us five without a guide. Nevertheless, we kept following them and went about half a league into the thick woods, into fens

ledict Donnacona monstré les peaulx de cinq testes d'homme estandus sur du boys cöme paulx de pchermin" (*Bref Recit.*, Tross ed., 29), and by Champlain's remark, p. 215 [104], above . His other references to scalping will be found below, p. 225 [109]; vol. II, pp. 2, 31, 160 [124, 137, 205].

[1] Champlain returned to France in the fall of 1609, setting out from Tadoussac Sept. 5 and arriving at Honfleur Oct. 13. He had interviews with De Monts and with the King, Henry IV, and set out on his return from Honfleur March 7. He arrived at Tadoussac April 26. Two days later he started for Quebec. A war party of Montagnais soon appeared at Quebec and reminded Champlain of his promises of the previous year. He kept his word, starting June 14, and in this narrative takes up the thread at his arrival at the mouth of the Richelieu. See *Voyages of Champlain*, II, 227-238; Laverdière, *Voyages, 1613*, 200-212.

and marshes, always with water to our knees, each armed with the corselet of a pikeman, which was very burdensome. Besides, there were quantities of mosquitoes so thick that they scarcely allowed us to catch our breath at all; they persecuted us so much and so cruelly that it was a strange experience. Nor did we know where we were until we noticed two savages crossing the woods. We called them, and told them that they must stay with us to guide us and conduct us to where the Iroquois were, and that otherwise we could not go there, and we should lose our way. This they did. After going a little way, we noticed a savage coming swiftly to look for us, to have us advance as quickly as possible. He gave me to understand that the Algonquins and the Montagnais had tried to force the barricade, and that they had been repulsed and the best men of the Montagnais had been killed and several others wounded. They had withdrawn to wait for us, and their hope was altogether in us. We had not gone more than an eighth of a league with this savage, who was the captain of the Algonquins, when we heard the yells and cries of both, calling one another names, and at the same time skirmishing lightly while they waited for us. As soon as the savages saw us, they began to shout in such a way that one would not have heard it thunder. I ordered my companions to follow me all the time, and not to separate from me at all. I went near to the barricade of the enemy to explore it. It was made of heavy trees set close together in a circle, which is the usual shape of their fortresses. All the Montagnais and Algonquins also approached this barricade. Then we began to discharge a great many musket shots through the foliage, since we could not see them as they could us. I was wounded as I was shooting the first time into the side of their barricade, by an arrow shot which slit the end of my ear and entered my neck. I took hold of it and pulled it out; it was barbed on the end with a very sharp stone. Another of my companions was wounded at the same time in the arm by another arrow, which I pulled out for him. Nevertheless, my wound did not prevent me from doing my duty, nor our savages from doing their part; and likewise the enemy, to such a degree that the arrows were seen flying from one side and the other as thick as hail. The Iroquois were astonished at the noise of our muskets, and especially at the fact that the balls pierced better than their arrows; and they were so frightened at the effect of them, when they saw several of their companions fall dead and wounded, that, on account of their fear, thinking these shots could not be cured, they threw themselves on the ground when they heard the noise; and we hardly missed a shot and fired two or three balls at a time, and most of the time we had our muskets resting on the edge of their barricade. When I saw that our ammunition was beginning to fail, I said to all the savages that they must overcome them by force and break their barricade; and to do this they must take their shields and cover themselves with them, and thus get so near that ropes could be tied to the posts which held them up, and then, by main strength, they could pull hard enough to throw them over, and by this means make a big enough opening to get into their fort; and that, meanwhile, we would keep back the enemy by musket shots when they came out to stop our men; and also that a certain number should go behind some big trees that were near this barricade, in order to throw them over on them to crush them; that others should protect them with their shields, to prevent the enemy from injuring them, which they did promptly. And as they were about to accomplish it, the bark, which was a league and a half from us, heard us fighting, through the echo of our muskets, which resounded as far off as they were; this led a young man from St. Malo, full of courage, called Des Prairies, who had his bark near us to trade in skins, to say to all those who were there that it was a great shame for them to see me fighting in this way with the savages, without coming to my aid, and that, for his part, he had too much regard for his honor, and did not wish any one to be able to reproach him in this way, and thereupon he decided to come to me in a shallop with some of his companions, and of mine, whom he took with him. As soon as he arrived he went toward the fort of the Iroquois, which was on the bank of the river. There he went ashore and came to find me. When I saw him I ordered the savages who were breaking down the fortress, to stop, so that the newcomers might have their part of the pleasure. I begged Sieur des Prairies and his companions to fire some salutes of the musket before our savages should take the enemy by storm, as they had decided to do; this they did, and they shot several times, each one doing his duty. When they had shot enough I addressed our savages and incited them to complete the work. Immediately approaching the barricade, as they had done before, with us on their flank, to shoot at any who should try to hinder the destruction, they bore themselves so well and so valorously that, with the help of our muskets, they made an opening in it, though it was one hard to get through, since it was the height of a man from the ground and there were the branches of the trees that had been felled, which were very troublesome. However, when I saw a sufficiently practicable entrance, I gave orders not to

SAMUEL DE CHAMPLAIN

fire any more, which were obeyed. At the same moment twenty or thirty, not only of savages, but our men, went in, sword in hand, scarcely meeting any resistance. At once all who were sound began to flee, but they did not go far, for they were cut down by those who were around the barricade, and those who escaped were drowned in the river. We took fifteen prisoners and the rest were killed by musket shots, by arrows and by swords. When this was done there came another shallop with some of our companions in it, who were too late, although in time enough to strip the booty. This did not amount to much, for there was nothing but robes of beaver on dead bodies covered with blood, which the savages would not take the trouble to plunder, and they laughed at those who did it, namely, those in the last shallop. Having gained the victory by the grace of God, they gave us much praise.

These savages scalped the heads of their dead enemies, as they are accustomed to do, as a trophy of their victory, and took them away. They returned with fifty of their own men wounded, and three of the Montagnais and Algonquins dead, singing, their prisoners with them. They hung these heads[2] on sticks in front of their canoes, and a dead body cut into quarters, to eat in revenge,[3] as they said; and they came in this way to where our barks were, near the mouth of the River of the Iroquois.

My companions and I set sail in a shallop, where I had my wound dressed. I asked the savages for an Iroquois prisoner, whom they gave me. I saved him from a good many tortures that he would have suffered, such as they inflicted upon his companions, whose nails they tore out, whose fingers they cut off, and whom they burned in many places. That day they killed three of them in this way. They took others to the edge of the water and fastened them all erect to a stake, then each one came with a torch of birch bark and burned him now in one place, now in another; and these poor wretches, when they felt the fire, shrieked so loud that it was a strange thing to hear them. After making them suffer in this way, they took some water and threw it over their bodies, to make them suffer more; then they applied the fire again in such a way that the skin fell from their bodies, and they continued to cry out loudly and to exclaim, dancing until these poor unfortunates fell dead on the spot.

[2] Here, meaning scalps.
[3] See Parkman's note, *Pioneers of France*, 359, on ceremonial or superstitious cannibalism among the Indians.

ALGONQUIANS, HURONS AND IROQUOIS

As soon as a body fell to the ground they beat it with heavy blows of a stick, then cut off the arms and legs and other parts of it, and he was not regarded as a man of importance among them who did not cut off a piece of the flesh and give it to the dogs. Nevertheless, all these tortures were endured with such firmness that those who look on are astonished.

As for the other prisoners who remained, whether to the Algonquins or the Montagnais, they were kept to be killed by the hands of their wives and daughters, who in this do not show themselves any less inhuman than the men, and they even surpass them in cruelty; for, by their cunning, they invent more cruel tortures and take pleasure in making them end their lives thus.

The next day Captain Iroquet arrived, and another Ochateguin, who had eighty men with him, and they were very sorry not to have been at the defeat. Among all these nations there were very nearly two hundred men who never had seen Christians before, and they wondered at them greatly.

We were together three days at an island of the River of the Iroquois; then each nation returned to his own country. I had a young fellow[4] who had passed two winters at Quebec, who had a wish to go with the Algonquins to learn their language, get acquainted with the country, see the great lake, observe the rivers, and what people inhabited it; also to explore the mines and the rarer things of this place, so that, on his return, he could give us information about all these things. I asked him if he was agreeable to it, for it was not my wish to force him to it. I went to find Captain Iroquet, who was very affectionate to me, and asked him if he wished to take this young fellow with him into his country, to pass the winter, and bring him back in the spring. He promised me to do it, and treat him like his son. He told it to the Algonquins, who were not too pleased, for fear some accident should befall him.

When I had shown them how much I wished it, they said to me that since I had that wish that they would take him and treat him like a child of their own. They obliged me also to take a young man in his place to carry to France, in order to report to them what he should see. I accepted the proposition gladly, and was very much pleased with it. He was of the tribe of the Ochateguins called Hurons. This gave them the

---

[4] Apparently Etienne Brulé. Laverdière, *Voyages, 1632*, part I, 178. For Brulé's later history see C. W. Butterfield, *Stephen Brulé*, Cleveland, 1898.

more reason for treating my boy well, whom I provided with what he needed; and we promised one another to meet again at the end of June.

Some days afterward this Iroquois prisoner, whom I had under guard, on account of the excess of liberty that I allowed him, got away and escaped, because of the fear and terror that he felt, in spite of the assurances given him by a woman of his tribe, whom we had at our settlement.

CHAPTER XII

Description of whaling in New France.

It[1] has seemed to me not inappropriate to give here a short description of whale fishing, which many people have not seen and believe to be done by cannon shots, since there are bold liars who affirm as much to those who know nothing of it. Many have obstinately maintained it to me, on account of these false reports.

Those, then, who are most skillful in this fishery are the Basques,[2] who, for the purpose, put their ships in a safe harbor, near where they think there are a good many whales, and fit out shallops manned by good men and provided with lines, which are small ropes made of the best hemp that can be found, at least 150 fathoms long; and they have a great many partisans as long as a short pike, with the iron six inches wide. Others are a foot and a half wide and two feet long, very sharp. They have in each shallop a harpooner, who is the most agile and adroit man among them and draws the biggest wages next to the masters, inasmuch as his is the most dangerous position. As soon as this shallop is out of port, they look in every direction, tacking from one side to the other, to see if they can see and discover a whale. If they do not see anything, they go ashore and climb the highest point that they can find, to get a farther view. There they leave a man on the watch. He descries the whale, which is discovered both by its size and by the water that it

---

[1] Champlain here omits the details of his return to Quebec and of his leaving there Aug. 8 and Tadoussac Aug. 13 for France. He takes up the thread with this description of whaling. Cf. *Voyages of Champlain*, II, 249-252.

[2] The hardy sailors of the Basque provinces in Spain had been engaged in fishing and whaling off Newfoundland since the time of the Cabot voyages.

spurts from its blow-holes, more than a hogshead at a time and to the height of two lances; and by the amount of water that it spurts they judge how much oil it can yield. There are some from which they draw as much as 120 barrels; from others it is less.

Upon seeing this tremendous fish they embark promptly in their shallops and, by means of oars or the wind, proceed until they are above him. Seeing him under water, the harpooner at once goes to the prow of the shallop and with a harpoon, which is an iron two feet long and half a foot wide at the barbs, attached to a stick as long as a short pike, having in the middle a hole to which the line is fastened; and as soon as the harpooner sees his opportunity he throws his harpoon at the whale and strikes him well in the front, and, at once, when he feels the wound, he goes to the bottom. And if by chance, in turning, he strikes sometimes the shallop with his tail, or the men, he breaks them like glass. This is all the risk of being killed that they run in harpooning. But as soon as they have thrown the harpoon into him they pay out their line until the whale is at the bottom; and, sometimes, as they do not go down straight, they drag the shallop more than eight or nine leagues, going as fast as a horse; and they are obliged more often than not to cut their line, lest the whale drag them under water. When it goes straight to the bottom it stays there only a little while and then returns very quietly to the surface; and as fast as it rises they take in the line gently, and then, when he is at the top, two or three shallops get around him with partisans, with which they give him several blows; and when he feels the blows he sounds again immediately, shedding blood and growing so weak that he has no strength or vitality any more; and when he rises again they succeed in killing him. When he is dead he does not go to the bottom again; and then they tie him with stout ropes and drag him ashore to the place where they do their trying out; that is, where they have the fat of this whale melted, to extract the oil from it.

This is the way in which they are caught, and not by cannon shots, as many think, as I have already said.

SAMUEL DE CHAMPLAIN

CHAPTER XIII

Departure of the author from Quebec. Mont Royal and its cliffs. Islands where potter's clay is found. Island of Ste. Hélène.

IN the year 1611[1] I took back my savage to those of his tribe, who were to come to Sault St. Louis,[2] intending to get my servant whom they had as a hostage. I left Quebec May 20 [21] and arrived at these great rapids on the 28th, where I did not find any savages, who had promised me to be there on the 20th of the month. I immediately went in a poor canoe with the savage that I had taken to France and one of our men. After having looked on all sides, not only in the woods, but also along the river bank, to find a suitable place for the site of a settlement, and to prepare a place in which to build, I went eight leagues by land, along the rapids through the woods, which are rather open, and as far as a lake,[3] where our savage took me. There I contemplated the country very much in detail. But in all that I saw I did not find any place at all more suitable than a little spot which is just where the barks and shallops can come easily, either with a strong wind or by a winding course, because of the strength of the current. Above this place (which we named La Place Royale), a league from Mont Royal, there are a great many little rocks and shoals, which are very dangerous. And near this Place Royale there is a little river running back a good way into the interior, all along which there are more than sixty acres of cleared land, like meadows,[4] where one might sow grain and make gardens. Formerly savages tilled there, but they abandoned them, on account of the usual wars that they had there. There are also a great number of other beautiful meadows, to support as many cattle as one wishes, and all the kinds of trees that we have in our

---

[1] Champlain arrived at Honfleur on his return Sept. 27, 1610. On March 1, 1611, he set sail from Honfleur on his return to New France. He here omits all details of the voyage, in particular the experiences with icebergs, told at some length in the earlier narrative. He reached Quebec May 21, on his way to the Sault St. Louis. Cf. *Voyages of Champlain*, III, 1-9.

[2] The Lachine Rapids.

[3] The Lake of Two Mountains. L.

[4] The place selected by Champlain is now called Pointe à Callières. "It is the centre of the present city of Montreal. The Custom House now stands upon the site he chose, and the Montreal ocean steamships discharge their cargoes there. A little river, now covered in and used for drainage, fell in at that point, and on its banks were the clearings cultivated by the Hochelagans of Cartier before the great war drove them westwards." S. E. Dawson, *The St. Lawrence*, 262.

forests at home, with a great many vines, walnuts,[5] plum trees, cherries, strawberries and other kinds which are very good to eat. Among others there is one very excellent, which has a sweet taste, resembling that of plantains (which is a fruit of the Indies), and is as white as snow, with a leaf like that of the nettle, and running on trees or the ground, like ivy. Fishing is very good there, and there are all the kinds that we have in France, and a great many others that we do not have, which are very good; as is also game of different kinds; and hunting is good: stags, hinds, does, caribous, rabbits, lynxes, bears, beavers and other little animals which so abound that while we were at these rapids we never were without them.

After having made a careful exploration, then, and found this place one of the most beautiful on this river, I at once had the woods cut down and cleared from this Place Royale, to make it level and ready for building. Water can easily be made to flow around it, making a little island of it, and a settlement can be made there as one may wish.

There is a little island twenty fathoms from this Place Royale, which is about 100 paces long, where one could put up a good, well-defended set of buildings. There are also a great many meadows containing very good potter's clay, whether for bricks or to build with, which is a great convenience. I had some of it worked up, and made a wall of it four feet thick and from three to four feet high and ten fathoms long, to see how it would last through the winter when the floods came down, which, in my opinion, would not rise to this wall, although the land is about twelve feet above that river, which is quite high. In the middle of the river there is an island about three-quarters of a league in circumference, where a good and strong town could be built, and I named it Isle de Ste. Hélène.[6] These rapids descend into a sort of lake, where there are two or three islands and some beautiful meadows.

While waiting for the savages I had two gardens made: one in the meadows and the other in the woods which I had cleared; and the second day of June[7] I sowed some seeds in them, which came up in perfect condition, and in a little while, which showed the goodness of the soil.

---

[5] Here, *noyers* probably describes butternuts.

[6] Laverdière suggests that this name occurred to Champlain from his recent marriage with Hélène Boullé, the daughter of Nicolas Boullé, secretary of the King's Chamber. *Voyages, 1613,* 245.

[7] 1611.

SAMUEL DE CHAMPLAIN

I resolved to send Savignon, our savage, with another, to meet those of his country, in order to make them come quickly; and they hesitated to go in our canoe, which they distrusted, for it was not good for much.

On the seventh.[8] I went to explore a little river,[9] by which sometimes the savages go to war, which leads to the rapids of the River of the Iroquois.[10] It is very pleasant, with meadows on it more than three leagues in circumference, and a great deal of land which could be tilled. It is one league from the great rapids[11] and a league and a half from Place Royale.

On the ninth our savage arrived. He had been a little way beyond the lake,[12] which is about ten leagues long, that I have seen before. He did not meet anything there, and could not go any farther, because their canoe gave out and they were obliged to return. They reported to us that above the rapids they saw an island where there were so many herons that the air was filled with them. There was a young man called Louis, who was a great lover of hunting, who when he heard that, wanted to go there to satisfy his curiosity, and earnestly begged our savage to take him there. This the savage consented to do, with a Montagnais chief, a very fine fellow, called Outetoucos. In the morning this Louis went to call the two savages, to go to this island of herons. They embarked in a canoe and went there. This island is in the middle of the rapids. There they took as many herons and other birds as they wished and re-embarked in their canoe. Outetoucos, against the wishes of the other savage, and such pressure as he could bring to bear, wished to pass through a place that was very dangerous, where the water falls nearly three feet, saying that formerly he had gone that way, which was false. He was a long time arguing with our savage, who wished to take him on the south side, along the mainland, where they had been oftenest accustomed to pass. Outetoucos did not want to do this, saying that there was no danger at all. When our savage saw that he was obstinate he yielded to his wish; but he told him that at least they must empty out some of the birds that were in the canoe, for it was too heavily loaded, or they would certainly fill with water and be lost. This he refused to do, saying that it would be time enough when they saw that there was danger for them. So they let

---

[8] Of June.

[9] The River St. Lambert.

[10] The Richelieu. The route was up the St. Lambert, then down the Montreal into Chambly Basin, then up the Richelieu. L.

[11] The Sault St. Louis, familiar to the modern tourist as the Lachine Rapids.

[12] The Lake of the Two Mountains.

themselves go in the current. When they reached the main fall of the rapids, they wished to get out of it and throw over their load; but there was no longer time, for the swiftness of the water overmastered them and they were immediately engulfed in the whirlpools of the rapids, which turned them around a thousand times, up and down, and did not release them for a long time. At last the violence of the water tired them out so much that this poor Louis, who did not know anything about swimming, lost his head, and as the canoe was under water he had to let go of it. When it came to the surface again the two others, who kept holding on to it, did not see our Louis any more, and so he died miserably.

When they had got beyond this fall, Outetoucos, being naked and having confidence in his power to swim, abandoned the canoe to get to the land, but as the water there was very swift he was drowned. For he was so tired out and overcome by the labor that he had had that it was impossible for him to save himself.

Our savage, Savignon, being more cautious, kept holding to the canoe firmly until it was in an eddy whither the current had carried it; and knew so well how to act, in spite of the effort and fatigue that he had undergone, that he came very quietly to land, where he threw the water out of the canoe. He returned in great fear that vengeance would be taken upon him, as they do toward one another; and he told us this story, which caused us sorrow.

The next day I went in another canoe to these rapids with this savage and another of our men, to see the place where they were lost, and also to try to recover their bodies. I assure you that when he showed me the spot my hair stood on end, and I was astonished that the dead men had been so rash and so lacking in sense as to pass through so terrible a place when they could go elsewhere; for it was impossible to pass there, for there are seven or eight falls where the water goes down as by steps, the lowest three feet high, and there is an extraordinary seething and boiling. A part of these rapids was all white with foam, and the noise was so great when the air resounded with the roar of the cataracts that it sounded like thunder. After having seen this place, and examined it in detail, we searched along the river for these bodies, while a rather light shallop was going on the other side, and we returned without finding them.

SAMUEL DE CHAMPLAIN

CHAPTER XIV

Two hundred savages return the Frenchman who had been entrusted to them, and take back the savage who had returned from France. Various remarks by the author.

On the 13th of this month[1] two hundred Huron savages, with the chiefs, Ochateguin, Iroquet, and Tregouaroti, brother of our savage, brought back my lad. We were very glad to see them, and I went to meet them with a canoe and our savage. Meantime, they advanced quietly in order, our men preparing to give them a salvo with the arquebuses and some small pieces. As they were approaching they began to shout all together, and one of the chiefs commanded their address to be made, in which they praised us highly, calling us truthful, in that I had kept my word to them, to come to find them at these rapids. After they had given three more shouts, a volley of musketry was fired twice, which astonished them so much that they asked me to tell them that there should not be any shooting, saying that the greater number of them never had seen Christians before, nor heard thunderings of that sort, and that they were afraid of its doing them harm. They were very much pleased to see our savage well, for they had supposed him dead, on account of reports which some Algonquins had made to them, who had heard it from the Montagnais savages. The savage warmly praised the good treatment that I had given him in France, and the curious things that he had seen there, at which he made them all wonder; and they went away quietly enough to their cabins in the woods, to wait for the morning, when I should show them the place where I wished them to encamp. I also saw my lad, who was dressed like a savage, and he also praised the treatment of the savages, according to the customs of their country; and explained to me all that he had seen in the winter, and what he had learned from them.

When the next day came I showed them a place for their cabins, with regard to which the elders and leading men consulted by themselves. And, after spending a long time doing this, they had me called alone with my servant, who had learned their language very well, and they told him that they desired to form a close friendship with me, in view of the courtesy that I had shown them in the past; and they again praised the treatment that I had shown to our savage as if he were a brother, and said that that put them under obligations to wish me so much good that

[1] June 13, 1611.

all that I desired of them they would try to provide me with. After a good deal of discourse they made me a present of one hundred beavers. I gave them in exchange some other kinds of merchandise; and they told me that there were more than four hundred savages who were to come from their country, and that what had detained them was an Iroquois prisoner who belonged to me, who had escaped and had returned to his country. He had given them to understand that I had given him his liberty and some merchandise, and that I was coming to the rapids with six hundred Iroquois to wait for the Algonquins and kill them all. The fear occasioned by this news had stopped them, and that but for that they would have come. I told them that the prisoner had stolen away without leave, and that our savage knew well in what way he had gone, and that there had been no thought of giving up their friendship, as they had been told, since we had gone to the war in company with them, and had sent my lad into their country to accept their friendship; and that this promise that I had kept so faithfully to them confirmed this fact still more. They replied that, as far as they were concerned, they never had thought it so, and that they understood well that all this talk was far from the truth; and that if they had thought otherwise they would not have come; and that it was the others who were afraid, as a consequence of never having seen a Frenchman, except my youth. They also told me that three hundred Algonquins were coming in five or six days, if we wished to wait for them, to go to war with them against the Iroquois, and that if I did not go they would return without doing it. I talked with them a great deal about the source of the great river,[2] and about their country, concerning which they discoursed in detail, not only with regard to the rivers, falls, lakes and lands, but also the peoples who inhabit it, and what is found there. Four of them assured me that they had seen a sea very remote from their country, and that the path thither was very difficult, not only because of the wars, but also because of the wilderness that it is necessary to cross in order to reach it. They also told me that the preceding winter some savages came from the region of Florida, beyond the country of the Iroquois; who lived in sight of our ocean sea and were on friendly terms with these savages. In fine, they gave me very exact descriptions, showing me by signs all the places where they had been, taking pleasure in recounting all these things to me; and I did not get tired of listening to them, in order to find out from them matters

[2] The St. Lawrence.

about which I had been uncertain. When all this talk was over I told them that they should trade off the few commodities that they had; which they did.

The next day, after having traded off all that they had, which was little, they made a barricade around their dwelling on the side where the woods were, and said that it was for their safety, in order to avoid being surprised by the enemy; which we took for gospel truth.[3] When night came, they called our savage, who was sleeping on my despatch boat, and my servant, and they went to them. After having talked some time they had me called, too, about midnight. When I came to their cabin I found them all seated in council, and they made me sit near them, saying that it was their custom when they wished to make a proposition to assemble at night, in order not to be diverted by looking at things, and that the daylight diverted the mind by things; but, in my opinion, they wished to tell me their wishes in secret, having confidence in me, as they have since given me to understand, telling me that they wanted very much to see me alone; that some of them had been beaten; that they were as well disposed toward me as toward their children, and had so much confidence in me that they would do what I said, but that they were very distrustful of other savages;[4] that if I should return I might take as many of their people as I wished, provided that they were under the leadership of a chief; and that they sent for me to assure me further of their friendship, which never should be broken, and to beg that I should not be ill-disposed toward them; that knowing that I had made up my mind to see their country, they would show it to me at the risk of their lives, aiding me with a goodly number of men who could go anywhere; and that in the future we should expect the same from them that they did from us. They at once sent for fifty beavers and four of their shell necklaces[5] (which they value as we do chains of gold). These presents, they said, were from the other captains, who never had seen me, and that they had sent them to me, and that they desired to be my

---

[3] Champlain explains, in his narrative of 1613, that he discovered later that these Indians were suspicious of the other Frenchmen and feared they would be attacked. *Voyages of Champlain*, II, 23 and 26.

[4] For *des autres sauvages*, the reading, to judge from the more detailed account in the narrative of 1613, should be either *des autres*, i. e., the other Frenchmen, or *des autres pataches*, the other boats, i. e., those belonging to the independent French traders who had followed after Champlain. Cf. Laverdière, *Voyages, 1613,* 251, 257.

[5] Necklaces of wampum.

friends always, but that if there were any Frenchmen who wished to go with them they should be very glad, and that they wished more than ever to maintain a firm friendship.

After much talk I proposed to them that, since they were willing to show me their country, I would ask His Majesty to aid us with forty or fifty men equipped with what was necessary for this journey, and that I would embark with them, provided that they supply us with what provisions we should need during this journey; that I would take something to them to make presents with to the chiefs of the country through which we should go, and that we should return to pass the winter in our settlement; that if I should find the country to be good and fertile, several settlements would be made there, and that by this means we should have communication with one another, living happily in the future in the fear of God, whom they would be taught to know.

They were much pleased with this proposition, and asked me to shake hands on it, saying that they, on their part, would do all that they could to carry it out; and that as for provisions we should not lack for them any more than they themselves; and they assured me once more that I should be shown what I wished to see. Upon that I took my leave of them at daybreak, thanking them for their willingness to favor my desire, and begging them always to continue to feel so.

The next day, the 17th of that month,[6] they decided to return and to take with them Savignon, to whom I gave some trinkets. He gave me to understand that he was going to lead a hard life in comparison with that which he had had in France. So he went off with great regret, and I was very glad to be relieved of him. Two captains told me that in the morning of the next day they would send to fetch me; which they did. I and my servant embarked with those who came. When we came to the rapids we went some leagues into the woods, where they were encamped on the lake, where I had been before. When they saw me they were very much pleased and began to shout, according to their custom, and our savage came to me to ask me to go into his brother's cabin, where he at once had meat and fish put over the fire to give me a feast.

While I was there a feast was held, to which all the leaders and I also were invited. And although I had already had a good meal, nevertheless, in order not to offend against the custom of the country, I went to it. After banqueting they went into the woods to hold their council, and,

[6] June 17, 1611.

meanwhile, I amused myself in looking at the landscape, which is very pretty. Some time afterward they sent for me, to tell me what they had resolved upon among themselves. I went to them with my servant. When I had seated myself near them they told me that they were glad to see me, and that I had not failed to keep my word as to what I had promised them; and that they realized my kind intentions more and more, which were to keep up my friendship further; and that before going away they wished to take leave of me; and that it would have been very disappointing for them if they had gone without seeing me again; and that they thought that, in that case, I should have been ill-disposed toward them. They begged me again to give them a man. I told them that if there was one among us who desired to go with them, I should be very glad of it.

After having made me understand their good-will for the last time, and I mine toward them, the case of a savage came up, who had been a prisoner of the Iroquois three times and had escaped very fortunately, and was resolved to go, with nine others, to avenge the cruelties that his enemies had made him suffer. All the captains begged me to dissuade him if I could, inasmuch as he was very brave, and they feared that if he should advance so far into the enemy with so small a force he never would return. I did so, to please them, by all the reasons that I could urge, which were of little effect upon him, as he showed me some of his fingers cut off and great cuts and burns on his body; and he said that it was impossible for him to live without killing his enemies and having his revenge; and that his heart told him that he must depart as soon as he could; which he did.

When I had finished with them I begged them to take me back in our despatch boat. To do this they prepared eight canoes to run the rapids, and stripped themselves naked, and made me take off everything but my shirt; for often it happens that some are lost in shooting the rapids; therefore, they keep close to one another, to aid one another promptly if a canoe should happen to capsize. They said to me: "If by chance yours should happen to turn over, as you do not know how to swim, on no account abandon it, but hold on to the little sticks that are in the middle, for we will save you easily." I assure you that those who have not seen or passed this place in these little boats that they have, could not pass it without great fear, even the most self-possessed persons in the world. But these people are so skillful in shooting these rapids that it is easy for them. I did it with them—a thing that I never had done, nor had any

ALGONQUIANS, HURONS AND IROQUOIS

Christian, except my youth—and we came to our barks, where I lodged a large number of them.

There was a young man among us who decided to go with the Huron savages, who live about 180 leagues from the rapids; and he went with Savignon's brother, who was one of the captains, and he promised me to show him all that he could.

The next day[7] a number of Algonquin savages came. They traded the little that they had, and made me a special gift of thirty beavers, for which I paid them. They begged me to continue in my good feeling toward them; which I promised to do. They talked to me very particularly in regard to some explorations in the north, which could be turned to use. And, in connection with this, they told me that if there was one of my companions who wished to go with them, they would show him something that I would be glad of, and that they would treat him like one of their children. I promised them to give them a young fellow,[8] and they were very glad. When he left me to go with them I gave him a detailed memorandum of things that he ought to observe among them.

After they had traded the little that they had, they separated into three groups—one to go to war, one to go up by the rapids, and the other by way of a small stream, which empties into the great rapids—and they set out on the 18th day of this month,[9] and we also.

On the 19th I arrived at Quebec, where I decided to return to France, and I reached La Rochelle on the 11th of August.[10]

---

[7] July 12. The next day after Pont Gravé started for Tadoussac. *Voyages of Champlain*, III, 31.

[8] Probably Nicolas de Vignau, L. For Vignau see below, vol. II, pp. 1 and 33, ff. [123 and 138, ff.]

[9] July 18, 1611.

[10] According to the narrative of 1613 Champlain left Tadoussac Aug. 11 and reached La Rochelle Sept. 16. *Voyages of Champlain*, III, 34. Soon after his arrival in France Champlain nearly lost his life by a fall from a horse. For the further details of his stay there see vol. III, 43, ff.

The Voyages of Sieur de Champlain

VOLUME II—BOOK IV

CHAPTER I

Departure from France; what took place up to the time of our arrival at St. Louis Rapids.

I LEFT Rouen on the 5th of March,[1] to go to Honfleur, where I set sail; and on May 7 I reached Quebec, where I found those who had passed the winter there in good spirits and having had no illnesses. They told us that the winter had not been severe, and that the river had not frozen. The trees were beginning, too, to reclothe themselves with leaves, and the fields to be decked with flowers.

On the 13th I left Quebec, to go to the Sault St. Louis,[2] where I arrived on the 21st. Then, as we had only two canoes, I could take only four men with me. Among them was one named Nicolas de Vignau, the boldest liar that had been seen for a long time, as the course of this narrative will make plain. He had formerly passed the winter with the savages, and I had sent him to make discoveries in preceding years. He reported to me on his return to Paris, in the year 1612, that he had seen the Northern Sea;[3] that the River of the Algonquins[4] came from a lake that emptied into it, and that in seventeen days' journey one could go and come between the Rapids of St. Louis and the sea. Further, he had seen the wreckage of an English ship that had been lost on this coast, on

---

[1] March 5, 1613.
[2] The Lachine Rapids at Montreal.
[3] La Mer du Nord here refers to Hudson Bay.
[4] The Ottawa.

which there had been eighty men who escaped to the land, whom the savages had killed, because these Englishmen wished to take their Indian corn and other provisions by force; and he had seen their heads,[5] which these savages had scalped (according to their custom), which they wished me to see, and also to give me a young English boy whom they had kept for me.[6] This news delighted me very much, for I thought that I had almost found what I had been seeking for so long a time. So I adjured him to tell me the truth, that I might notify the King of it; and warned him that if he was letting me believe some lie he was putting a rope around his neck; also that, if the story were true, he could rest assured of being well rewarded. He assured me again of it with stronger oaths than ever. And, in order to play his part better, he gave me a description of the country, which be said that he had made to the best of his ability. He seemed so confident and so full of sincerity that the narrative that he had gotten up—the story of the wreckage of the ship and the matters mentioned above—had a very plausible appearance, taken in connection with the voyage of the English toward Labrador in the year 1612, where they found a strait through which they sailed as far as the 63d degree of latitude and the 290th[7] of longitude, and passed the winter at the 53d degree and lost some ships, as their report proves. These things making me believe what he said was true, I then made a report of it to the Chancellor; and showed it to Marshal de Brissac, President Jeannin and other Seigneurs of the Court, who told me that I must see it myself. That was why I asked Sieur Georges, a merchant of La Rochelle, to give him a passage in his ship, which he willingly did; and when he was there he questioned him as to why he was making the voyage. And, since it was of no advantage to him, he asked him if he expected some salary, to which he answered that he did not, and that he did not expect anything except from the King, and that he undertook the voyage only to show me the Northern Sea, which he had seen; and he made an affidavit of this at La Rochelle before two notaries.

[5] Les testes qu'iceux sauvages avoient escorchées." See note above, vol. I, 218 [105].

[6] The suggestion for this yarn may have come from some Indian rumor in regard to Hudson's Voyage in the years 1610-12. After spending the winter of 1610-11 in the Bay he and eight others were set adrift in a small boat and never again heard of. Hudson's map of his discovery was brought to England by the mutineers of 1612, and Champlain saw a cut of it published that same year and incorporated it in a small map which may be found in *Voyages of Champlain*, III, 228. S.

[7] East of Ferro. The longitudes are so given on the small map just mentioned.

SAMUEL DE CHAMPLAIN

Now, as I was taking leave, on Whitsunday,[8] of all the principal men, to whose prayers I commended myself, and of all the rest, I said to him, in their presence, that if what he had told me before was not true, he must not give me the trouble of undertaking the journey, to make which one must run many risks. Once more he asserted over again all that he had said, on peril of his life.

So, our canoes being loaded with some provisions, with our arms and merchandise, with which to make presents to the savages, I set out—Monday, May 27—from the Isle de Ste. Hélène with four Frenchmen and a savage, and an adieu was given me from our bark with a few shots from small pieces. This day we went no farther than the Sault St. Louis, which is only one league up the river, because of the bad weather, which did not permit us to go any farther.

On the 29th we passed the rapids, partly by land, partly by water. We had to carry our canoes, clothes, provisions and arms on our shoulders, which is no slight task for those who are not accustomed to it. After having gone two leagues beyond the rapids, we entered a lake,[9] about twelve leagues in circumference, into which three rivers empty—one coming from the west, from the direction of the Ochateguins,[10] who live 150 to 200 leagues from the great rapids; another from the south,[11] the country of the Iroquois, the same distance off; and the third from the north,[12] coming from the country of the Algonquins and Nebicerini,[13] also about the same distance. This river from the north (according to the account of the savages) comes from farther off, and passes by tribes unknown to them, about 300 leagues from them.

This lake is filled with beautiful large islands consisting of meadows only, where it is pleasant to hunt, deer and game being abundant. There is also plenty of fish. The country surrounding it is full of big forests. We stopped for the night at the entrance of this lake, and set up barricades, on account of the Iroquois who prowl about these places to surprise their enemies; and I am sure that if they had got hold of us they would have given us the same treatment. Therefore we kept good watch all night. The next day I took the altitude of this place, which is in

---

[8] May 26 in 1613. L.
[9] Lake St. Louis.
[10] The Hurons. This was the St. Lawrence.
[11] The Chateauguay.
[12] The Ottawa.
[13] The Nipissings.

latitude 45° 18'. About three o'clock in the afternoon we entered the river that comes from the north,[14] and passed a small rapid by land, in order to spare our canoes, and spent the rest of the night in a little island waiting for the day.

On the last of May we passed by another lake,[15] seven or eight leagues long and three wide, where there are some islands. The country about is very level, except in some places where there are some hills covered with pines. We passed a rapid[16] which is called by the inhabitants, Quenechouan. It is full of stones and rocks, and the water flows through them with great swiftness. We had to get into the water and drag our canoes along the shore with a rope. Half a league from there we passed some small rapids by rowing, which cannot be done without sweating. It takes great skill to shoot these rapids and avoid the whirlpools and breakers which are in them, and the savages do this with a dexterity that cannot be surpassed, looking for side passages and the easiest places, which they recognize at a glance.

On Saturday, the first of June, we passed two other rapids—the first half a league long and the second a league—where we had a great deal of trouble; for the rapidity of the current is so great that it makes a terrible noise, and in pouring down from one layer of rock to another it makes so much white foam everywhere that the water cannot be seen at all. These rapids are strewn with rocks, and there are some islands here and there covered with pines and white cedars. It was there that we had difficulty from not being able to carry our canoes by land, because the woods were so thick, and we had to drag them in the water with ropes. As I was drawing mine I thought I was lost, because it swerved into one of the whirlpools, and if I had not, fortunately, fallen between two rocks, the canoe would have dragged me in, because I could not undo the rope that was wound around my hand, quickly enough, which hurt me very much and had like to have cut it off. In this danger I cried to God, and began to pull my canoe, which was returned to me by a back current, such as is found in these rapids. Having escaped, I praised God, begging Him to preserve us. Our savage came afterward to rescue me, but I was out of danger. It is not to be wondered at that I was interested in saving

---

[14] The Ottawa.

[15] The Lake of Two Mountains.

[16] The first of a series of rapids called the Long Sault, "now overcome by the Carillon and Grenville canals—twelve miles of very turbulent water." Dawson, *The St. Lawrence*, 266.

our canoe, for if it had been lost we should have had to stay there, or wait for some savages to pass by there, which is a slight hope for those who have nothing on which to dine and who are not accustomed to such weariness. As for our Frenchmen, they did not have any better luck, and several times they expected to lose their lives, but the Divine Goodness kept us all safe. The rest of the day we spent in repose, for we had toiled enough.

The next day we met fifteen canoes of savages, called Quenongebin, in a river, after we had passed a little lake four leagues long and two wide. They had been warned of my coming by those who had passed the Rapids of St. Louis coming from the war with the Iroquois. I was very glad to meet them again, and they also to meet me. They were surprised to see me with so few men and with only one savage. After we had exchanged greetings in the fashion of the country, I begged them not to go any farther, in order that I might explain my wishes, and we encamped on an island.

The next day I informed them that I had come to their country to see them, and to fulfill the promise that I had made them before; and that if they were resolved to go to the war it would be very agreeable to me, inasmuch as I had brought some men with that intention. With this they were much pleased. And having told them that I wished to go farther, to inform some other tribes, they wanted to divert me from it, saying that the way was bad, and that what we had seen was nothing to it. On that account I begged them to give me one of their men to steer our second canoe, and also to guide us, for our leaders did not know the way any farther. They did so willingly, and in exchange I made them a present and gave them one of our Frenchmen, the least necessary, whom I sent back to the rapids, with a leaf of my notebook, in which, for want of paper, I gave news of myself.

Thus we separated; and, continuing our course up this river, we found another one very beautiful and broad, which comes from a nation called Ouescharini, who live north of it four days' journey from its mouth. This river[17] is very attractive, because of the beautiful islands in it and the lands decked with beautiful open woods which border it; and the land is good to till.

On the fourth day we passed near another river which comes from the north,[18] where some tribes named Algonquins live. It empties into

[17] Rivière de Petite Nation, Little Nation River.
[18] The Gatineau.

the great St. Lawrence River, three leagues below the Rapids of St. Louis, thus forming an island of nearly forty leagues.[19] It is not wide, but filled with a vast number of rapids which are very difficult to pass. Sometimes these people go down this river to avoid meeting their enemies, knowing that they will not look for them in places so difficult of access.

At the mouth of this river there is another which comes from the south, at the entrance of which there is a fine waterfall; for it falls with such vehemence from a height of 20 or 25 fathoms that it makes an overhanging curtain[20] nearly 400 paces wide. The savages pass under it for pleasure without getting wet, except with the spray that this water makes. There is an island in the middle of this river, which, like all the country around, is filled with pines and white cedars. When the savages want to enter the river, they climb the mountain, carrying their canoes, and go half a league by land. The region about is filled with all sorts of game, which often causes the savages to stop there. The Iroquois come there also sometimes to surprise them while they are making the passage.

We passed a fall a league from there, which is half a league wide[21] and descends from a height of six or seven fathoms. There are many little islands, which are nothing but cliffs, ragged and inaccessible, covered with poor brushwood. At one place the water falls with such violence upon a rock that, in the course of time, there has been hollowed out in it a wide and deep basin, so that the water flows round and round there and makes, in the middle, great whirlpools. Hence, the savages call it Asticou, which means Kettle. This waterfall makes such a noise in this basin that it can be heard more than two leagues off. The savages who pass by it have a ceremony which we shall describe in its place. We had

---

[19] This passage, as it reads, is very perplexing. Laverdière suggests that a clause has been left out, and proposes: "This river (i. e., the Gatineau) in the back country connects with another which empties 30 (instead of 3) leagues below the Sault St. Louis into the St. Lawrence." *Voyages, 1613,* 299.

[20] Rideau (Curtain) Falls, in the Rideau River. The height of the falls is greatly overstated. It is 30 feet. Possibly Champlain wrote *brasses* instead of *pieds* through a lapse of memory. Champlain was now at the site of the city of Ottawa, which lies in the angle made by the Ottawa and Rideau rivers to the west of the Rideau.

[21] The Chaudière (Kettle) Falls. The width given by Champlain includes the islands and minor channels. The main stream at the falls is now about 200 feet wide; the height is 50 feet. Baedeker's *Canada,* 154. Dawson gives the height as 40 feet. The Chaudière Falls supply the power today to run many sawmills and paper-mills in Ottawa and Hull, on the other side of the river.

SAMUEL DE CHAMPLAIN

great difficulty here in going up against a strong current by paddling, in order to reach the foot of this fall, where the savages took their canoes, and our Frenchmen and I took our arms, provisions and other commodities, in order to pass over the rough rocks about a quarter of a league, the extent of the fall; and almost as soon as we had to embark we had to go ashore again and go about 300 paces through some copsewood; and then again, after entering the water, to get our canoes by some sharp rocks, with an amount of trouble that can be imagined. I took the altitude of the place and found that it was 45° 38'.

In the afternoon we entered a lake,[22] five leagues long and two wide, where there are very beautiful islands filled with vines, walnuts[23] and other fine trees; and 10 or 12 leagues from there, up the river, we passed several islands covered with pines. The soil is sandy, and a root is found there which makes a crimson dye, with which the savages paint their faces and then they put on little gew-gaws in their own way. There is also a range of mountains along this river, and the country around seems to be rather rough. We spent the rest of the day on a very pleasant island.

The next day we continued our course as far as some big rapids, about three leagues wide, where the water descends about 10 or 12 fathoms over a slope and makes a marvelous noise.[24] It is filled with countless islands covered with pines and cedars. In order to pass it we had to make up our minds to give up our maize or Indian corn and the few other provisions that we had, with the least necessary luggage; reserving only our arms and lines, to afford us something to live on, according as places and luck in hunting might allow. Thus lightened we passed, sometimes rowing, sometimes by land, carrying our canoes and arms by three rapids, which are a league and a half long, where our savages, who are untiring in this work and accustomed to endure such hardships, helped us very much.

Pursuing our course we passed two other rapids; one by land, the other by rowing, and with poles, standing up; then we entered a lake[25] six or seven leagues long, into which empties a river[26] coming from the south. On this river, at a distance of five days' journey from the other river, there are people living, called Matouoüescarini. The land about

[22] Lake des Chênes.
[23] Butternuts.
[24] The Des Chats Rapids.
[25] Lac Des Chats.
[26] The Madawaska.

this lake is sandy and covered with pines, which have almost all been burned by the savages. There are some islands, in one of which we rested and saw beautiful red cedars, the first that I had seen in this country, from which I made a cross, which I set up at one end of the island on a high place, well in sight, with the arms of France, as I have done in other places where we have stopped. I named this island St. Croix.

On the 6th we left this island of St. Croix, where the river is a league and a half wide, and having gone eight or ten leagues we passed a little rapid by rowing, and a great many islands of different sizes. Here our savages left their sacks with their provisions and the least necessary things, in order to be less burdened in going by land to avoid several rapids that we had to pass. There was a great discussion among our savages and our impostor, who affirmed that there was no danger by the rapids, and that we ought to go that way. Our savages said to him: "You are tired of living"; and to me, that I ought not to believe him, and that he did not tell the truth. So, as I had several times noticed that he had no acquaintance with these places, I followed the advice of the savages, which was a lucky thing for me, for he was looking for difficulties, in order to ruin me, or to disgust me with the enterprise, as he confessed subsequently (which shall be mentioned later). So we crossed the river to the west, its course being from the north. I took the altitude of this place, which is in latitude 46⅔ degrees.[27] We had a great deal of trouble in following this trail by land, though I, for my part, was loaded only with three arquebuses, as many oars, my cloak and some little things. I encouraged my men, who were a little more heavily loaded and found the mosquitoes a worse burden than their loads.

Thus, after having passed four little ponds and gone two leagues and a half, we were so tired that we could not go any farther, for the reason that it was nearly twenty-four hours since we had eaten anything except a little broiled fish without any seasoning; for we had left our provisions, as I have already said. We rested on the shore of a pond, which was rather pleasant, and made a fire to drive off the mosquitoes, which tormented us greatly. Their persistency is so remarkable that it is impossible to give a description of it. We cast our lines to catch some fish.

The next day[28] we passed this pond, which is about a league long, and then we went by land three leagues, by a harder country than we had ever seen, in that the winds had beaten down the pines on top of

---

[27] It should be 45⅔ degrees.
[28] June 7.

SAMUEL DE CHAMPLAIN

one another, which is no slight obstacle, for it is necessary to pass sometimes over and sometimes under these trees. In this way we came to a lake,[29] six leagues long and two wide, very full of fish; and the people of the country about come there to fish. Near this lake there is a settlement of savages who till the soil and raise maize. The chief is named Nibachis. He came to see us, with his followers, and was surprised that we had been able to pass the rapids and bad roads that it was necessary to traverse to reach them. And, after having given us some tobacco, according to their fashion, he began to address his companions, saying to them that we must have fallen from the clouds, for he knew not how we could have got through the country; and that they who lived in the region had a great deal of trouble in going over these bad trails. He told them, in addition, that I was accomplishing all that I wished to; in short, that he believed of me what the other savages had told him about me. And, knowing that we were hungry, they gave us some fish, which we ate; and having dined, I made him understand, through Thomas, my interpreter, the pleasure that I felt in having met them; that I had come to this country to assist them in their wars, and that I wished to go farther, to see some other chiefs for the same purpose; at which they rejoiced and promised me help. They showed me their gardens and fields, where there was maize. Their soil is sandy, and for that reason they devote themselves more to the chase than to tilling the soil, in contrast to the Ochataiguins.[30] When they wish to prepare a piece of land for cultivation they cut and burn the trees, and they do this very easily, for there are only oaks and elms. When the wood is burned they stir up the ground a little and plant their maize, kernel by kernel, as people do in Florida.[31] It was only four inches high when I was there.

---

[29] Muskrat Lake. See Slafter's note in *Voyages of Champlain,* III, 64-66, for an account and a picture of the astrolabe found in this neighborhood in 1867, which is supposed to have been lost by Champlain.

[30] The Hurons.

[31] Used in the Spanish sense, which included what is now the Southern States of the Union.

ALGONQUIANS, HURONS AND IROQUOIS

CHAPTER II

Continuation. Arrival at Tessoüat's, and the kind reception he gave me. Character of their cemeteries. The savages promise me four canoes to continue my way. Soon afterward they refuse me them. Speech of the savages to dissuade me from my undertaking, showing the difficulties. Response with regard to these difficulties. Tessoüat accuses my guide of lying, and of not having been where he said he had. The guide maintains that what he says is true. I urge them to give me some canoes. Several refusals. My guide convicted of lying, and his confession.

NIBACHIS had two canoes equipped to take me to see another chief, named Tessoüat, who lived eight leagues from him on the shore of a great lake,[1] through which flows the river that we had left, which extends northward. So we crossed the lake[2] in a west northwesterly direction nearly seven leagues, where, having gone ashore, we went one league northeast in a rather beautiful country, where there are well-trodden footpaths, by which one may go easily; and we reached the shore of the lake,[3] where Tessoüat's settlement was. He was there with another neighboring chief, and was thoroughly astonished to see me, and told us that he thought it was a dream and that he did not believe what he saw. From there we went to an island,[4] where their cabins were pretty poorly covered with the bark of trees. The island is full of oaks, pines and elms, and is not flooded in high water, like the other islands in the lake.

This island is in a strong situation, for at its two ends and at the place where the river flows into the lake there are troublesome rapids, and their roughness makes the island a stronghold; and they have made their settlement there to avoid the pursuit of their enemies. It is in latitude 47°[5] as is the lake, which is ten leagues long and three or four wide. It is full off fish, but the hunting there is not very good.

When I visited the island I examined their cemeteries, and there I was greatly astonished to see sepulchres shaped like a bier, made of pieces of wood crossed at the top and fixed in the ground three feet or so apart. On the interlaced tops they put a large piece of wood, and in front

---

[1] Allumette Lake.
[2] Muskrat Lake.
[3] Allumette Lake is formed by an expansion of the Ottawa. The river is here divided by Allumette Island. On the shore of the lake opposite the island is the town of Pembroke.
[4] Allumette Island.
[5] Actually 45° 47'. S.

another piece upright, on which is rudely carved the face of the man or woman who is buried there. If it is a man, they put in a shield, a sword attached to a handle, according to their method; a club and bows and some arrows. If it is a chief, there will be a plume on the head and some other trinket or ornament. If a child, they give it a bow and an arrow. If a woman or a girl, a kettle, an earthen pot, a wooden spoon and a paddle. The whole tomb is six or seven feet long at most and four wide. Others are smaller. They are painted yellow and red, with much work as delicate as the tomb.[6] The deceased is buried in his robe of beaver-fur, or other furs which he used in his life, and they put all his riches close by him, such as hatchets, knives, kettles and awls, in order that these things may serve him in the country whither he is going; for they believe in the immortality of the soul, as I have said elsewhere. These sepulchres of this kind are made only for warriors; for others they do not put in more than they do for women, as being useless people; and so, little is found in their graves.

After having observed the poorness of this soil, I asked them how they enjoyed cultivating so poor a country, in view of the fact that there was some much better that they left deserted and abandoned, like that at the Rapids of St. Louis. They answered me that they were obliged to do so to keep themselves secure, and that the roughness of the place served them as a bulwark against their enemies. But they said that if I would make a settlement of Frenchmen at the Rapids of St. Louis, as I had promised to do, they would leave their dwelling-place to come and settle near us, being assured that their enemies would not do them harm while we were with them. I told them that this year we should make preparations with wood and stones to make a fort next year and cultivate the land. When they heard this they gave a great shout, as a sign of applause. This conference finished, I asked all the chiefs and leaders among them to meet the next day on the mainland, in Tessoüat's cabin. He wished to give me a tabagie.[7] I said that I would tell them my plans there. This

[6] The word *tombeau* is repeated by inadvertence. The narrative of 1613 has *la sculpture*, "the carving," in this place. *Voyages, 1613*, 308.

[7] An Algonquin word for "feast." It was introduced into French by Champlain, Lescarbot and others. The French lexicographers all derive it from, or connect it with, "tobacco." There is no connection of etymology or meaning. "Tobacco" is a West Indian word, and originally meant a kind of pipe or cigar used in smoking the herb. See Las Casas, *Historia de las Indias*, I, 332. The Algonquin word for tobacco is *petun*. Owing to this misconception of the lexicographers, *tabagie*, in French, came to mean "smoker," or smoking-room, tobacco pouch. In the first sense it is familiar to readers of Carlyle's

they promised to do; and then they sent to their neighbors and asked them to come there.

The next day all the guests came, each with his wooden bowl and his spoon, and they sat down, without order or ceremony, on the ground in Tessoüat's cabin. He distributed to them a kind of broth made of maize crushed between two stones, with meat and fish cut into small pieces, all cooked together without salt. They also had meat broiled over coals and fish boiled separately, which he also distributed. And as for me, inasmuch as I did not care for any of their broth, because they cook it in a very dirty way, I asked them for some meat and some fish, to prepare in my own way, and they gave it to me. To drink we had beautiful clear water. Tessoüat, who gave the tabagie, entertained us without eating, according to their custom.

When the tabagie was over, the young men, who are not present at the speeches and councils, and who, at the tabagies, remain at the door of the cabins, went out; and then each of those who remained began to fill his pipe, and one and another offered me one; and they spent a good half hour in this exercise, without saying a single word, as is their custom.

After having smoked sufficiently during this long silence I told them, through my interpreter, that the reason of my voyage was only to assure them of my affection and of my desire to aid them in their wars, as I had done before; that what had prevented me from coming the year preceding, as I had promised them to do, was that the King had occupied me in other wars; but that now he had commanded me to visit them and to assure them of these things, and that, with this object, I had a number of men at the Rapids of St. Louis; that I had come to go through their country to examine the fertility of the soil, the lakes, the rivers and the sea, that they had told me were in their country; and that I wished to see a tribe six days' journey from them—named Nebicerini[8]—to invite them also to the war. For this purpose I asked them to give me four canoes with eight savages to guide me to that country. And, inasmuch as the Algonquins are not great friends of the Nebicerini, they appeared to listen to me with greater attention.

My discourse over, they began again to smoke and to confer together in a very low voice with regard to my propositions. Then Tessoüat spoke

Frederick the Great, where frequent reference is made to the *tabagie*, "tobacco parliament," of the King, Frederick's father. Cf. also p. 157, below [204].

[8] The Nipissings, on Lake Nipissing.

for all and said that they had always thought me more attached to them than any Frenchman that they had seen; that the proofs that they had had of it in the past made their belief of it in the future easy. Moreover, I had thoroughly shown myself their friend, in that I had gone through so much danger in order to come see them and to invite them to the war; and that all these things obliged them to feel as kindly toward me as toward their own children. But still, he went on, I had broken my promise the preceding year and two hundred savages had come to the Rapids, expecting to find me and to go to the war, and to make me presents; and not having found me, they were very much saddened, thinking that I was dead, as some people had told them; and, further, that the Frenchmen who were at the Rapids would not aid them in their wars, and they had resolved among themselves not to go to the Rapids any more. This, he said, had been the reason for their going to war alone (not expecting to see me any more); and, in fact, two hundred[9] of them had gone. And, inasmuch as most of their warriors were away, they asked me to postpone the expedition to the following year, saying that they would tell the decision to everybody in the country. As for the four canoes for which I asked, they gave them to me, but with great reluctance, saying that they were greatly displeased with such an undertaking, because of the hardships that I should endure in it; that these people were sorcerers, and that they had killed a great many of their people by charms and poisoning, and that, on that account, they were not friends. Moreover, with regard to war, I had no business with them, inasmuch as they were a people of small spirit; and they wished to deter me from my purpose with several other considerations.

I, on the other hand, who had no other wish but to see these people and establish a friendship with them, in order to see the Northern Sea, took their difficulties lightly, saying to them that it was not far to that country; that, as for the bad trails, they could not be worse than those that I had already passed over, and that, as for their sorceries, they would have no power to harm me, and that my God would preserve me from them. I added that I was acquainted with their herbs and would, therefore, be careful about eating them; that I desired to make them all friends together, and that I was making them presents with that object, feeling sure that they would do something for me. In response to these reasons

---

[9] The figure in the 1613 narrative is 1200, and in the case of the 200, just above, 2000. *Voyages of Champlain*, III, 73.

they granted me, as I have said, four canoes, at which I was very glad, forgetting all past hardships in the hope of seeing the sea so much longed for.

To pass the rest of the day, I walked in the gardens, which were filled with nothing but squashes, beans and our peas, which they were beginning to cultivate. There Thomas, my interpreter, who understood the language very well, came to find me to warn me that the savages, after I had left them, had got the idea that if I should undertake this voyage I should die and they also; and that they could not give me those promised canoes, since there was no one among them who would guide me, but that they wished me to postpone the voyage to the next year, when they would take me there with a good equipment, in order to defend themselves against those people, in case they wished to do them harm, since they are bad.

The news made me feel very bad, and I went to them at once and said to them that until that day, I had regarded them as men and trustworthy, and that now they showed themselves children and liars; and that if they would not carry out their promise they would not show their friendship to me. If, however, they felt it an inconvenience to give me four canoes, they might give me only two, and four savages.

They described to me again the difficulty of the roads, the number of rapids, the wickedness of those tribes, and that it was for fear of losing me that they gave me this refusal. I answered them that I was sorry that they showed themselves so little my friends, and that I would never have thought it; that I had a young fellow with me (showing them my impostor) who had been in their country, and had not observed all the difficulties that they described, or found these people so bad as they said. Then they began to look at him, and especially Tessoüat, the old chief, with whom he had spent the winter; and, calling him by name, he said to him, in his language: "Nicolas, is it true that you said that you had been among the Nebicerini?" It was a long time before he spoke; then he said to them, in their language, which he spoke a little: "Yes; I have been there." They at once looked askance at him, and threw themselves on him, with loud cries, as if they would eat him or tear him to pieces; and Tessoüat said to him: "You are a bold liar; you know well that every night you slept at my side with my children, and every morning you got up there. If you have been among these people, it was while you were asleep. How have you been so barefaced as to tell your chief such lies, and so wicked as to be willing to risk his life among such dangers? You are a scoundrel, and he ought to put you to death more cruelly than we do our enemies. I am not surprised that he should be so insistent, on the assurance of your words."

I at once told him that he must reply, and that if he had been to that country he must give me some descriptions, to make me believe it, and to relieve me from the anxiety in which he had involved me; but he remained silent and altogether distracted. Then I drew him apart from the savages and exhorted him to tell me if he had seen this sea, and if he had not seen it to tell me that. Again, with oaths, he affirmed all that he had already said, and that he would show it to me, if these savages would give some canoes.

After this conversation Thomas came to warn me that the savages of the island had sent a canoe secretly to the Nebicerini, to inform them of my arrival. And, in order to profit by the opportunity, I went to these savages to tell them that I had dreamed that night that they were going to send a canoe to the Nebicerini without telling me of it; at which I was warned [surprised],[10] in view of the fact that they knew that I wished to go there. To this they answered me, saying that I did them a great wrong in trusting more to a liar, who wished me to lose my life, than to so many brave chiefs who were my friends and who cherished my life. I replied to them that my man (speaking of our impostor) had been in the country with one of Tessoüat's relatives, and had seen the sea and the wreckage of an English ship, together with eighty heads[11] that the savages had, and a young English boy whom they kept prisoner and whom they wished to present to me.

When they heard of the sea, the ships, the scalps of the Englishmen and the prisoner, they shouted more than before that he was a liar; and so they afterward called him, as if it were the greatest insult that they could have offered him, all saying together that he ought to be put to death, or that he should tell with whom he had been there, and that he should mention the lakes, rivers and roads by which he had gone. To this he answered that he had forgotten the name of the savage, in spite of the fact that he had named him to me more than twenty times, and even the day before. As to the characteristics of the country, he had described them in a paper that he had given to me. Then I presented the map, and

---

[10] The reading is "estonné" in the narrative of 1613 and "adverty" in the narrative of 1632. The latter is apparently a printer's or copyist's error, repeating the form from the immediately preceding phrase, "sans m'en advertir."

[11] Here, obviously, scalps; see note, vol. I, 217 [105].

had it interpreted to the savages, who questioned him upon it. To this he made no reply, and so, by his sullen silence, revealed his villainy.

As my mind was wavering in uncertainty, I went off by myself and called to mind the details of the voyage of the English that has already been mentioned, and the accounts of our liar were sufficiently in conformity to it; also that there was little probability that this fellow had invented all that, and that he would not have wished to undertake the journey; but that it was more credible that he had seen these things and that his ignorance did not permit him to reply to the questions of the savages. Besides, if the account of the English were true, the Northern Sea could not be more than 100 leagues in latitude from this country, for I was in latitude 47° and in longitude 296°. But it was possible that the difficulty of passing the rapids, and the roughness of the mountains covered with snow, was the reason why these people had no knowledge of this sea. To be sure, they had told me that from the country of the Ochateguins it was only thirty-five or forty days' journey to the sea, which they see in three places. Of this they again that year assured me. But no one had spoken to me of this Northern Sea, except this liar, who had greatly delighted me by reason of the shortness of the way.

Now, when this canoe was getting ready, I had him summoned before his companions and, explaining to him all that had taken place, I told him that he must not deceive me any more, and that he must say if he had seen the things spoken of, or not; that I wished to improve the opportunity that presented itself; that I had forgotten all that had taken place, but that if I went farther I would have him hanged and strangled.

After some reflection he fell on his knees and asked my pardon, saying that all that he had said, both in France and in this country, about this sea was false; that he never had seen it, and that he had not been farther than Tessoüat's village, and had said these things in order to get back to Canada. Beside myself with anger, I had him taken away, being unable to have him any longer before my eyes.[12] I also charged Thomas to inquire into everything in detail. He finally told him that he had not believed that I would take the journey, on account of the dangers, believing that some difficulty would present itself which would prevent me from going, such as the unwillingness of the savages to give me ca-

---

[12] Dr. Dawson remarks that this "is the only instance in Champlain's record when his even temper was ruffled." *The St. Lawrence*, 269. It will be recalled that this exploration to Hudson Bay was the principal object of the year's work when Champlain left France. See above, pp. 1-4 [123-124].

noes; that, in this way, the journey would be postponed until another year, and that when he returned to France he would be rewarded for his discovery; and if I would leave him in this country he would go until he found it, even if he should die. These were his words, which were reported to me by Thomas; but they did not please me very much, astonished as I was at the barefacedness and wickedness of this liar. Nor was I able to imagine how he had fabricated this deception, unless he had heard a report of the voyage of these English mentioned before and, in hopes of having some reward, as he said, had had the rashness to risk it.

Soon afterward I went to inform the savages, to my great regret, of the malice of this liar, and to tell them that he had confessed the truth to me, at which they were delighted, reproaching me for the lack of confidence that I had felt in them, who were chiefs and my friends, and who always spoke the truth; and they said that this liar must be put to death, for he was extremely malicious, saying to me: "Do you not see that he wished to cause your death? Give him to us and we promise you that he will never lie again." When I saw that they and their children were shouting after him, I forbade them to do him any harm, and told them to prevent their children from doing so, for I wished to take him back to the Rapids, in order to make him give his report; and that when I got there I would consider what I should do with him.

As my journey was ended in this way, and without any hope of seeing the sea in that quarter, except in my mind's eye, I regretted not having employed the time better, and also the trouble and labor that I had had to endure patiently. If I had gone in another direction, following the description of the savages, I should have outlined an undertaking which now had to be postponed until another time.

Having no other desire, for the moment, than to return, I asked the savages to come to the Sault St. Louis, where they should receive good treatment; which they announced to all their neighbors.

Before starting, I made a cross of white cedar, which I set up on the shore of the lake in a conspicuous place, with the arms of France; and I begged the savages kindly to preserve it, as also those that they would find along the roads where we had passed. They promised me to do so, and that I should find them when I should return to them.

ALGONQUIANS, HURONS AND IROQUOIS

CHAPTER III

Our return to the Rapids. False alarm. Ceremony at the Chaudière Falls. Confession of our liar before each one. Our return to France.

ON June 10[1] I took leave of Tessoüat, to whom I made several presents, and I promised him that, if God kept me in health, I would come the next year with an equipment to go to war; and he promised me to assemble a great number of people for that time, saying that I should see nothing but savages and arms, which would please me; and he gave me his son to keep me company. So we set out with four[2] [40] canoes, and went down the river that we had left, which turns to the north, at the place where we went ashore to take our way through the lakes. On our way we met nine large canoes of the Ouescharini with forty strong, powerful men, who came at the news that they had heard; and we met others also, making, together, sixty canoes, and twenty others who had set out before us, each one with a good quantity of merchandise.

We ran six or seven rapids between the island of the Algonquins[3] and the little rapids, a very disagreeable country. I saw very well that if we had come that way we should have had a great deal more trouble and could hardly have got along; and that it was not unreasonable for the savages to withstand our liar, whose only object was to make me lose my life.

Continuing our course ten or twelve leagues below the island of the Algonquins, we rested on a very pleasant island covered with vines and walnuts, where we caught some beautiful fish. About midnight two canoes came up from fishing farther off, which reported having seen four canoes of their enemies. At once three canoes were despatched to reconnoitre, but they returned without having seen anything. Relying upon this, each one took his repose, except the women, who decided to pass the night in their canoes, not feeling safe on land. An hour before dawn a savage, having dreamed that the enemy were upon him, jumped up with a start and began running to the river to escape, crying: "They are killing me!" Those of his band awoke, not knowing what was the matter; and, thinking that they were pursued by their enemies, they threw

---

[1] June 10, 1613.
[2] The narrative of 1613 says 40, *Voyages of Champlain*, III, 81, and the sum total a few lines below indicates the same.
[3] Allumette Island.

themselves into the water; as did also one of our Frenchmen, who thought that he was being knocked in the head. At this noise, the rest of us, who were at a distance, were also soon awakened, and, without asking anything more, ran toward them. But, seeing them wandering here and there in the water, we were very much astonished, for we did not see them pursued by their enemies, or in a condition to defend themselves. After I had inquired of our Frenchman the cause of this excitement, and he had told me how it had happened, it all passed off in laughing and ridicule.

Continuing our course, we arrived at the Chaudière Falls, where the savages had the accustomed ceremony, which is as follows: after having carried their canoes below the falls, they get together in one place, where one of them, with a wooden plate, takes up a collection, and each one of them puts into this plate a piece of tobacco. The collection made, the plate is put into the middle of the band, and all dance round it, singing in their fashion; then one of the chiefs makes a speech, showing that for a long time they have been accustomed to make this offering, and that by this means they are guaranteed against their enemies; that otherwise misfortune would befall them, as the devil has persuaded them; and they live in this superstition, as in several others, as we have said elsewhere. That done, the speaker takes the plate and goes and throws the tobacco into the middle of the caldron, and they raise a great cry all together. These poor people are so superstitious that they do not expect to have a good journey if they have not had this ceremony in this place, for their enemies await them in this passage, not daring to advance farther because of the bad trails; and sometimes they surprise them there.

The next day we arrived at an island at the entrance to the lake, seven or eight leagues from the great Rapids of St. Louis, where resting at night, we had another alarm, the savages having thought that they saw some canoes of their enemies. This made them make several big fires, which I had them put out, explaining the trouble that could come of them, namely, that instead of hiding themselves they would show where they were.

On June 17 we reached the Rapids of St. Louis, where I gave them to understand that I did not wish them to trade any merchandise without my permission; and that, as for provisions, I would have some given to them as soon as we should arrive; which they promised me, saying that they were my friends. So, continuing our course, we reached the barks, and were saluted by some discharges of cannon, at which some of the savages were delighted, and others very much astonished, never having heard such music. Having landed, Maisonneuve[4] came to me with the passport from Monseigneur the Prince. As soon as I had seen it, I let him and his men enjoy the benefit of it, like ourselves, and had the savages told that they might trade the next day.

When I had told all those on the bark about the details of my journey, and the malice of our liar, they were very much astonished; and I begged them to assemble, so that in their presence, and that of the savages and his companions, he might acknowledge his villainy; which they willingly did. So being assembled, they had him come, and asked him why he had not shown me the Northern Sea, as he had promised me. He answered them that he had promised something impossible, for he never had seen this sea; but that the desire to make the voyage had made him say that; also that he did not believe that I would undertake it. Wherefore he begged them to please pardon him, as he had begged me; confessing that he had done very wrong, but that if I would please leave him in the country long enough to repair the fault, he would see this sea, and report positive information in regard to it the next year. For certain reasons I pardoned him, on this condition.[5]

After the savages had traded their merchandise and had resolved to go back, I begged them to take with them two young men, to take care of them in a friendly way, show them the country, and pledge themselves to bring them back; to which they made great objections, pointing out to me the trouble that our liar had given me, and expressing the fear that they would make false reports to me, as he had done. I replied that if they would not take them, they were not my friends, and on that account they resolved to do so. As for our liar, none of the savages would have him, no matter how much I begged them, and we left him to the protection of God.

Seeing that we had no more to do a this country, I decided to return to France, and we arrived at Tadoussac on July 6.

[4] Paul de Chomedy, Sieur de Maisonneuve, founded Montreal on this spot in 1642, acting for "La Compagnie de Montréal." The original name was Ville-Marie de Montréal. Between 1611 and 1642 it was only a summer trading-station. Dawson, *The St. Lawrence*, 270.

[5] At this point in the narrative of 1613 are a few descriptive details of hunting, etc., while at the trading-station. *Voyages of Champlain*, III, 85-86.

SAMUEL DE CHAMPLAIN

On August[6] 8 the weather was suitable for sailing, and on the 26th of the same month[7] we arrived at St. Malo.

CHAPTER IV

The author goes to Sieur de Monts, who gives him the authorization to join the company. This he shows to the Count de Soissons. The commission that he gives him. The author addresses himself to the Prince, who takes him under his protection.

AFTER my return to France[1] I went to Sieur de Monts, at Pons in Saintonge, where he was Governor, and I told him of the success of the whole affair and the remedy that it was necessary to apply. He approved of all that I said about it, and, as his affairs would not permit him to come to court, he committed to me the execution of the matter and left me in full charge, with power of attorney to join the company, with such a sum as I should think suitable for him. When I arrived at court I made out some statements, which I gave to the late President Jeannin, who thoroughly approved of them and encouraged me to carry out the project, and even wished to do me the favor of taking these statements and showing them to the Council. But, clearly perceiving that those who love to fish in troubled waters[2] would find these regulations annoying, and would make an effort to hinder their being carried out, as they had done in the past, it seemed best to put myself in the hands of some great man whose authority could repel envy.

Since I had known the late Count de Soissons[3] (a Prince who was pious and kind in all virtuous and holy undertakings) through the help of some friends of mine who were of his Council, I explained to him the importance of the affair; the way to regulate it; the evil that disorder had caused in the past; and that it would bring on a complete ruin, to the great dishonor of the name of France, if God did not raise up some one who would restore it.

[6] Laverdière proposed to substitute July 8, on the ground that there was nothing to keep Champlain a month in Tadoussac, and that Maisonneuve's vessel, on which he sailed, was all ready. Cf. *Voyages, 1613*, p. 325; text and Laverdère's note.

[7] August 26, 1613.

[1] That is, in 1611. The first ten pages of this chapter, according to the chronological order, should precede chapter I of this volume, and follow p. 254 of vol. I. [p. 122]

[2] An idiom, meaning to take advantage of a confused state of affairs.

[3] Charles de Bourbon, Count de Soissons, was the youngest son of Louis de Bourbon, first Prince of Condé.

ALGONQUIANS, HURONS AND IROQUOIS

When he was informed of the whole affair, he looked at the map of the country and promised me, subject to the good pleasure of the King, to give the matter his protection. Meanwhile, Sieur the President Jeannin showed the articles to the gentlemen of the Council, through whom we asked His Majesty kindly to give us the Count as a patron. This was granted by the gentlemen of his Council. In addition, they sent the articles to the late Duke d'Anville, Peer and Admiral of France, who highly approved of this project, promising to do all that lay in his power to favor this enterprise. When I was on the point of having the letters patent of his commission published in all the ports and harbors of the kingdom, and was honored with an appointment as his lieutenant, in order to form such a company as seemed to me good, as is shown by the commission already mentioned and inserted here, a serious illness overtook the Count at Blandy, of which he died. This postponed this undertaking; a result which those who envied us did not dare attempt until after his death, when they thought that the whole matter had fallen through.

"Charles de Bourbon, Count de Soissons, Peer and Grand Master of France, Governor for the King in the provinces of Normandy and Dauphiné and his Lieutenant-General in the country of New France. To all those who shall see these present letters, Greeting: Be it known, to all to whom it may concern, that on account of the good and entire confidence that we have in the person of Sieur Samuel de Champlain, captain-in-ordinary for the King, in the navy, and because of his good sense, competence, practical knowledge and experience in seamanship, and great diligence and knowledge that he has of this country, on account of the various negotiations, voyages and visits that he has made there, and in other places adjacent: this Sieur de Champlain, on these accounts, and in virtue of the power given us by His Majesty, we have commissioned, ordered and deputed, and we do commission, order and depute, by these presents, to represent our person in this country of New France; and to this end we have commanded him to go and settle with all his people, in the place called Quebec, on the Saint Lawrence River, otherwise called the Great River of Canada, in this country of New France; and both in this place, and in other places that the Sieur de Champlain shall deem good, there to have constructed and built such other forts and fortresses as shall be necessary and needful to him for his preservation and that of his men; which fort, or forts, we shall keep in his control in this place of Quebec and other places to the extent of our power; and as much and as far as possible to establish, extend and make known the name, power and authority of His Majesty, and make all the peoples of this land, and those adjacent to it, subject themselves to it, submit to it and obey it; and that by means of this, and of all other lawful ways, he shall call, instruct, provoke and move them to the knowledge and service of God, and to the light of the faith and the Catholic, Apostolic and Roman religion; establish it there, and, in the exercise and profession of it, maintain, preserve and keep these places in obedience to His Majesty, and under his authority. And that he may have there more consideration, and act with more assurance, we have, in virtue of our power, permitted this Sieur de Champlain to commission, establish and appoint such captains and lieutenants as shall be necessary. And, likewise, to commission officers for the dispensation of justice, and for the maintenance of civil order, regulations and ordinances, and to carry on trade and to make contracts for that purpose, and for peace, alliance and confederation, good friendship, correspondence and intercourse with these peoples, and their princes, or others having power and rule over them; to maintain, keep and carefully preserve the treaties and alliances which he shall make with them, provided that they give satisfaction on their part. And, in default of this, to make open war with them, to restrain them and bring them to reason, as far as he shall judge necessary, for the honor, obedience and service of God, and the establishment, maintenance and preservation of the authority of His Majesty among them; at the least to live, dwell, resort and go in and out among them in all confidence, liberty, intercourse and communication; to negotiate and trade there in a friendly and peaceful way; to carry on, to this end, the discovery and exploration of these lands, and especially from this place called Quebec, to as far as they can reach above it of the regions and rivers that are tributary to this St. Lawrence River; to try to find a route easy to traverse through this country to the countries of China and the East Indies, or elsewhere, as far as possible, along the coasts and on the mainland; to have all the mines of gold, silver or copper, or other metals and minerals, carefully sought out and explored; to have the metals mined, extracted, purified and refined, to be converted and disposed of as is prescribed by the edicts and regulations of His Majesty, and as shall be commanded by us. And where this Sieur de Champlain finds Frenchmen, and others, trading, negotiating and communicating with the savages and people between this place Quebec and places beyond it, as was said above, for whom no reservation has been made by His Majesty, we have authorized him, and do authorize him, to seize and apprehend such persons, together with their ships, merchandise and all that is found belonging to them, and to have them brought and sent to France, to the harbors of our Government of Normandy, to the hands of justice, to be prosecuted according to the severity of the Royal ordinances, and what has been accorded us by His Majesty. And, this done, this Sieur de Champlain shall manage, carry on business and bear himself in the performance of his duties as our lieutenant, in the manner that he thinks will advance this conquest and settlement; the whole for the good, service and authority of His Majesty, with the same power, sway and authority that we should have if we were there in person, and as if the whole matter were expressly specified and declared in greater detail. And, in addition to all this already stated, we have given this Sieur de Champlain permission, and we now give him permission, to associate and take with him such persons, and to make use of such sums of money, as he thinks best for the carrying out of our undertaking. For its management, even for the embarkation and other things necessary to this object that he will do in the cities and harbors of Normandy and other places, where you will judge it appropriate, we have, moreover, given, and we now do give, you, by these presents, all the responsibility, power, commission and special command; and for this we have substituted and delegated you in our place and office with the duty of observing, and causing to be observed by those under your charge and rule, all that has been stated; and of making for us a good and faithful report, on all occasions, of all that shall have been done and accomplished, that we may give a prompt explanation to His Majesty. So we pray and request all Princes, Potentates and foreign Lords, their lieutenant-generals, admirals, governors of their provinces, chiefs and leaders of their soldiers, whether by sea or by land, captains of their cities and coast forts, harbors, shores, havens and straits, to give to this Sieur de Champlain, for the whole carrying out and execution of these presents, all support, succor, assistance, shelter, help, favor and aid, if there be need of it, and in whatever may be required by him.

"In witness whereof, we have these presents signed with our own hand, and countersigned by one of our secretaries-in-ordinary; and upon these we have had the seal of our arms set and attached.

"Paris, the fifteenth day of October, one thousand six hundred and twelve.

SAMUEL DE CHAMPLAIN

"Signed   CHARLES DE BOURBON.
"And on the other side, by Monseigneur
the Count,   BRESSON."

But this condition of things did not last any longer than was necessary, for I resolved to address myself to the Prince, who, when I had explained the importance and merit of the affair to him, which the Count had taken up as protector, was very willing to continue it on his authority, which caused me to have his commissions drawn up, His Majesty having given his protection. When the commissions were sealed, the Prince continued to honor me with the lieutenancy of the late Count, with the administration of it, in order to take into partnership such persons as I thought good, and capable of aiding in the carrying out of the enterprise.

As I was preparing to publish in all the ports and harbors of the realm the commissions of the Prince, some busybodies, who had no interest in the matter, asked him to annul it, on the pretence that such a step would be for the interest of all the merchants in France, who had no reason to complain, since each one of them was received into the association and, therefore, could not justly take offence; for this reason, when their malice was recognized, they were rejected, receiving permission only to become members of the company.

During these altercations I could not do anything for the settlement in Quebec, and I had to be satisfied, for this year, to go there without forming any organization and only with the passports of the Prince, which were made out for five ships, namely: three from Normandy, one from La Rochelle and another from St. Malo; on condition that each should furnish me six[4] men, together with what was necessary to aid me in the discoveries which I hoped to make beyond the great Rapids, and the twentieth of what they should be able to make from furs, to be employed in repairs of the settlement, which was going to destruction. That is all that can be done this year, until the company shall be formed.

All these ships were getting ready, each in its port and harbor, and I went to set sail at Honfleur[5] with Sieur du Pont Gravé, who was acting for the associates who had not disbanded. Once on board, we went

---

[4] Four in narrative of 1613.
[5] April 6, 1613.

directly to Tadoussac,[6] and from there to Quebec, where we arrived in good health.[7] This was in the year 1613.

Continuing our course from there to the great Rapids of St. Louis, where each one traded in skins, I looked for the ship that was first ready, to return in it.[8] It was that of St. Malo, in which I embarked; and, weighing anchor and spreading sails, we had such favorable winds that in a few days we arrived in France. When we were there I explained to several merchants how profitable and useful a well-organized company would be, if conducted under the authority of a great prince, who could support it, in spite of any amount of envy; and that they should consider what they had lost by the lack of regulations in the past, and even in the present year, from mutual envy. And, realizing all these faults, they promised me to come to court to form a company, under certain conditions. When this was agreed I went to Fontainebleau, where the King was, and also the Prince, to whom I gave a faithful report of my voyage.

Some days afterward the ships of St. Malo and of Normandy were ready, but those of La Rochelle were not. Meanwhile I did not relax my efforts to organize the company at Paris, reserving one-third of the shares for those of La Rochelle, with the understanding that, in case they did not wish to join it within a certain time, they would not thereafter be received. They were so dilatory in this affair that they did not come in time and were, consequently, excluded; and those of Rouen and St. Malo took up the whole, sharing equally.

At that time one had to make arrows of all kinds of wood,[9] for the incessant appeals to the Prince forced me to do a great many things at his command. Finally, the company was formed and the agreements made, and I had them ratified by the Prince and His Majesty for eleven years. When this company had existed some time in peace there arose some dissension between them and those of La Rochelle, who were angry at having been excluded for not having presented themselves at the time set. This resulted in a great lawsuit, which was hung up until they obtained from the Prince a passport by a trick for a ship which, by the

[6] Champlain arrived at Tadoussac April 29.

[7] May 7.

[8] The narrative now passes over the exploration of the Ottawa, given above in chs. I-III, pp. 1-42 [123-143], and takes up the events of 1613 where they were dropped at the close of ch. III.

[9] I. e., resort to every kind of expedient.

will of God, was lost fifteen leagues below Tadoussac, on the north shore. For without this stroke of fortune there is no doubt at all that, as it was well armed, it would have fought, wishing to enjoy the passport unjustly acquired, contrary to ours, in which the Prince pledged himself not to give any passports except to those of our company, and that if any others should be found, in whatever manner or way they were obtained, he declared them null and void henceforward, as well as from the date of issue. For this reason it would have been right to seize those of La Rochelle, which could not have been done except with the loss of a number of men. A part of the merchandise of this ship was saved and taken by our men, who got good profit from it with the savages, which caused them a very good year. On their return they had a great lawsuit against La Rochelle, which was at last settled in favor of this organization.

Continuing this enterprise under the authority of the Prince, and seeing that we had no clergy, we got some through the intervention of Sieur Hoüel,[10] who had a particular affection for this holy plan, and told me that the Recollect fathers would be the right ones there, both for residence at our settlement and for the conversion of the infidels. I agreed with this opinion, as they are without ambition and live altogether in conformity to the rule of St. Francis. I spoke of them to the Prince, who heartily approved, and the company offered voluntarily to support them until they could have a seminary, which they hoped to get through the charitable alms that would be given them, to take charge of and instruct the young.[11]

Certain individuals of St. Malo, urged by others as envious as themselves at not being members of the company (although there were some of their fellow-citizens in it), wished to attempt something: but, not daring to go to the Prince, or to find councillors of State who would be willing to undertake their petition against his authority, continued to have it inserted in the *cahier général*[12] of the Estates that it be permitted to have the trade in furs free throughout the province, as a very impor-

---

[10] Louis Hoüel, secretary of the King and comptroller-general of the salt works at Broüage. *Voyage, 1619*, 3.

[11] This was the beginning of Catholic missions in Canada. Among the merchants trading in Canada the Huguenots were prominent, but the Huguenot influence lost ground from now on. Cf. Dawson, *The St. Lawrence*, 271.

[12] A memorial containing a list of grievances, or proposed changes, submitted to the Estates General. This meeting of the Estates General, in 1614, was the last ever held until that in 1789, at the opening of the French Revolution.

tant thing. It was a very serious article, and those who worded it should be pardoned, for they did not understand the matter, which was explained to them contrary to the truth.

This shows how the most famous assemblies make mistakes when they act without investigation. These envious persons thought that they had made a great stroke, and that in this assembly of the Estates held in Paris, miracles would be accomplished in regard to this matter, as if they had no other threads to wind. Having got wind of this, I spoke of it to the Prince and showed him the interest that he had in this prohibition, which was so just, contained in this article, and that if he would please do me the honor of securing me a hearing, I would make it clear that Brittany had no interest in the matter, except the people of St. Malo, the most important of whom had been admitted into that company, and that others had refused to enter, and, in their ill-will, had had this article inserted in the *cahier* of the province. He told me that he would have me speak to these gentlemen; which was done, and I then made clear the truth of the matter. By this means the article came to be fully understood and was not annulled.

CHAPTER V

Departure of the author for New France. New discoveries in the year 1615.

WE left Honfleur on August [April[1]] 24, 1615, with four fathers and set sail with a very favorable wind and went on our way without meeting ice or any other dangers, and in a short time arrived at Tadoussac, the 25th of May, where we rendered thanks to God for having brought us so seasonably to the harbor of safety.[2]

We began to set men to work to fit up our barks, in order to go to Quebec, the place of our settlement, and to the great Rapids of St. Louis, the gathering-place of the savages who come there to trade. Immediately upon my arrival at the Rapids, I visited these people, who were very anxious to see us and delighted at our return, from their hopes that we would give them some of our number to help them in their wars against their enemies. They explained that it would be hard for them to come to

---

[1] The context five lines below and elsewhere shows that April is the correct reading.
[2] The narrative of 1619 contains additional details at this point. *Voyages of Champlain*, III, 106-109.

us, if we did not assist them, because the Iroquois, their old enemies, were always along the trail and kept the passage closed to them. Besides, I had always promised them to aid them in their wars, as they gave us to understand through their interpreter. Whereupon I perceived that it was very necessary to assist them, not only to make them love us more, but also to pave the way for my undertakings and discoveries, which, to all appearances, could not be accomplished except by their help; and also because this would be to them a sort of first step and preparation to coming into Christianity; and to secure this I decided to go thither and explore their country and aid them in their wars, in order to oblige them to show me what they had so many times promised to.

I had them all gather to tell them my intention, upon hearing which they promised to furnish us 2500 men of war, who would do wonders, while I, on my part, was to bring, for the same purpose, as many men as I could; which I promised them, being very glad to see them come to so wise a decision. Then I began to explain to them the methods to follow in fighting, in which they took a singular pleasure; and they showed a good hope of victory. When all the matters were decided upon, we separated, with the intention of returning to carry out our undertaking. But before making the journey, which could not occupy less than three or four months, it was fitting for me to make a trip to our settlement to make such regulations for matters there as would be necessary during my absence. And the next day[3] I left there to return to the Rivière des Prairies with two canoes of savages.

On the ninth of this month[4] I embarked with two others, namely, one of our interpreters and my man, with ten savages, in the two canoes, which was all they could carry, since they were heavily loaded and weighed down with clothes, which prevented me from taking more men.

We continued our journey up the St. Lawrence River about ten leagues and went by the Rivière des Prairies,[5] which empties into this river. We left the St. Louis Rapids, five or six leagues higher up on the left, where we passed several little rapids in this river, and then entered a lake,[6] beyond which we entered the river,[7] where I had been formerly, which

[3] Apparently June 23. Cf. Laverdière, *Voyages, 1619*, 243.
[4] July 9, 1615.
[5] The Rivière des Prairies, or Black [Back] River, is the branch of the Ottawa that goes east of the Island of Montreal.
[6] The Lake of Two Mountains.
[7] The Ottawa.

ALGONQUIANS, HURONS AND IROQUOIS

leads to the Algonquins, eight to nine[8] leagues from the St. Louis Rapids, of which river I have given a full description already.[9] Continuing my journey as far as the lake of the Algonquins[10] we entered a river[11] which flows into this lake and went up it about thirty-five leagues and passed a great number of rapids, either by land or by water, through an unattractive country full of firs, birches and some oaks, a great many rocks and, in many places, somewhat mountainous. It was, moreover, a very barren waste and hardly inhabited, except by some Algonquin savages—called Otaguottouemin—who live in the country and support themselves by their hunting and by the fishing which they carry on in the rivers, ponds and lakes with which the country is pretty well provided. It is true that God seems to have wanted to give to these frightful desert regions something in its season to serve for the refreshment of man and for the inhabitants of these places, for I assure you that there are along the rivers a great quantity of blueberries, a small fruit very good to eat, and a great many raspberries and other small fruits, and in such quantities that it is wonderful. These fruits the inhabitants dry for their winter, as we do prunes in France for Lent. We left this river, which comes from the north[12] and is that by which the savages go to the Saguenay to exchange their furs for tobacco. This place is in latitude 46°; it is rather pretty to look at, but otherwise of little importance.

Pursuing our route by land, leaving the river of the Algonquins,[13] we passed several lakes, where the savages carry their canoes, until we entered the lake of the Nipissings, in latitude 46¼°. This was on the twenty-sixth day of the month,[14] after having gone not only by land, but by the lakes, twenty-five leagues or thereabouts. Then we arrived at the cabins of the savages,[15] where we tarried two days with them. They gave us a kind welcome, and there was a considerable number of them. They are people who do not cultivate the soil much. *A* shows the dress of these

---

[8] Accepting Laverdière's emendation, reading "8 à 9" for "89," which takes the distance to be that from the rapids to where the des Prairies River branches off from the Ottawa.

[9] See above, pp. 6-14 [126-129].

[10] Allumette Lake.

[11] This section of the Ottawa is called La Rivière Creuse, or Deep River.

[12] The junction of the Ottawa from the north and the Mattawa from the northwest, which Champlain followed some distance.

[13] The Mattawa.

[14] July 26, 1615.

[15] The Nipissings. The actual distance is about 32 miles. S.

Indian Costumes
[See pp. 152, 154, 155, 184]

people going to war; *B,* that of the women, which differs in no particular from that of the Montagnais and Algonquins, great peoples, who extend far into the interior. While I was with them the chief of these people, and others of their oldest men, entertained us with several feasts, according to their custom; and took the pains to go fishing and hunting, in order to treat us in the most polite way possible. There were fully 700 or 800 of them who live ordinarily on the lake, where there are a great number of very pleasant islands; and, among others, one which is more than six leagues long, where there are three or four pretty ponds and a number of fine meadows with very beautiful woods surrounding them. There is a great abundance of game which frequent these little ponds, where the savages fish. The northern side of this lake is very pleasant. There are fine meadows for pasturing cattle and several little rivers which flow into them.

At that time they were fishing in a lake very full of various sorts of fish; among others one very good, which is a foot long, and also other kinds, which the savages take to dry for provisions. This lake, in its extent, is about eight leagues wide and twenty-five long.[16] Into it flows a river which comes from the northwest,[17] by which they go to barter the merchandise that we give them in exchange for their furs, with those who live in that region, who live by hunting and by fishing, because the country is very full of animals, birds and fish.

When we had rested two days with the chief of these Nipissings, we embarked in our canoes and entered a river[18] into which this lake empties, and went by it about thirty-five leagues, and went down by several little rapids, partly by land and partly by water, as far as Lake Attigouantan.[19] All this country is still more unpleasing than that before it, for I did not see, along this river, ten acres of tillable land, but rather rocks and mountains. To be sure, near Lake Attigouantan, we

[16] Lake Nipissing is 55 miles long and 10-20 wide. North Bay, near where Champlain was, is now a junction point between the Grand Trunk and Canadian Pacific railroads.
[17] Sturgeon River.
[18] French River.
[19] Georgian Bay, Lake Huron. The route Champlain had just pursued "continued to be the fur traders' high road to the west until the days of steamboat navigation. In the early days of the Colony it was beyond the usual reach of Iroquois war parties, and it is, in fact, the shortest and most direct route to Lake Superior, for from the Strait of Machilimackinac to the head of tidewater, at Lake St. Peter, below Montreal, is an absolutely due east line—the parallel of 46° N." Dawson, *The St. Lawrence,* 273. The name is uniformly Attigouantan in the 1632 narrative, but Attigouautan in that of 1619.

found some Indian corn, but in small quantity; and there our savages gathered some squashes, which seemed good to us, for our provisions had begun to fail through the bad management of the savages, who ate so much at first that at the last very little was left, although we had only one meal a day. The blueberries and raspberries helped us a great deal (as I have already said); otherwise we should have been in danger of want.

We met 300 men of a tribe that we named Cheveux Reléves,[20] because they wear their hair dressed very high and better combed than our courtiers, beyond comparison, however many irons and forms they may use. This seems to give them a fine appearance. *A* and *C* show how they are armed when they go to war. They have nothing for arms but the bow and arrow, made in the way that you see depicted, which they ordinarily carry, and a round shield of dressed leather from an animal like the buffalo.[21] When they go out from their homes they carry the club. They wear no breeches and they have their bodies pinked in many patterns, and they paint their faces with various colors. Their nostrils are pierced and their ears adorned with beads. When we had visited them and formed a friendship with them I gave a hatchet to their chief, who was as much pleased and delighted with it as if I had given him some rich gift. When I asked him what was his country, he indicated it to me with a piece of charcoal on the bark of a tree, and informed me that they came to this place to dry some of the fruit called blueberries, to serve them for manna in winter, when they cannot find anything else.

The next day we separated, and continued our way along the shore of the lake of the Attigouantan, which contains a great number of islands, and went about forty-five leagues, keeping, all the time, along this lake. It is very large and is nearly 300 leagues long from east to west and 50 wide;[22] and, because of its great extent, I named it The Fresh Sea.[23] It abounds in several kinds of very good fish, not only those that we have, but also some that we do not have, and chiefly in trout, which are monstrously large. I saw some that were as much as four and a half feet long, and the smallest that were seen were two and a half feet. Pike of similar

---

[20] The "High Hair."

[21] The bison.

[22] It is not unlikely that Champlain gives, as the length of Lake Huron, what the Indians gave as the combined length of Superior and Huron, omitting or not making clear the existence of the St. Mary's River. Lake Huron is about 250 miles long and from 50 to 200 wide.

[23] La Mer Douce.

ALGONQUIANS, HURONS AND IROQUOIS

size also are plentiful, and a certain kind of sturgeon, a very large fish and extraordinarily good. The country bordering this lake is partly rough, on the north side, and partly flat and inhabited by savages, and somewhat covered with woods and oaks. Afterward we crossed a bay,[24] which forms one end of the lake, and went about seven leagues, until we arrived at the country of the Attigouantan,[25] at a village called Otoüacha, on the first day of August, where we found a great change in the country, this being very beautiful and, for the most part, cleared, and with many hills and several rivers, which make this region pleasant. I went to examine their Indian corn, which was then far advanced for the season.

These places seemed very pleasant to me, in comparison with a country so poor as that from which we had just come. The next day I went to another village called Carmaron, one league from this one, where they received us very kindly, giving us a feast of their bread, squashes and fish. As for meat, it is very scarce there. The chief of the village strongly urged me to stay there, which I could not grant him, and so I returned to our village.

The next day I went away from this village to another called Touaguainchain, and to another called Tequenonquiaye, in which we were received in a very friendly way by the inhabitants of these places who made good cheer for us as well as they could with their Indian corn in different ways. The country is beautiful and fertile, and traveling through it is fine.

From there I had myself guided to Carhagouha, which was enclosed by a triple palisade of wood, thirty-five feet high, for their defence and preservation. When I was here—August 12—I found there thirteen or fourteen Frenchmen who set out before me from the Rivière des Prairies.[26] When I saw how slow the savages were in assembling their army, and that I had time to visit their country, I decided to go by short days' journeys from village to village to Cahiagué, where the whole army was to have its rendezvous, about fourteen leagues distant from Carantouan.[27] I left this village the 14th of August with ten of my companions. I visited five of the principal villages, fortified by palisades of wood, and reached Cahiagué, the principal village of the country, where there are 200 pretty large cabins, where all the men of war were to gather. In all

[24] Matchedash Bay.
[25] The region between Georgian Bay and Lake Simcoe.
[26] These Frenchmen were accompanied by Father Joseph Le Caron.
[27] Read Carhagouha. L.

these villages they received us very courteously and kindly. This country is very beautiful. It is in latitude 44½°, and there are very many clearings where they plant a great quantity of Indian corn, which grows there finely; as is also the case with squashes and sunflowers, from the seed of which they make oil, with which they rub their heads. It is much intersected by brooks, which flow into the lake; and there are a great many vines and plums, which are very good; raspberries, strawberries, little wild apples,[28] nuts and a kind of fruit which has the form and color of small lemons, about the size of an egg. The plant that bears it is two and a half feet tall and has three or four leaves, at the most, of the form of the fig-leaf, and each plant bears only two apples.[29] Oaks, elms and beeches are found in abundance, likewise many forests of firs, which are the common resort of partridges and rabbits. There are also a quantity of small cherries and wild cherries, and the same kinds of wood that we have in our forests in France are to be found in this country. To tell the truth, the soil seemed to me a little sandy, but it is, notwithstanding, good for their kind of wheat. In this little stretch of country I discovered that the population consisted of an infinite number of souls, to say nothing of the other regions where I did not go, which are (by common report) as much or more populous than these; and it came over me that it was a great pity that so many creatures live and die without the knowledge of God, and even without any religion, or law, either divine, political, or civil, established among them. For they do not worship or pray in any way, as far as I could observe from their conversation. They have, indeed, a certain kind of ceremony among them, which I will describe in its place, for any one who is sick, or to find out what is going to happen to them, even in regard to the dead; but these ceremonies are performed by certain persons who want to impose on people, just as they did, or as it was done, in the time of the ancient pagans who allowed themselves to be carried away by the persuasions of enchanters and diviners; nevertheless, the most of the people do not believe in anything that they do and say. They are kind enough to one another, as far as food is concerned, but in other respects very avaricious, and do not give anything for nothing. They wear deer- and beaver-skins, which they get from the Algonquins and Nipissings in exchange for Indian corn and Indian meal.

[28] Probably the American crab-apple. S.
[29] Probably the May-apple. S.

ALGONQUIANS, HURONS AND IROQUOIS

CHAPTER VI

Our arrival at Cahiagué. Description of the beauty of the country: character of the savages who inhabit it, and the inconveniences that we suffered.

ON the 17th day of August I arrived at Cahiagué,[1] where I was received with great delight and thankfulness by all the savages of the country. They heard that a certain nation of their allies, who lived three good days' journey beyond the Entouhonorons,[2] with whom the Iroquois are also at war, wished to assist them in this expedition with 500 good men, and make an alliance, and swear friendship toward us. They had a great desire to see us, and for us all to fight together; and showed that they were glad of our acquaintance, and I was equally glad to have found this opportunity, because of the desire that I had to get some news of this country.[3] This nation is very warlike, according to the belief of the nation of the Attigouantans. There are only three villages,[4] which are in the middle of more than twenty others, with which they are at war; without the assistance of their friends, for they are obliged to pass through the country of the Chouontouaroüons, which is thickly settled, or else make a very long circuit.

When I had arrived at this village it was best for me to stay there until the men of war should come from the neighboring villages, so that we might go on as soon as possible; during which time they kept having feasts and dances, because of the joy that they felt to see us so determined to aid them in their war, just as if they were already confident of the victory.

When most of our men had assembled, we left the village, on the first day of September, and passed along the shore of a little lake[5] three leagues from the village, where they catch a great deal of fish, which they cure for the winter. There is another lake very near, twenty-six leagues in circumference,[6] flowing into the small one at a place where the great

---

[1] Near the town of Orillia, near the lower end of Lake Simcoe. Parkman, *Pioneers of France*, 399.
[2] The western portion of the Five Nations in Champlain's usage. See *Voyages of Champlain*.
[3] I. e., the present State of New York.
[4] I. e., of this tribe of allies of the Attigouantans.
[5] Lake Couchiching.
[6] Lake Simcoe.

catch of this fish is made by means of a great many stakes, which almost close the strait, leaving only some little openings where they set their nets in which the fish are caught. These two lakes empty into the Fresh Sea.[7] We stayed in this place a little while, to wait for the other savages. When they had all come with their arms, meal and necessary things, we decided to choose some of the most resolute men in the band to go to give notice of our starting to those who were to help us with 500 men, so that they might join us and we might arrive at the same time before the stronghold of the enemy. When we had made this decision they sent two canoes with twelve of the strongest savages and one of our interpreters,[8] who begged me to let him make the journey; which I granted readily, since he wished it, and, in this way, would see the country, and would find out about the people who inhabit it. The danger was not slight, since it was necessary to pass through the midst of the enemy. We continued our way toward the enemy, and went about five or six leagues through these lakes, and then the savages carried their canoes about ten leagues by land, and we came upon another lake extending about six or seven leagues in length[9] and three in width. From it flows a river which empties into the great lake of the Entouhonorons.[10] When we had crossed this lake we passed a rapid, and, continuing our course, still going down this river, about sixty-four leagues—that is, to the entrance of this lake of the Entouhonorons—we passed five rapids by land, some of them four or five leagues long, where there are several lakes of rather large size. These lakes, as well as the river which flows from one to the other, abound in fish, and the whole country is very beautiful and attractive. Along the river bank it seemed as if the trees had been planted there in most places for pleasure, and also as if all these regions had once been inhabited by savages who since had been obliged to abandon them, for fear of their enemies. The vines and walnuts are very plentiful, and grapes ripen there, but they always leave a sharp, acid taste, which comes from not being cultivated; for the clearings in these places are rather attractive.[11]

    Hunting for stags and bears is very common here. We hunted there and took a goodly number of them as we journeyed down. To do this they station 400 or 500 savages in line in the woods, with the line touching

[7] Lake Huron.
[8] Étienne Brulé. L.
[9] Sturgeon Lake.
[10] Lake Ontario.
[11] I. e., from the standpoint of a settler, implying a fertile soil and a sunny exposure.

certain points that project into the river, and then marching in order, with the bow and arrow in the hand, shouting and raising a great noise to surprise the animals, they keep going until they reach the end of the point on the river. Then all the animals that are between the point and the hunters are driven to throw themselves into the water, unless they try to run the gauntlet of the arrows which are shot at them by the hunters. Meanwhile, the savages who are in the canoes, posted and arranged on purpose along the shore of the river, approach the stags and other animals hunted and worried and greatly frightened. Then the hunters kill them easily with spearheads attached to the end of a stick, like a half-pike. This is how they hunt, and they follow the same method in the islands, where there is a great deal of game. I took special pleasure in watching them hunt in this way, observing their skill. Many animals were killed by shots of the arquebus, at which they were greatly amazed. But it unfortunately happened that, as some one was shooting at a stag, a savage who chanced to come in range was wounded by a shot of an arquebus, without any one intending it, as may be assumed. Thereupon, there arose a great commotion among them, which was, however, quieted by giving some presents to the wounded man, which is the usual way of pacifying and settling quarrels. And, if the wounded man dies, the presents and gifts are given to the relatives of him who was killed. As for game, there is a great deal of it in the season. There are also many cranes, as white as swans, and several other kinds of birds such as those in France.

We went, by short days' journeys, as far as the shore of the lake of the Entouhonorons, hunting all along, as I have said. When we arrived there we went across at the eastern end, which is the entrance to the great River St. Lawrence, at latitude 43°, where there are some beautiful and very large islands in this passage. We went about fourteen leagues to get to the other side of the lake, in a southerly direction, toward the territory of the enemy. The savages hid all their canoes in the woods near the shore.[12] We went about four leagues by land, along a sandy beach, where I observed a very agreeable and beautiful country crossed by several little brooks and two small rivers which empty into this lake; and a great many ponds and meadows, where there were an unlimited amount of

[12] "On or near the point of land west of Hungry Bay." Parkman, *Pioneers of France*, 401. Mr. O. H. Marshall thought the most probable location of the landing place to be in Henderson Bay, under the shelter of Stony Point. *Historical Writings of the late Orsamus H. Marshall*, 53.

game, many vines and beautiful woods, and a great number of chestnut trees, of which the fruit was still in the burr. The nuts are very small, but taste good. All the canoes being thus concealed, we left the shore of the lake, which is eighty leagues long and twenty-five wide.[13] The most of this region is inhabited by savages living on its shores. We continued our way by land twenty-five or thirty leagues. For four days' journey we crossed a great many brooks and a river coming from a lake which empties into that of the Entouhonorons.[14] This lake is 25 or 30 leagues in circumference. There are some pretty islands in it, and it is the place where the Iroquois' enemy catch fish, which are abundant there.

The 9th of the month of October our savages, as they were exploring, met, four leagues from the enemy's stronghold, eleven savages whom they took prisoners, namely: four women, three boys, one girl and three men, who were going fishing. Now it must be noted that one of the chiefs, upon seeing these prisoners, cut off the finger of one of these poor women as a beginning of their usual punishment. Whereupon I interfered, and blamed the chief—Iroquet—showing him that it was not the act of a warrior, as he represented himself to be, to be cruel to the women, who have no defence but their tears, and who, on account of their helplessness and weakness, should be treated kindly. I told him that, on the contrary, this act would be thought to come from a low and brutal courage, and that if he did any more of these cruel things he would not give me any courage to assist them, or to favor them in their war. To which his only answer was, that their enemies treated them in the same way; but that since this sort of thing was displeasing to me, he would do nothing more to the women, but he certainly would to the men.

The next day at three o'clock in the afternoon we arrived in front of the stronghold of their enemies,[15] where the savages got into some skirmishes with one another, although our plan was not to reveal ourselves until the next day; but the impatience of the savages would not allow it,

---

[13] Lake Ontario is 197 miles long and 30 to 60 miles wide.

[14] Oneida River and Oneida Lake.

[15] The site of this fort has been placed in the town of Fenner, on Nichols Pond, Madison County, N. Y., a little south of Oneida Lake, by Parkman, *Pioneers of France*, 403; Dawson, *The St. Lawrence*, 279; and Mr. Slafter's note in his *Voyages of Champlain*, I, 130. Mr. O. H. Marshall, on the other hand, made out a strong case for locating it "on or near Onondaga Lake, four leagues or ten miles from the great Iroquois fishery at the foot of Oneida Lake." *The Historical Writings of the late Orsamus H. Marshall*, 19-66. The sentence quoted is on p. 59.

both on account of their desire to see their enemies shot, and also that they might rescue some of their men who had got in too close. At that moment I drew near and was on the spot, but with very few men; nevertheless, we showed them what they had never seen or heard. For, as soon as they saw us, and heard the arquebus shots, and the balls whistling by their ears, they withdrew promptly to their forts, carrying their dead and wounded; and we also, in a like manner, retreated to our main body with five or six of our men wounded, one of whom died there.

When this was done we retreated about a cannon shot out of sight of the enemy, but against my advice and what they had promised me. This moved me to speak to them rather roughly and angrily, in order to stir them up to do their duty, for I foresaw that if everything went according to their notions, and following the guidance of their advice, nothing could result but harm leading to their undoing and ruin. Nevertheless, I did not give up sending to them and proposing means that should be used to overcome their enemies. This was to make a wooden platform with walls,[16] which should overlook their palisades. Upon this should be stationed four or five of our arquebusiers, to fire over their palisades and galleries, which were well supplied with stones; and in this way the enemy, who might harass us from their galleries above, might be dislodged. Meantime, we would give orders to provide some boards to make a kind of mantelet, to cover and protect our men from arrows and from stones. These things, namely: this cavalier and the mantelets, could be carried along by a large number of men. One was made in such a way as to prevent water from being used to put out any fire which might be set to the fort; and those who were on the cavalier would be doing their duty, with some arquebusiers to be stationed there. By this means we should defend ourselves in such a way that they could not draw near to put out the fire that we should apply to their ramparts. Approving this suggestion, the next day they set about building and equipping these cavaliers and mantelets; and they worked with such diligence that they were done in less than four hours. They hoped that that day the promised 500 men would come, but there was some doubt about them, because they had not appeared at the rendezvous, as they had been bidden to do and had promised. This troubled our savages very much. But, perceiving that there were enough of them to take the fort and, as I thought, for my part, that delay in all affairs is always detrimental, at least in many re-

---

[16] Called a "cavalier" in the French.

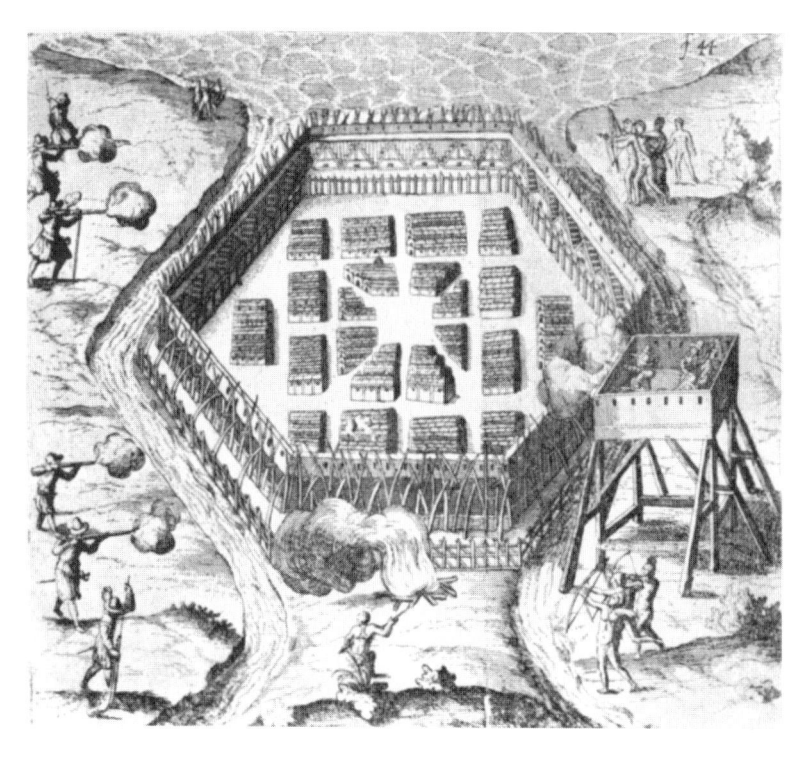

The Attack on the Iroquois Fort

spects, I urged them to attack this fort, explaining to them that the enemy, having found out about their forces and the effect of our arms, which pierced what was proof against arrows, would barricade themselves and be covered; a safeguard they were already resorting to, for their village was enclosed within four good palisades of logs of wood interlaced, so that there was not more than half a foot of opening between any two. These palisades were thirty feet high, and had galleries after the fashion of a parapet, which were furnished with [a front wall of] pieces of wood set double—proof against our arquebus shots. They were near a pond, where the water never failed. There were a good many gutters, one placed between each pair of loopholes, by which water was poured outside, and they had water inside, under cover, to extinguish fire. This is their method of fortification and of defence, and they are stronger than the villages of the Attigouantans.

Now, we approached to attack this village, having our cavalier carried by 200 of the strongest men, who set it down before the palisades at the distance of a pike's length. I had four arquebusiers mount upon it. They were well protected from the arrows and stones which could be shot and thrown at them. Meanwhile, the enemy did not cease, on that account, to shoot and throw a great number of arrows and stones from over their palisades. But the many arquebus shots fired upon them forced them to move and to abandon their galleries. Now, when the cavalier was brought up, instead of bringing up the mantelets, according to orders, and, in particular, the one under which we were to set the fire, they left them and began to yell at their enemies while they shot arrows into the fort, which (in my opinion) did not do much execution. They must be excused, for they are not soldiers and, besides, they do not want any discipline or correction, and only do what seems good to them. This is why one of them thoughtlessly set fire to the fort quite in the wrong way and against the wind, so that it had no effect. When the fire was out, most of the savages began to carry wood to the palisades, but in so small a quantity that the fire did not have much effect. The disorder, too, which arose among these people was so great that we could not hear one another. I shouted after them in vain, and remonstrated with them, as well as I could, as to the danger to which they exposed themselves by their lack of intelligence, but they heard nothing, on account of the great noise that they were making. Seeing that I was like to burst my head with shouting, and that my protests were vain, and that there was no way to remedy the disorder, I decided to do what I could with my men, and to shoot at those whom we could discover and get sight of. Meanwhile, the enemy took advantage of our disorder; they went to the water and threw it on in such abundance that one would have said that it was brooks which flowed through their spouts; so much that in less than no time the fire was all out; and they kept up shooting arrows, which fell upon us like hail. Those who were on the cavalier killed and maimed many of them. We were about three hours in this fight. Two of our chiefs and leaders were wounded, namely, one named Ochateguain, the other Orani, and about fifteen other warriors. The others on our side, seeing their men wounded and some of their chiefs, began to talk of retreat, without further fighting, to wait for the 500 men, who could hardly delay coming any longer; and so they withdrew, for no reason save this freak of disorder. But then, the chiefs have no absolute control at all over their companions, who follow their own inclination and do as they please, which is the cause of their disorder, and which ruins all their affairs. For, having determined upon something among themselves, it only needs a rascal to destroy their resolution and make a new plan. So they accomplish nothing for one another, as may be seen from this expedition.

As I was wounded by two arrow shots—one in the leg and the other in the knee—which discommoded me a great deal, we withdrew to our fort. Now, when all were assembled, I remonstrated with them several times with regard to the disorder that had taken place, but all my talk was to no purpose and did not move them at all, for they replied that a great many of their men had been wounded, as well as myself, and that it would cause a great deal of fatigue and annoyance to those who were retreating to carry them; that there was no way of returning against their enemies, as I proposed to them; but that they would be glad to wait four days longer for the 500 men who were to come, and when they came they would make a second attempt against their enemies; and would carry out what I told them better than they had done in the past. That was as far as I could get, to my great regret. The foregoing shows how they fortify their towns, and by this picture one may understand and see that those of their friends and enemies are similarly fortified.

The next day there was a very violent wind which lasted two days, very favorable for setting fire again to the enemy's fort; which I urged them strongly to do; but, afraid of getting the worst of it and, besides, pleading their wounds, they found excuse for not wishing to do anything.

ALGONQUIANS, HURONS AND IROQUOIS

We were in camp until the 16th of this month,[17] and during this time there were some skirmishes between the enemy and our men, who very often got caught by the enemy, rather through their rashness than lack of courage; and I can assure you that it was necessary, every time they went to the charge, to go and get them out of the throng, since they could get back only under cover of our arquebus shots, which the enemy greatly feared and dreaded. For, as soon as they caught sight of one of the arquebusiers, they withdrew at once, saying to us, in a persuasive manner, that we should not interfere in their fights, and that their enemies had very little courage to require us to assist them, with a great deal more talk of that kind.

Seeing that the 500 men did not come, they planned to set out and to make their retreat as soon as possible; and they began to make a sort of baskets to carry the wounded, who are put into them, huddled up in a bunch, bent over and bound in such a way that it is impossible for them to stir any more than a baby in its swaddling clothes; and it cannot help making them feel great pain. I can certify to this, having been carried some days, on the back of one of our savages, thus tied and bound, which wore out my patience. As soon as I had the strength to stand up, I got out of this prison, or, to express it better, off the rack.

The enemy pursued us about half a league, to try to catch some of those who formed the rear-guard; but their efforts were useless, and they fell back.

The only good feature that I noticed about their warfare is that they make a retreat with great security, putting all the wounded and the aged in the centre, with well-armed men in front, on the wings and at the rear, and they keep up this arrangement until they are in a safe place, without breaking their ranks. Their retreat was very long, say 25 or 30 leagues, which was a source of great weariness to the wounded and to those who carried them, although the latter changed from time to time.

On the 18th of the month a great deal of snow fell, which lasted a very short time, with a high wind that inconvenienced us very much; nevertheless, we did so well that we arrived at the shore of the lake of the Entouhonorons, and the place where our canoes were hidden, which we found all whole. We had been afraid that the enemy might have broken them up. When they were all together and ready to go back to their village, I begged them to send me back to our settlement; which they

---

[17] October 16, 1615.

SAMUEL DE CHAMPLAIN

did not wish to grant me at the beginning, but at last they resolved to do so, and looked for four men to guide me. These volunteered. For (as I have already said) the chiefs have no control over their companions, which is the reason why they often fail to do what they would like to have them. When the four men were ready, there was no canoe, each one needing his own. This did not afford me pleasure; on the contrary, it distressed me very much, for they had promised to take me back and guide me, after their war, to our settlement. Besides, I was very poorly prepared to spend the winter with them; except for that, I should not have been concerned about it. Some days afterward I perceived that their plan was to keep me, and my companions also, not only for their own security, for they feared their enemies, but also for us to hear what passed in their councils and assemblies, and to help determine what to do in the future.

The next day, the 28th of this month, each one began to make preparations—some to hunt deer; others bear and beaver; others to go fishing; others to go back to their villages. And to provide me with a retreat and lodging, one of the principal chiefs, called Darontal, offered me his cabin, provisions and accommodations. He himself went off deer-hunting, which is regarded by them as the most noble form of the chase. After having crossed the end of the lake, from the island before mentioned, we went up a river[18] about twelve leagues; then they carried their canoes by land half a league, at the end of which we entered a lake,[19] some ten or twelve leagues in circumference, where there was a great quantity of game, such as swans, white cranes, bustards,[20] wild geese, ducks, teal, thrushes, larks, snipe, geese and several other kinds of birds too numerous to mention, of which I killed a great number, which stood us in good stead while we waited for some deer to be caught. From there we went to a certain place ten leagues off, where our savages thought there were a great many of them. Twenty-five savages got together and set about building two or three cabins of logs of wood, laid one upon another, and they stopped up the chinks with moss, to prevent the air from coming in, covering them with the bark of trees. When this was

---

[18] The Cataraqui. Dawson, *The St. Lawrence,* 281.

[19] Loughborough Lake, or some neighboring one of the group.

[20] Outardes, bustards. The early French travelers called the brant goose a bustard. See *Voyages of Champlain,* III, 48, and Baxter, *Jacques Cartier,* 158, n. Newton's *Dictionary of Birds,* on the other hand, gives the ordinary wild goose, *Bernicla canadensis,* as the outarde of the early explorers.

done, they went into the woods near a grove of firs, where they made an enclosure in the form of a triangle, closed on two sides and open on one. This enclosure was made by a stockade eight or nine feet high and about 1500 paces long on each side; at the apex of this triangle there was a little yard, which grew narrower and narrower, covered in part by branches, leaving an opening of only five feet, about the width of an ordinary door, by which the deer were to enter [this yard]. They did so well that in less than ten days they had their enclosure ready. Meanwhile, some other savages had gone fishing for such fish as trout and pike of immense size, which were all that we needed. When everything was ready, they started half an hour before daylight to go into the woods about half a league from their enclosure, separated from one another eighty paces, each having two sticks, which they beat together, marching slowly in this order until they came to their enclosure. When the deer hear this noise, they flee before them until they reach the enclosure, into which the savages drive them, and gradually they come together at the opening of their triangle, where the deer run along the sides of the stockade until they reach the end, toward which the savages pursue them sharply, with bow and arrow in hand, ready to shoot. And when they reach the end of their triangle, they begin to shout and to imitate wolves, which are plentiful and which dvour the deer. The deer, hearing this frightful noise, are obliged to enter the small yard by the narrow opening, whither they are pursued in a very lively fashion by arrow shots, and there they are easily caught; for this yard is so well enclosed and so confined that they cannot get out of it. There is great sport in such hunting, which they continued every two days so successfully that in thirty-eight days they captured 120 deer, from which they feasted well; reserving the fat for the winter, which they use as we do butter, and a little of the flesh, which they carry off to their houses to have for feasts with one another; and from the skins they made themselves clothes.

There are other devices for catching deer, such as the snare, with which they take the lives of many. Thus you see depicted opposite a representation of their hunt, enclosure and snares. This is how we passed the time while waiting for it to freeze, so that we might go back more easily, since the country is very marshy.

In the beginning, when we set out for the hunt, I went off too far into the woods in pursuing a certain bird, which seemed strange to me. It had a beak like that of a parrot, and was as big as a hen and yellow all over, except for its head, which was red, and its wings, which were blue.

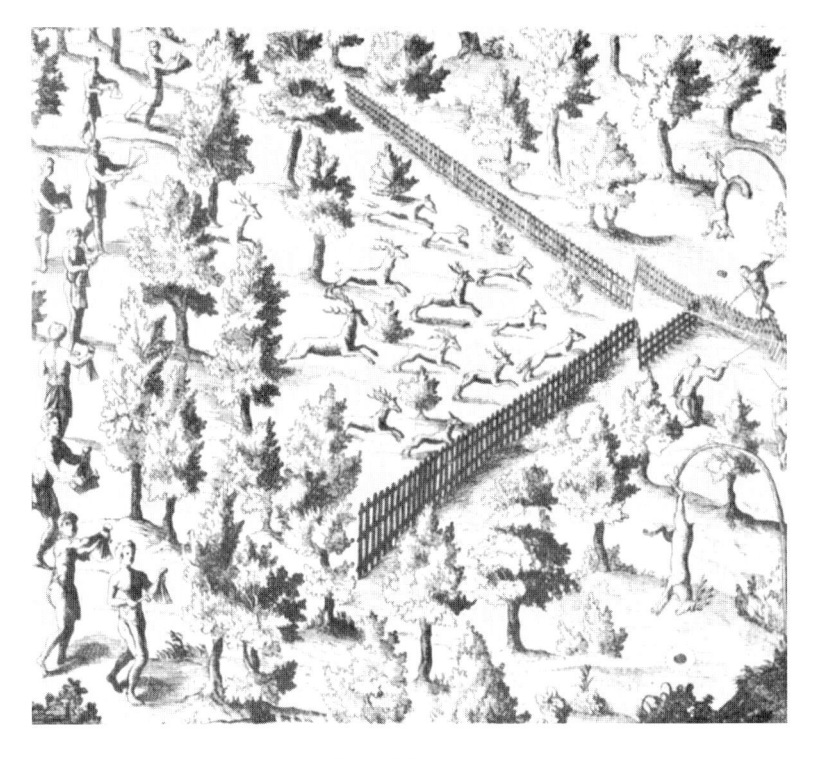

Deer Hunting

ALGONQUIANS, HURONS AND IROQUOIS

It made short flights, like a partridge. My desire to kill it led me to follow it from tree to tree a very long time, until it flew away. Then, losing all hope, I wished to return upon my steps, where I found none of our hunters, who had been constantly gaining upon me until they had reached their enclosure. In trying to catch up with them, going, as it seemed to me, straight to where the enclosure was, I lost my way in the forest—going now one way, now another—without being able to see where I was. As night was coming on, I passed it at the foot of a large tree. The next day I set out and walked until three o'clock in the afternoon, when I found a little stagnant pond, and seeing some game there, I killed three or four birds. Tired and worn out, I prepared to rest and to cook these birds, from which I made a good meal. My repast over, I thought to myself what I ought to do, praying God to aid me in my misfortune in this wilderness; for, during three days, there was nothing but rain mingled with snow.

Committing all to His mercy, I took courage more than before, going hither and thither all day without catching a glimpse of any footprint or trail, except those of wild beasts, of which I generally saw a good number; and so I passed the night without any consolation. At dawn of the next day, after having a scant meal, I resolved to find some brook and follow it, judging that it must needs empty into the river on whose banks our hunters were. This resolution once made, I put it through with such success that at noon I found myself on the shore of a small lake about a league and a half long, where I killed some game, which helped me very much; and I still had eight or ten charges of powder. Walking along the bank of this lake to see where it discharged, I found a rather large brook, which I followed until five o'clock in the afternoon, when I heard a great noise. Listening, I could not discern what it was until I heard the noise more distinctly, and then I concluded that it was a waterfall in the river that I was looking for. Going nearer I saw an opening,[21] and when I had reached it, I found myself in a very large, spacious meadow, where there were a great many wild animals. And, looking on my right, I saw the river, wide and big. Wishing to examine this place, and walking in the meadow, I found myself in a little path where the savages carry their canoes. When I had examined this place well, I recognized that it was the same river, and that I had been that

---

[21] The word in the text is *écluse*, which makes no sense. In the 1619 narrative it is *éclasie*, which is not given in the dictionaries consulted. In both cases the reading should be *éclaircie*, a glade, or opening in a wood.

way. Well pleased at this, I supped on the little that I had and lay down for the night. When morning came, and I had studied the place where I was, I inferred, from certain mountains that are on the border of that river that I was not mistaken and that our hunters must be higher up[22] than I by four or five good leagues, which I covered at my leisure, going along the bank of this river, until I caught sight of the smoke of our hunters. I reached their place, greatly to their happiness as well as to my own. They were looking for me, and had lost hope of seeing me again; and they begged me not to separate from them any more, and to take my compass with me, which I had forgotten, which could have put me back on my way. They said to me: "If you had not come, and we could not have found you, we should not have gone to the French any more, for fear of their accusing us of having taken your life." After this, Darontal was very careful of me when I went hunting, always giving me a savage to accompany me.

To return to my subject, they have a certain superstition about hunting, namely, that if they should have some of the meat taken in this way roasted, or if any of the fat should fall into the fire, or if any of the bones should be thrown into it, they would not be able to catch any more deer; and, for this reason, they begged me not to have any of it roasted. In order not to shock them, I refrained from it while I was with them. Afterward, when I told them that I had had some roasted, they would not believe it, saying that, if that were true, they would not have caught any deer if such a thing had been done.

CHAPTER VII

How the savages traverse the ice. Concerning the Tobacco People. Their way of living. People called the Neutral Nation.

ON the fourth day of December we set out from this place, walking on the river, which was frozen, and on the frozen lakes and ponds, and through the woods, nineteen days, which was not without much trouble and labor, both for the savages, who were each loaded with 100 pounds weight, and for myself, who carried a load of 20 pounds. It is very true that I was sometimes relieved by our savages; but, nevertheless, I did not avoid a great deal of discomfort. As for them, in order to traverse the ice

---

[22] In the 1619 narrative the reading is "lower down" *dessous*, instead of *dessus*.

more easily, they are accustomed to make a sort of wooden sled[1] on which they put their loads. Then they draw them behind them, going very quickly. Some days afterward there came a great thaw, which distressed us very much; for we had to go through fir forests full of brooks, ponds, marshes and swamps. Here were a great many trees overthrown upon one another, which made us no end of trouble, and other difficulties, causing us great discomfort, for we were all the time wet up above our knees. We traveled four days in this condition, because in most places the ice did not bear us. We traveled so well that we arrived at our village[2] on the twenty-third day of this month. There Captain Iroquet came to winter with his companions, who are Algonquins, and his son, whom he brought to have treated and his wound dressed, because, while he was hunting, he had been very seriously hurt by a bear that he was trying to kill. After resting some days, I decided to go to see the peoples, in winter, whom the summer and the war had not allowed me to visit. I left this village on the fourteenth of the following January,[3] after having thanked my host for the kind entertainment that he had given me. Taking some Frenchmen with me; I traveled to the Tobacco Nation,[4] where I arrived on the seventeenth of this month of January. These people plant maize, called Turkish corn in France, and have a fixed dwelling-place, like the others. We went to seven other villages of their neighbors and allies, with whom we made a pledge of friendship; and they promised us to come in large numbers to our settlement. They made us very good cheer and gave us a present of flesh and fish to make a feast, as is their custom. All the people ran in from every direction to see us, making us a thousand demonstrations of friendship, and they accompanied us most of the way. The country is full of hills and little fields, which make the landscape pleasant. They were beginning to build two villages, through which we passed, in the midst of the woods, because they find such a place convenient for building and fortifying them. These people live like the Attigouantans and have the same customs, and are near the

[1] The familiar toboggan.
[2] Cahiagué.
[3] Jan. 14, 1616.
[4] La Nation de Petum (read Petun); otherwise, the Petuneux. *Petun* was the Algonquin word for tobacco. They lived southwest of the Hurons, with whom Champlain had been staying, a region corresponding to the present counties of Dufferin and Grey. Dawson.

SAMUEL DE CHAMPLAIN

Neutral Nation,[5] which is powerful and occupies a large extent of country three days' journey from them.

After visiting these people, we left that place and went to a nation of savages which we named the Cheveux Reléves,[6] who were very much delighted to see us again. We established a friendship, and they, in turn, promised to come to see us at our settlement. In this place it has seemed to me suitable to describe them and give an account of their country, customs and manners. In the first place, they are at war with another tribe of savages called Asistagueroüon which means Fire People,[7] who live ten days' journey from them. I informed myself very much in detail about their country[8] and the tribes that inhabit it, what they are like and how many of them there are. This tribe is very large and most of its members are great warriors, hunters and fishers. They have several chiefs, each of whom commands in his own region. Most of them plant Indian corn and other grains. There are hunters who go in troops to various regions and countries, where they trade with other tribes more than 400 or 500 leagues distant. They are the cleanest savages in their households that I have seen, and they work the most industriously at various patterns of mats, which are their Turkish rugs. The women keep the body covered; the men uncovered, without anything except a fur robe which they put on their bodies. It is a kind of cloak, which they leave off ordinarily, especially in summer. The women and the girls are no more moved at seeing them in this way than if they saw nothing out of the ordinary. The women live very happily with their husbands. They have the following custom when they have their menses: they withdraw from their husbands, or the daughters from their fathers and mothers and other relatives, and go into little houses, where they stay in retirement while the illness lasts, without having any association with men, who have provisions and articles carried to them until their return. Thus, it is known who is in that condition, and who is not. These people have great feasts—even more than other tribes. They made us good cheer and received us very kindly, and asked me earnestly to aid them against their enemies, who are on the border of the Fresh Sea, 200 leagues off. To this

---

[5] The Nation Neutre lived in that part of Ontario north of Lake Erie. They received their name from their attempt to be neutral in the wars between the Hurons and the Iroquois.

[6] The Ottawas.

[7] The Algonquin name for the Gens de Feu was Mascoutins. S.

[8] I. e., the country of the Cheveux Reléves.

I answered that I would do so at another time, for I did not have what was necessary then. There is also, in a southerly direction, at two or three days' journey from these, another tribe of savages who make a great deal of tobacco. They are called the Neutral Nation, and a great many of them are warriors. They live to the south of the Fresh Sea and assist the Cheveux Reléves against the Fire People. But with the Iroquois and our men they are at peace, and maintain neutrality. I had a great desire to see this nation, but they dissuaded me from doing so, saying that the preceding year one of our men had killed one of them when we were at war with the Entouhonorons,[9] and that they were offended by it. And we were told that they are much given to revenge, not considering at all who made the attack, but inflicting the penalty upon the first man of the tribe that they catch, or even on one of their friends, when they can catch one of them, unless beforehand some agreement has been made with them, and gifts and presents have been given to the relatives of the deceased. This prevented me from going at this time, although some of this tribe assured us that they would not do us any harm on this account. This gave us the reason for returning by the same way by which we had come.

Continuing my journey, I went to find the nation of the Pisierinii,[10] who had promised to conduct me further in the continuation of my plans and explorations. I was, however, diverted from this by the news that came from our great village and from the Algonquins, where Captain Iroquet was, to the effect that the nation of the Attigouantans had placed in their hands a prisoner of a hostile nation, with the hope that Captain Iroquet would inflict on this prisoner the revenge common among them. But, instead of this, he had not only set him at liberty, but, having found him skillful and an excellent hunter, had treated him like a son, at which the Attigouantans had become jealous, and resolved to take the vengeance themselves; and, in fact, had appointed a man to undertake to go and kill this prisoner, although he was allied to them. As he was executed in the presence of the principal men of the Algonquin nation, they, indignant at such an act and moved by anger, immediately killed this rash man who had undertaken murder. The Attigouantans, in turn, being offended by this murder and insulted by this act, where they saw one of their companions dead, seized their arms and betook them-

---

[9] The expedition of 1615 against the Iroquois. Entouhonorons was the Huron name of the Iroquois.

[10] Nipissings.

SAMUEL DE CHAMPLAIN

selves to the tents of the Algonquins (who winter near their village). They attacked this Captain Iroquet severely, and he was wounded by two arrow shots. At another time they plundered some of the cabins of the Algonquins before the could get ready to defend themselves, so that the two sides did not have an equal chance. In spite of this, these Algonquins had not settled the score, for they were obliged to come to terms and were compelled, in order to have peace, to give the Attigouantans some[11] necklaces of wampum,[12] with 100 fathoms of it,[13] which is regarded of great value among them; and, besides, a number of kettles and axes, with two women prisoners in place of the dead man. In brief, they were in a great quarrel. These Algonquins had to suffer this great rage patiently, and expected that all would be killed, for they would not be very secure, notwithstanding their gifts, until they should find themselves in another situation. This news troubled me very much, for I imagined the difficulties that could arise from it, not only for them, but for us who were in their country.

I soon met two or three savages of our village, who urged me to go there to get them to come to terms, telling me that if I did not go there none of them would return any more to the French, for they were at war with these Algonquins, and looked upon us as their friends. Seeing this,

---

[11] The number 50 is mentioned in the narrative of 1619. *Voyages of Champlain*, III, 149.

[12] Pourceline. This is translated wampum, as this Indian name has been adopted in English usage. In French the primary use of "porcelaine" is as the name of the Porcelain or Venus shell: Cypraea Porcellana. In English, the secondary meaning only, i. e., as the name of chinaware, is familiar. Hence it is misleading to translate Champlain's "pourcelaine" by "porcelain" as Mr. Otis does in the *Voyages of Champlain*.

[13] *Brasses*, which is used in a somewhat special sense in the description of wampum. In the later writers *branches* is commonly used. Charlevoix gives the following description of this wampum, or shell-work: "There are two sorts of these shells, or, to speak more properly, two colours—one white and the other violet. The first is most common, and perhaps on that account less esteemed. The second seems to have a finer grain when it is wrought; the deeper the colour is, the more it is valued. Small cylindrical beads are made of both, which are bored through and strung upon a thread, and of these the *branches* and collars of shell, or wampum, are made. The branches are no more than four or five threads, or small straps of leather about a foot in length, on which the beads of wampum are strung. The collars are in the manner of fillets or diadems formed of these branches, sewed together with thread, making a tissue of four, five, six or seven rows of beads, and of proportionable length; all which depends on the importance of the affair in agitation, and dignity of the person to whom the collar is presented." Charlevoix, *Journal of a Voyage to North America, etc.,* London, 1761, I, 319. One or two verbal changes have been made in the translation.

ALGONQUIANS, HURONS AND IROQUOIS

I set out as soon as possible, and in passing I visited the Nipissings to find out when they would be ready for the journey to the north, which I found they had given up, on account of these quarrels and fights, as our interpreter explained to me. He told me, also, that Captain Iroquet had come to all these tribes to find me, and to wait for me. He begged them to be at the camp of the French at the same time that he was, to see what agreement could be made between them and the Attigouantans, and to postpone the journey to the north until another time. For this purpose this Iroquet had given some wampum to break off the journey, and they promised us to come to our camp at the same time with us. If ever any one was in distress it was I, who had been waiting patiently to see, this year, that for which during several years preceding I had searched with a great deal of care and labor.

These people go to traffic with others who live in those northern regions, a great part of them being in a district where the hunting is very good and where there are a great many large animals, of which I have seen several skins. When I formed an idea of their shape, I judged that they were buffaloes.[14] The fishing too is very abundant there. It takes forty days to make this journey, either going or returning.

I started out for our village, mentioned above, on the fifteenth day of February, taking with me six of our men. When we got there the inhabitants were very much pleased, as were also the Algonquins, whom I sent our interpreter to visit, in order to find out how everything had happened, not only on one side, but on the other. I did not wish to go, in order not to give either side any suspicion. Two days were spent in finding out from both sides how it all took place. This done, the principal men and elders of the place came away with us and we all went together to the Algonquins; and, in one of their cabins, after some speeches, they agreed to accept and abide by all that I should say, as umpire in the matter, and said that they would put into execution whatever I should propose. Collecting and seeking out the wishes and inclinations of both parties, and judging that all that they wanted was peace, I explained to them that the best course was to be at peace, and to remain friends, so as to resist their enemies more easily; and when I went away I begged them not to call upon me at all to do this for them, if they did not intend to follow, point for point, the advice that I should give them with regard to this dispute, since they had asked me to give my opinion. Whereupon

---

[14] The American bison.

they told me at once that they had not desired my return for any other purpose. I, for my part, felt sure that if I did not reconcile and pacify them they would part ill-disposed toward one another, each one thinking that he had the right of it; also that they would not have gone to their cabins if I had not been with them, or even to the French, if I had not embarked in the matter and taken, as it were, charge and conduct of their affairs. Thereupon I said to them that, for my part, I had no other intention than to go with my host, who had always treated me well, and that I should with difficulty find one so good, for he was the one whom the Algonquins blamed, saying that he was the only captain who had had arms taken up. Much talking was done on both sides, and the conclusion was that I should give them my advice and tell them what seemed best to me.

Seeing that they referred the whole matter to my will, as if I were their father, and promised that in the future I might do with them as seemed good to me, I answered them that I was very glad to see them so inclined to follow my counsel, and I assured them that it should be only for the good and advantage of the tribes. On the other hand, I was very much troubled to hear other sad news, namely, the death of one of their relatives and friends, whom we regarded as one of our own, and that this death had been able to cause such great distress, from which nothing but perpetual wars with each other would have resulted, with many great disasters and a change in their friendship; that, in consequence, the French would have been deprived of seeing them and visiting them, and would have been obliged to go in search of other nations; and this, too, when we were loving one another like brothers, leaving to our God the punishment of those who should merit it.

I explained to them that such actions between two nations, friends and brothers as they called themselves, was unworthy of reasonable men, but rather like brute beasts; moreover, that they had difficulty enough to repel their enemies who pursued them, generally routing them to their villages and taking them prisoners; that these enemies, seeing such a division and civil wars among them, would rejoice and derive profit from it; and that they would be impelled and encouraged to make and carry out new plans, in the hope that they would soon see their ruin, or at least their enfeeblement, through themselves, which would be the true and easy way for them to conquer them and triumph over them, and make themselves masters of their country, since they no longer helped one another; that they did not appreciate the evil that could come to them in this way, or that for the death of one man they put 10,000 men in danger of dying, and the others of being in perpetual slavery; that, in truth, one man was of great consequence, but that it must be considered how he had been killed, and that it was not with deliberate purpose, or to begin a civil war among them, it being only too obvious that the dead man had committed the first offence in that he had pounced upon and killed the prisoner in their cabin, having undertaken a thing that was too audacious, even if the latter were an enemy.

This stirred up the Algonquins, and, seeing that a man had been bold enough to kill another in their cabin, when they had given him his liberty and had treated him like one of themselves, they were beside themselves at once; and some, whose blood was up more than others, could not control themselves, nor restrain their anger, and had killed the man in question; but, not-withstanding this, they had no ill-feeling toward the nation as a whole, and had no further purpose than the dealing with this rash man. They thought that he fully merited what he had got, since he had himself sought it.

And, besides, it was noted, that the Entouhonoron, feeling himself wounded by two blows in the stomach, wrenched from his wound the knife which his enemy had left there and gave him two stabs with it, as I had been told positively; so that one could not know for certain if it were the Algonquins who had committed the murder. And to prove to the Attigouantans that the Algonquins did not love the prisoner, and that Iroquet did not bear so much affection for him as they had supposed [I said that], they had eaten him,[15] all the more since he had inflicted stabs of the knife upon his enemy; a thing, however, unworthy of man, but rather of brute beasts. Moreover, the Algonquins were very sorry for all that had taken place, and that if they had thought that such a thing would occur they would have given this Iroquois as a sacrifice. As for the other side, now that recompense had been made for this death and offence (if it should be called so) with fine presents and two prisoners, they had no reason, at present, to complain, and ought to conduct themselves more mildly toward the Algonquins, who are their friends; and that, since they had promised me to arbitrate with regard to everything, I begged them both to forget all that had occurred between them, and never to think of it again, nor bear any hatred or ill-will. If they did this we should be under obligations to love and aid them, as I had done

---

[15] Cf. Parkman, *Pioneers of France,* 359; also vol. I, p. 226 [109].

in the past. And if they were not pleased with my advice I begged as many of them as could to come to our settlement, where, before all the captains of vessels, our friendship might be confirmed anew and counsel might be taken to arrange to secure them from their enemies—a thing to be thought of.

Then they said that they would adhere to all that I had said to them, and they returned to their cabins, to all appearances very happy, except the Algonquins, who broke up to retreat to their village; but, according to my opinion, they did not seem to be entirely happy, inasmuch as they said to one another that they should not come any more to pass the winter in these places. The death of these two men had cost them too much. I returned to my host, whom I encouraged as much as I could, in order to persuade him to come to our settlement, and to bring there all the inhabitants of his country.

During the four months of winter I had enough leisure to observe their country, manners, customs, way of living, and the form of their assemblies, and other things, which I shall describe presently. But, first, it is necessary to speak of the situation of the country,[16] and its divisions, not only with regard to the tribes, but also the distances between them. As to its extent, from east to west it is nearly 450 leagues long, and, in places, 200 leagues wide from north to south, from latitude 41° to 48° or 49°. This land is a sort of island, surrounded by the great River St. Lawrence, which passes through several lakes of great extent,[17] on the shores of which live various tribes who speak different languages and have fixed abodes; some are fond of tilling the soil, and others do not love it. They, nevertheless, have different ways of living and different customs, some better than others. On the north shore of this great river, extending in a southwesterly direction about 100 leagues toward the Attigouantans, the country is partly mountainous, and the air there is rather temperate, more so than in any other place in these regions, in latitude 41°. All these parts of the country are abundant in game, such as stags, caribous, elks,[18] does, buffaloes,[19] bears, wolves, beavers, foxes, minks, martens and several other kinds of animals which we do not

---

[16] I. e, of all Eastern Canada.

[17] Champlain had seen Lake Huron and Lake Ontario, and from this passage it would seem that he had been told of Lake Erie.

[18] I. e., moose.

[19] Champlain, misled by seeing buffalo robes secured by trade, has perhaps placed the range of the buffalo at this time too far east.

have on this side of the water. Fish of various sorts and kinds are caught there in great abundance, not only the kinds that we have, but others that we do not have on the coasts of France. As for hunting for birds, there is plenty of that, for they come there in their time and season. The country is traversed by plenty of rivers, brooks and ponds connecting with one another and, at last, emptying into the River St. Lawrence and into the lakes through which it passes. The country is very pleasant, being covered with large and high forests, full of trees similar to the species that we have in France, although it is true that, in several places, there is a great deal of cleared land, where they plant their Indian corn. The country also abounds in meadows, marshes and swamps, which supply food for the animals just mentioned. The country north of this great river is not so pleasant as that to the south. Between latitude 47° and 49° it is full of big rocks in some places, as far as I could make out, which are inhabited by savages who live a wandering life about the country, not tilling the soil nor cultivating anything—at least, practically nothing. They are nomads—now in one place and now in another. The country there is cold and disagreeable enough. The extent of this northern region along latitude 49° is 600 leagues in width, and it includes the places of which we have ample knowledge. There are also many fine, large rivers which come from this quarter and empty into this river, and others which (in my opinion) empty into the sea, going through the regions to the north, between latitude 50° and 51°, according to the report and account that have been given me by those who go to traffic and trade with the people who live there.

With regard to the regions farther west, we cannot really know their extent, inasmuch as the peoples have no knowledge of it beyond 200 or 300 leagues or more toward the west, whence comes this great river; which goes, among other places, through a lake extending nearly thirty days' journey by canoe, to wit, the one that we named the Fresh Sea[20] on account of its great extent, which is forty days' journey in the canoes of the savages to whom we have access. They are at war with other nations westward of this great lake, which is why we cannot have fuller knowledge of them, except that we have been told various and sundry times that certain prisoners from these places had reported that there were

---

[20] Lake Huron, including also Lake Superior, or Lake Michigan; for, as remarked above (p. 67) [155], the distances given imply it. The Indians, in mentioning the extent they could go to the west on the Fresh Sea, might not emphasize, or even mention, the St. Mary's River, or the Strait of Mackinac.

some people there like ourselves in being white, and that they had seen their hair, which is very blond.[21] I hardly know what to think about this, except that they were people more civilized than they. Really, to know the truth of the matter, it would be necessary to see them, but it requires assistance, such as is afforded only by the time and courage of men of means who could or would undertake this enterprise.

As for the country south of this great river, it is very thickly peopled, much more so than on the north side, with various tribes who are at war with one another. The country there is very delightful, much more so than that on the north side, and the air is more mild. There are many kinds of trees and fruits there that are not found north of this river, but, on the other hand, there is not so much profit and gain in the south from the trade in furs. As for the character of the regions on the east, they are well enough known, for the great ocean sea borders these places, namely, the coasts of Labrador, Newfoundland, Cape Breton, La Cadie,[22] and the Almouchiquois.[23] And the people who inhabit them are also well known, for I have given ample description of them heretofore.

The country of the nation of the Attigouantans is in latitude 44° 30' and 230 leagues long toward the west.[24] It contains eighteen villages, of which eight are enclosed and walled with palisades of wood in triple rows, interlaced with one another, with galleries on top provided with stones and water for throwing and for putting out any fire that their enemies might set against them. This country is beautiful and charming, and most of it is cleared. It has the same shape and situation as Brittany,[25] being almost surrounded and enclosed by the Fresh Sea. These eighteen villages, according to their account, are peopled by 2000 warriors, not including the ordinary people, who might number 20,000 souls. Their cabins are in the form of tunnels, or arbors, covered with

---

[21] This Indian rumor refers, no doubt, to the Spaniards of New Mexico; perhaps to the expedition of Oñate 200 or 300 leagues to the east or northeast of Sante Fé in 1601, or possibly to Indian traditions of the De Soto or Coronado expeditions. Scalps taken at that time might have been preserved. On the expedition of Oñate, see H. H. Bancroft, *History of Arizona and New Mexico*, 149-150.

[22] I. e., Acadie.

[23] New England.

[24] The text is evidently corrupt here. Probably 230 stands for 20 à 30, which would not be far out of the way, although still too high for the land between Lake Simcoe and Lake Huron. For a discussion of the reading, see Laverdière, *Voyages de Champlain, 1619*, p. 73, and *1632*, I, 288.

[25] I. e., it is a peninsula.

the bark of trees; from 25 to 30 fathoms, more or less, long and 6 wide. They have a passageway through the middle from 10 to 12 feet wide, extending from one end to the other. On the two sides there is a kind of bench, 4 feet high, where they sleep in summer to avoid being pestered by fleas, which are very common; and in winter they sleep on the ground on mats, near the fire, so as to be warmer. They store up dry wood and fill their cabins with it, to keep themselves warm in winter. At the end of these cabins there is a space in the middle of their dwelling, where they preserve their Indian corn, which they put into large barrels made of the bark of trees. There are pieces of wood suspended, on which they put their clothes, provisions and other things, for fear of the mice, which abound. In such a cabin there will be twelve fires, which means twenty-four households. The fire smokes in good earnest in winter, so that many are attacked with serious ailments of the eyes from it, to which they are liable even to the extent of losing their sight toward the close of life. There is no window or opening, except the one that is on top of their cabins, by which the smoke goes out. They sometimes move their village at intervals of 10, 20 or 30 years, and transport it 1, 2 or 3 leagues, for their soil becomes worn out in producing corn without being fertilized; and so they go to clear another place, and also to have wood more accessible, if they are not obliged, by their enemies, to pull up and go away farther; as did the Entouhonorons, who went some 40 to 50 leagues. This is the form of their dwellings, which are separated from one another, say 3 or 4 paces, for fear of fire, which they dread very much.

Their life is wretched in comparison with ours, but a happy one for them, who have not tasted better and believe that there is none more excellent. Their principal food and ordinary provision is Indian corn and Brazilian beans,[26] which they prepare in various ways. They pound it in wooden mortars and reduce it to meal, from which they extract the meal dust by means of certain winnowing fans made from the bark of trees; and then from this meal they make bread, with beans. These beans they have first boiled into soup, like the Indian corn, so as to be easier to beat, and they put the whole together. Sometimes they add blueberries, or dried raspberries, sometimes pieces of deer's fat. Then, having steeped the whole in lukewarm water, they make bread in the form of cakes, which they bake under the ashes. And when they are baked, they wash them, and wrap them in leaves of Indian corn, which they fasten to

[26] The kidney bean. See above, vol. I, p. 101 [50].

them, and put them into boiling water. But this latter is not the ordinary kind. They make also another kind, which they call *migan*, as follows: they take the pounded Indian corn, without winnowing out the dust, and put two or three handfuls of it in an earthen pot full of water, set it boiling, stirring it from time to time, for fear it should burn or stick to the pot; then they put into this pot a little fish, fresh or dry, according to the season, to give flavor to this *migan*, which is the name that they give it. And they make this very often, although it is a bad-smelling thing, principally in winter, either because they do not know how to prepare it, or because they do not wish to take the trouble to do so. They make two kinds of it, and prepare it well enough when they wish to; and when there is fish in it, this *migan* does not smell bad, but only when venison is used. When the whole thing is cooked, they take out the fish and pound it very fine, not going into such detail as to remove the bones, scales or entrails, as we do; and put the whole into a pot, which often causes a bad taste. Then, when it is made in this way, they give to each one his portion. This *migan* is very thin, and has not much substance, as one can easily judge. As for drink, there is no need of it, for this *migan* is thin enough itself. They have another kind of *migan*, namely: they parch new corn before it is ripe, which they preserve, and they cook it whole with fish, or flesh, when they have it. Another way: they take very dry Indian corn, parch it in the ashes, then pound it and reduce it to meal, like the other kind already mentioned, and preserve it for their journeys here and there. The *migan* made in this way is the best, according to my taste. To make it, they have a great deal of meat and fish cooked, which they cut up into pieces, then put it into great kettles, which they fill with water, making it boil very hard. This done, they take off from the surface, with a spoon, the fat that comes from the meat and the fish; then they put in this meal made from the roasted corn, stirring it all the time, until the *migan* is cooked and thickened like soup. They give and distribute to each one a plateful, with a spoonful of the fat. They are accustomed to make this dish at banquets. Now, this corn, freshly roasted, is greatly esteemed among them. They also eat beans, which they have boiled with a large proportion of roasted meal, mixing in a little fat and fish. Dogs are in request at their feasts, which they often make together, especially during the winter, when they are at leisure. In case they go hunting for deer, or fishing, they reserve what they get for these feasts, nothing remaining in their cabins except the thin *migan* as a rule. It resembles hog-wash, which is given to hogs to

ALGONQUIANS, HURONS AND IROQUOIS

eat. They have another way of eating the Indian corn. To prepare it they take ears of it and put them in water, under the mud, leaving them two or three months in this state, until they think it is decayed. Then they take it out and boil it with meat or fish; then eat it. They also roast it, and it is better so than boiled. There is nothing that smells so bad as this corn when it comes out of the water all muddy, yet, nevertheless, the women and children suck it, as one does sugarcane,[27] and have nothing that seems to them to taste better, as they show. Ordinarily, they have only two meals a day.

They also fatten bears, which they keep two or three years to feast on. I saw that if they had domestic animals they would be careful with them, and would keep them very well, if I should show them how to feed them. That would be an easy thing for them, since they have good pasturage and a great deal of it, whether for horses, oxen, cows, sheep, swine or any other kinds. For lack of these, one considers them poor, as they seem to be. Nevertheless, with all their poverty in various respects, I regard them as happy among themselves, for they have no other ambition than to live and to take care of themselves; and they are more certain of that than those who wander about the forests like brute beasts. They also eat many summer squashes, which they boil and roast under the ashes.

As to their clothes, they are made in various ways and styles, of different skins of wild animals; not only those that they catch, but those that they get in exchange for their Indian corn, meal, wampum and fishing-nets from the Algonquins, Nipissings and other tribes, who are hunters and have no fixed abodes. They dress and fit the skins tolerably well, making their breeches of a rather large deer-skin and their leggings of another piece. They go clear up to the belt and are in many folds. Their shoes are of deer-, bear- and beaver-skins, of which they use a good number. Besides, they have a robe of the same fur in the form of a cloak, which they wear in the Irish, or gipsy, style; and they have sleeves which are attached with a string in the back. That is how they are dressed in winter, as is seen in Figure *D*. When they go abroad they gird their robe about the body; but in the village they leave off their sleeves and do not gird themselves at all. Instead of lace from Milan for the adornment of their garments, they use the odds and ends of these skins,[28] of which

---

[27] A reminiscence of Champlain's early voyage to the West Indies.
[28] The French reads: "Les passements de Milan pour enrichir leurs habits sont de colle, et de la raclure des dites peaux." Otis has "are made of glue and the scrapings of the

they make bands in various styles, according to taste. In some places they put stripes of reddish brown paint among the bands of fur trimming, which always look whitish, not losing their shape, no matter how dirty they may be. There are some among these tribes who are much more skillful than others in dressing the skins and more ingenious in inventing designs to put on their clothes. Above all others, our Montagnais and Algonquins take the most pains about it. They put on their robes bands of porcupine quills, which they dye a very beautiful scarlet color. They think a great deal of these bands among themselves and detach them to make them serve for other robes when they wish to change. Besides, they use them to adorn their faces and to appear more comely. When they wish to appear in fine array they paint their faces black and red, which colors have been mixed with oil made from the seed of the sunflower, or with grease of the bear or other animals. They also dye their hair, which some wear long, others short, and still others on one side only. As for the women and girls, they always wear it in the same way. They are dressed like the men, except that their robes always are girt around them. They come down to the knee. They are not at all ashamed to expose the body; that is, from the waist up and from the middle of the thigh down. The rest is always covered. They wear a great deal of wampum, both as necklaces and chains, which they put on the front of their robes, or hanging from their belts, or as bracelets, or as pendants from the ears. They have their hair well combed, colored, and greased. Thus arrayed, they go to dances with their hair in a bunch behind bound with eel-skins, which they prepare and use as a cord. Sometimes they attach to this plates a foot square covered with wampum, which hangs down behind, and, so, decked in this way and sprucely dressed, they show themselves gladly at dances, whither their fathers and mothers take them, sparing nothing to beautify and adorn them. I

before-mentioned skins"; and, just below, "bands of red and brown color amid those of glue." Cotgrave's Dictionary, which was prepared by a contemporary of Champlain, gives as the meaning of *colle*: 1st, glue; 2d, solder; 3d, "also the unprofitable corners of before-mentioned skins"; and, just below, "bands of red and brown color amid those of glue." Cotgrave's Dictionary, which was prepared by a contemporary of Champlain, gives as the meaning of *colle*: 1st, glue; 2d, solder; 3d, "also the unprofitable corners of hides and skins cut off in the dressing"; and for *raclure*, besides "scrapings," "remnants." The two words, *colle* and *raclure*, are covered by the phrase, "odds and ends." The editor is not sure that the version in the text is correct. It is, however, offered with this explanation, for it seems more in accord with other descriptions of Indian garments. If it is accepted, it would follow that the text should read "de la colle."

can assure you that I have seen at dances many a girl who had more than twelve pounds of wampum on her, not to mention the other trinkets with which they are loaded and attired. The illustration, *F*, shows how the women are dressed; *G*, the girls going to the dance. There is also an illustration of how the women pound their Indian corn (letter *H*).

These people are of a rather merry disposition, although there are many of them who have a gloomy and saturnine expression. They are well-formed and proportioned in body, some of the men being very strong and robust. And there are also women and girls who are very beautiful and attractive in figure, coloring (although it is olive) and in features, all in proportion; and their breasts hang down hardly at all, unless they are old. Some of them are very powerful and of extraordinary height. They have almost all the care of the house and the work; for they till the ground, plant the Indian corn, lay up wood for the winter, beat the hemp and spin it, make fishing-nets from the thread, catch fish, and do other necessary things. They also harvest their corn, store it, prepare it to eat, and attend to their household affairs. Moreover, they follow their husbands from place to place in the fields, where they serve as mules for carrying the baggage.

As to the men, they do nothing but hunt for deer and other animals, catch fish, make cabins and go to war. When they have done these things they go to other tribes, to whom they have access, and whom they know, to trade and exchange what they have for what they have not. When they come back they do not stir from the feasts and dances which they make for one another, and when these are over they go to sleep, which is the best employment of all.

They have a sort of marriage among them, which is like this: when a girl is 11, 12, 13, 14 or 15 years old, she will have several suitors, according to her good graces, who will woo her and ask the consent of her father and her mother, although often the girls do not accept their consent. Those who are the best and most discreet submit to their wishes. This lover, or suitor, gives the girl some necklaces, chains and bracelets of wampum. If the girl finds the suitor agreeable, she accepts this present. This done, he comes to sleep with her three or four nights without saying a word, when they gather the fruit of their affections. And it often happens that after having spent a week or a fortnight together, if they cannot agree, she will quit her suitor, who forfeits his necklaces and other gifts made by him. Frustrated in his hope, he will seek another woman, and she another suitor; and thus they continue until a satis-

Indian Costumes

factory union is made. There are many girls who pass their entire youth thus with several husbands, who are not alone in the enjoyment of the creature, married though they are; for, when night comes, the young women run from one cabin to another, as do the young men, on their part, visiting any girls they please. They do so without violence, however, referring the whole matter to the wish of the woman. The husband will do the same thing to a woman neighbor, without there being any jealousy among them on that account, or, in any case, very little; and they incur no ill-repute or insult for it, for it is the custom of the country.

When the women have children, the preceding husbands return to them, to show them the friendship and affection that they had borne them in the past, saying that it is more than that of any other man, and that the child who is to be born is his and of his begetting. Another will tell her the same thing; and so it is at the choice and option of the woman to take and accept him who pleases her most. Having gained by her loves a great deal of wampum, she remains with him without leaving him any more; or, if she leaves him, it must be for some important reason, other than impotence, for he is on trial. Nevertheless, while she is with this husband she does not cease to indulge herself freely; yet she keeps herself at home and busy always with the household, making a good appearance. The result is that children that they have together cannot be sure of being legitimate. They have a custom, however, which provides against this risk that they may never succeed to their property, by constituting the children of their sisters, whom they know to have been born of them, their heirs and successors.[29] Coming now to the feeding and bringing-up of their children: they put them, during the daytime, on a little wooden board, and dress and wrap them up in furs, or skins, and bind them on this little board. Then they set it up on end, leaving a little opening through which the baby may do its little duties. If it is a girl they put a leaf of Indian corn between the thighs, which presses against her person, and they have the end of this leaf come outside and turn down, and in this way the child's water runs off on this leaf, without her being irritated by the water. They also put under the babies, down made from certain reeds that we call hare's-foot, on which they rest very softly. They also clean them with the same down. To adorn

---

[29] A feature of the custom of reckoning descent through the female line which was widely prevalent among the North American Indians.

them, they trim the board with beads, and put some on the baby's neck, no matter how little it is. At night they put it to bed entirely naked, between the father and mother, where it must be considered providential that it is preserved from being suffocated, except very rarely. These children are extremely spoiled, as a result of not being punished, and are of so perverse a nature that they strike their fathers and mothers, which is a sort of curse that God sends them.

They have no laws among themselves, nor anything like them, there being neither any correction nor censure of evil-doers, but merely the rendering evil for evil, which is the reason why they are so often involved in quarrels and wars on account of their differences.

Similarly, they do not recognize any divinity, and do not believe in any god, or anything whatever, but live like brute beasts. They have some respect for the devil, or something like it, for to the word that they use various significations are attached, and it embraces in itself several things; so that it is hard to know and discern whether they mean the devil, or something else. But what makes one think it is the devil is that, when they see a man do something extraordinary, or prove more skillful than the common run, a valiant warrior, or one who is in a rage and beside himself, they call him *Oqui;* as we should say, a great spirit, or a great devil. There are certain persons among them who are the *Oqui,* or *Manitous,* so called by the Algonquins and Montagnais, who have the care of healing the sick, binding up the wounded, and predicting future things. They persuade the sick to make feasts, or have them made, with the intention of taking part in them, and they make them go through various other ceremonies, in the hope of a prompt recovery. The sick believe and hold true all that these *Oqui* tell them.

These people have not the malicious spirit of other savages more remote than they, which makes one think that they would be converted to the knowledge of God if their country were inhabited by persons who took pains and care to teach them, by good examples and right living. For, to-day, they have the desire to improve themselves; to-morrow, when it will be thought best to suppress their foul customs, their dissolute ways and their uncivilized habits, this wish will change. Now, when I talked to them about our belief, laws and customs, they listened to me with great attention in their councils; then they said to me: "You say things that are above our minds and our reason, and that we cannot understand in words. But if you wish us to understand them, it is necessary to bring to this country women and children, in order that we may learn your ways of living, how you worship God, how you obey the laws of your King, how you cultivate and plant the ground and feed animals. For, if we see these things, we shall learn more in one year than in twenty of talk, for we shall find our life wretched in comparison with yours." Their discourse seemed to me good common-sense, and to show the desire that they have to know God.

When they are ill they send for the *Oqui*, and he, after having asked about the malady, sends for a great number of men, women and girls, with three or four old women, just as may be commanded by this *Oqui*. They go into their cabins and dance, each one having a bear-skin, or the skin of some animal, on the head. The bear-skin is most often used, for it is the most frightful. There are two or three other old women about the patient, or sick person, who often is sick only in imagination. But they are soon cured of this sickness, and they make feasts at the expense of their relatives or friends, who give them something to put into their kettle, besides the gifts and presents that they receive from the dancing men and women, such as wampum and other trinkets. This is what cures them quickly. For when they see that they have nothing more to hope for, they get up, with what they have been able to amass. But those who are very ill are not easily cured by such play, dances and doings. The old women who are about the sick person receive the presents, each one singing in turn. Then they stop singing. And when all the presents are given they begin to lift their voices with one accord, singing all together and beating time with sticks on pieces of dried bark of trees. Then all the women and girls place themselves at the end of the cabin, as if they wanted to perform the opening scene of a ballet, with the old women walking first, their bear-skins on their heads. They have only two styles of dance that have any harmony—one of four steps, and the other of twelve, as in the *trioly* of Brittany. They are rather graceful. Young men often take part with them. After dancing an hour or so, the old women take hold of the sick person, who pretends to get up sadly, then goes to dancing. Once having begun to dance, he continues and enjoys himself like the others.

Sometimes the medicine-man[30] gets a reputation from this, when his patient is seen to be cured and about so soon; but those who are very ill and failing die oftener than they get cured. For they make such a noise and din from morning until two o'clock at night that it is impossible for

---

[30] Le medicin, the physician.

A Medicine Dance

the patient to endure it without a great deal of pain. If the patient takes a notion to have the women and girls dance together it must be by order of the *Oqui*. For he and the *Manitou* accompanied by some others, go through monkey tricks and incantations, and writhing, in such a way that often they are beside themselves, as if they were mad and out of their senses. They throw the fire from one side of the cabin to the other, now eating burning coals—having held them some time in their hands, then throwing red-hot ashes into the eyes of the spectators. One would say, to see them acting in this way, that the devil—*Oqui* or *Manitou*, if one must call him that—possessed them and made them writhe in that fashion. When the noise and din are over, each one goes away to his cabin. But the wives of those who are possessed, and the inmates of their cabin, are in great fear lest they burn all that is in it, so they take out everything that is there. For when they come in they are perfectly wild, their eyes flashing and terrible. Sometimes they stand and sometimes they sit just as the impulse moves them. They grab everything that they find, or run up against and fling these things about from one side of the cabin to the other. Then they lie down and sleep for a while; then, waking up with a start, they grab some fire and stones, which they hurl about on all sides without any regard. This fury passes off in the sleep that comes upon them. Then they take a sweat and call their friends to take one, too; for they think it the true cure by which to recover health. They cover themselves with their robes and some big pieces of bark of trees, and have in their midst a good many stones which have been heated red-hot in the fire. While they are in the sweat, they sing all the time. And since they get very thirsty, they drink a great quantity of water, and gradually change from madmen to sober ones. It happens, rather from chance than from science, that three or four of these sick people get well, which confirms them in their false belief that they are healed by means of these ceremonies; not noting that, for so many cured, ten others die.

There are also women who go into these rages, and walk on their hands and feet like animals, but they do not do so much harm. When the *Oqui* sees one, he begins to sing; then, with some grimaces, he blows upon her, ordering her to drink of certain waters, and to make a feast, either of flesh or of fish, which must be found. When the yelling is over, and the banquet finished, each one returns to her own cabin. She stays there until the next time that he comes to visit her, blowing on her, and singing, with several others who have been called for this purpose. They hold in the hand a dry tortoise-shell filled with little pebbles, which they rattle in the ears of the sick person, directing her at once to have three or four feasts, with singing and dancing, when all the girls come adorned and painted, with masquerades, and people in disguise. Assembled thus, they go and sing near the bed of the sick person, then walk through the village while the feast is being prepared.

With regard to their housekeeping and living, each one lives on what he can get from fishing and from the harvest in as much land as is needed. They clear it with great difficulty, as they have no proper tools for the purpose. They strip the trees of all their branches, which they burn at their base, in order to kill them. They clean up the ground between the trees, then plant their corn at distances of a pace, putting about ten grains in each place; and so they continue until they have enough for three or four years' provision, for fear lest some bad year, barren and unfruitful, should come upon them.

If any girl marries in winter, each woman and girl is expected to carry to the bride a load of wood for her provision; for each household is furnished with what is necessary, inasmuch as she could not do it alone, and also that she may have time enough to attend to other things which are in time and season.

Their government is as follows: the elders and principal men assemble in council, where they decide and propose all that is necessary for the affairs of the village. This is done by vote of the majority, or by the advice of certain ones among them who are esteemed to be of excellent judgment. Such advice so given is scrupulously followed. They have no particular chiefs who command with absolute authority, but they show respect to the oldest and bravest, who are called captains. As for penalties, they do not resort to them, but everything is done through the entreaties of the old men and by dint of speeches and remonstrances. They have a general conference, and if some one in the assembly offers to do something for the good of the village, or to go somewhere for the common service, and he is thought capable of doing what he promises, he is encouraged and persuaded by inspiring words that he is a daring fellow just fitted for such undertakings, and that he will gain a great reputation. If he wishes to accept, or refuse, this duty, he is allowed to do so, but there are few who refuse it.

When they wish to undertake wars, or go into the enemy's country, two or three of the older or valiant captains undertake the leadership for that time, and go to the neighboring villages to make their intention known; making presents to them, to put them under obligations to accompany them. Then they decide upon the place where they wish to go, the disposition of the prisoners who may be captured, and other things of importance. If they do well they receive praise for it; if they do badly they are blamed. They have a general meeting each year in some village that they name, whither an ambassador comes from each province. There they have great feasts and dances for a month or five weeks, according as they decide together; make a new compact of friendship; decide what must be done for the preservation of their country, and give presents to one another. This done, each one goes back to his own section.

When any one dies, they wrap the body in furs and cover it very neatly with the bark of trees; then they place it high up on four posts in a little cabin, which is covered with bark and is just the length of the body. These bodies are buried in these places only a certain length of time, say eight or ten years, when those of the village recommend the place where their ceremonies should be held, or rather a general council, which all the people of the country attend. This done, each one returns to his own village, and then takes all the bones of the dead, which they clean and make very smooth, and guard carefully. Then all the relatives and friends take them, with their necklaces, furs, axes, kettles and other things of value, with a great many provisions which they bring to the prescribed place. When all are gathered there, they put the provisions where the people of that village direct; and then have feasts and dances without interruption for ten days—the length of time that the festival lasts—during which other tribes gather there from all parts to see the ceremonies which are taking place. By means of these ceremonies they form new ties of friendship, saying that the bones of their relatives and friends are to be all put together, as a symbol that, as they are all together in one place, so ought they, too, to be united in friendship and harmony, like relatives and friends, without being able to part from one another. These bones being thus mingled, they make many speeches on the subject; then, after some grimaces or acting, they dig a big grave, into which they throw the bones, with the necklaces, belts of wampum, axes, kettles, sword-blades, knives and other trifles, which they prize highly. Then they cover the whole with earth and with many logs of wood. Then they enclose it with stakes, on which they place a covering. Some of them believe in the immortality of the soul, saying that after their death they go to a place where they sing like crows.

It remains to describe the way in which they fish. They make several round holes in the ice, and the one through which they are to draw the

Burial Place

seine is about five feet long and three wide. Then they begin at this opening to place the net, which is attached to a wooden rod six or seven feet long. They put the rod under the ice and push it from hole to hole, at each of which one or two men put their hands into the holes, catching hold of the rod, to which is attached an end of the net, until they come to meet each other at the opening of five or six feet. This done, they let the net drop to the bottom of the water. It sinks by means of certain little stones which are fastened to the end of it. When it is at the bottom they draw it up again with their arms by its two ends, and so they take the fish that are caught in it.

After having fully discussed the habits, customs, government and manner of life of our savages,[31] we will take up our narrative. When they had assembled to come with us, and take us back to our settlement, we set out from their country on May 20,[32] and we were forty days on the way. We caught a great quantity of fish of various kinds, and we also captured several varieties of animals and game, which gave us special pleasure besides the sustenance that we derived from them. We reached our Frenchmen at the end of the month of June. I found there Sieur du Pont, who had come with two vessels from France. He had almost despaired of seeing me again, on account of the bad news that he had heard from the savages, that I was dead.

We also saw all the holy fathers, who had remained at our settlement, and they were very glad to see us, and we to see them. Then I prepared to set out from the St. Louis Rapids, to go to our settlement, taking with me my host, Darontal. Taking leave, on this account, of all the savages, and assuring them of my affection, I told them that I should see them again some day to assist them, as I had done in the past, and that I would bring them presents, to keep up their friendship with one another. I begged them to forget the quarrels that they had had together, when I set them in harmony; which they promised to do. We left on the 8th of July, and reached our settlement on the 11th of the same month. There I found every one in good condition, and we all, with our holy fathers, returned thanks to God for His care in preserving and keeping us from the many perils and dangers to which we had been exposed.

[31] For other contemporary accounts of the Hurons see Thwaites's edition of the *Jesuit Relations*, index. Parkman, on the basis of this material, has given a detailed description of Huron manners in his *Jesuits in North America*, XXIV-XLII.

[32] May 20, 1616.

During this time I made the best cheer I could for my host, Darontal. He admired our buildings, conduct and way of living, and said to me in private that he never should die content until he had seen all his friends, or at least a good number of them, come to make their abode with us, in order to learn to serve God, and to understand our way of living, which he deemed infinitely happy, in comparison with theirs. He said that what he could not understand of it by what we said, he could much better and more easily get hold of by associating with us. He suggested that, for the advancement of this work, we should make another settlement at the St. Louis Rapids, so as to give them a safe passage of the river, for fear of their enemies; and said that at once they would come in great numbers to us, to live there like brothers. I promised him to do this as soon as I could. So, after we had remained four or five days together, and I had given him some valuable presents, with which he was much pleased, he returned to the St. Louis Rapids, where his companions awaited him.

During my sojourn at the settlement I had some of the common corn cut—that is, the French corn that had been planted there—which was very beautiful, in order to carry some to France, to show that this soil is very good and fertile. There was also some very fine Indian corn and some grafts and trees that we had brought thither.

We set sail in our barks on the 20th day of July, and arrived at Tadoussac on the 23d of the same month. There Sieur du Pont was waiting for us with his ship ready and equipped. We embarked in it and left on the third day of the month of August, and had so favorable a wind that we arrived at Honfleur the 10th day of September, 1616. There we returned praise and thanksgiving to God for preserving us from all the perils and dangers to which we had been exposed, and for having brought us back in safety to our country. To Him, then, glory and honor forevermore. Amen.[33]

[33] This narrative ends on page 309 of Laverdière, *Oeuvres de Champlain*, vol. V.

THE END

THE VOYAGE OF SAMUEL CHAMPLAINE

of Brouage,

made unto Canada in the yeere 1603, dedicated to CHARLES DE MONTMORENCIE, &c., High Admirall of France

The Translation published in Hakluytus Posthumus, or Purchas His Pilgrims.

LONDON: 1625.

Edited by

EDWARD GAYLORD BOURNE.

CHAPTER I

Short account describing the voyage from Honfleur, in Normandy, to the Port of Tadoussac, in Canada.[1]

We departed from Honfleur, the fifteenth day of March 1603. This day we put into the Roade of New Haven,[2] because the winde was contrary. The Sunday following being the sixteenth of the said moneth, we set saile to proceed on our Voyage. The seventeenth day following, we had sight of Jersey[3] and Garnsey,[4] which are Iles betweene the Coast of Normandie and England. The eighteenth of the said moneth, wee discryed the Coast of Britaine.[5] The nineteenth, at seven of the clocke at night, we made account that we were thwart of Ushent.[6] The one and twentieth, at seven of clocke in the morning, we met with seven ships of Hollanders, which to our judgement came from the Indies. On Easter day, the thirtieth of the said moneth, wee were encountered with a great storme, which seemed rather to be thunder then winde, which lasted the space of seventeene dayes, but not so great as it was the two first dayes; and during the said time we rather lost way then gained.

The sixteenth day of April the storme began to cease, and the Sea became more calme then before, to the contentment of all the Company; in such sort as continuing our said course untill the eighteenth of the said moneth, we met with a very high Mountaine of Ice. The morrow after we discried a banke of Ice, which continued above eight leagues in length, with an infinite number of other smaller peeces of Ice, which hindred our passage. And by the judgement of our Pilot, the said flakes

---

[1] The chapter headings in this narrative have been translated and inserted by the editor from Laverdière's text.
[2] Havre.
[3] D'Orgny, i. e., Aurigny; in English, Alderney.
[4] Guernsey.
[5] Brittany.
[6] Ouessant. An island off Cape Finisterre, the westernmost point of Brittany.

ALGONQUIANS, HURONS AND IROQUOIS

of Ice were one hundred, or one hundred & twenty leagues from the Country of Canada, and we were in 45. degrees and two third parts; & we found passage in 44. deg. The second of May, at eleven of clocke of the day, we came upon The Banke in 44. degrees one[7] third part. The sixt of the said moneth, we came so neere the land that we heard the Sea beate against the shore, but we could not descrie the same through the thicknesse of the fogge, whereunto these coasts are subject; which was the cause that we put farther certain leagues into the Sea, untill the next day in the morning, when we descried land, the weather being very cleere, which was the Cape of Saint Marie.[8] The twelth day following we were overtaken with a great flaw of winde, which lasted two dayes. The fifteenth of the said moneth, wee descried the Isles of Saint Peter. The seventeenth following we met with a banke of Ice neere Cape de Raie,[9] sixe leagues in length, which caused us to strike saile all the night, to avoide the danger we might incurre. The next day we set saile, and descried Cape de Raie, and the Isles of Saint Paul, and Cape de Saint Laurence,[10] which is on the South side. And from the said Cape of Saint Laurence unto Cape de Raie, is eighteene leagues, which is the breadth of the entrance of the great Gulfe of Canada.[11]

The same day, about ten of the clocke in the morning, we met with another Iland of Ice, which was aboue eight leagues long. The twentieth of the said moneth, we discried an Isle, which containeth some five and twenty or thirty leagues in length, which is called the Isle of Assumption,[12] which is the entrance of the River of Canada. The next day we descried Gachepe,[13] which is a very high land, and began to enter into the said River of Canada, ranging the South coast unto the River of Mantanne,[14] which is from the said Gachepe sixtie five leagues; from the said River of Mantanne we sailed as far as the Pike,[15] which is twenty leagues, which is on the South side also: from the said Pike we sailed

---

[7] It should be two-thirds.

[8] Cape St. Mary, on the southern coast of Newfoundland on the eastern side of Placentia Bay.

[9] Cape Ray.

[10] Cape North, Cape Breton Island.

[11] The Gulf of St. Lawrence.

[12] Champlain wrote Anticosty. Cartier named Anticosti, *Isle de Assomption*, and apparently that was the name familiar in England in Purchas's time.

[13] Gaspé.

[14] Matane.

[15] Du Pic. Corrected by Laverdière to du Bic. Bic is 170 miles east of Quebec.

over the River unto the port of Tadousac, which is fifteene leagues. All these Countries are very high, and barren, yeelding no commoditie. The foure and twentieth of the said moneth[16] we cast anker before Tadousac, and the six and twentieth we entred into the said Port, which is made like to a creeke in the entrance of the River of Saguenay, where there is a very strange currant and tide, for the swiftnesse and depth thereof where sometimes strong windes do blow because of the cold which they bring with them; it is thought that the said River is five and forty leagues unto the first fall, and it commeth from the North North-west. The said Port of Tadousac is little, wherein there cannot ride aboue ten or twelve Ships: but there is water enough toward the East, toward the opening of the said River of Saguenay along by a little hill, which is almost cut off from the maine by the Sea: The rest of the Countrie are very high Mountaines, whereon there is little mould, but rockes and sands full of woods of Pines, Cypresses,[17] Fir-trees,[18] Burch, and some other sorts of trees of small price. There is a little Poole neere unto the said Port, enclosed with Mountaines covered with woods. At the entrance of the said Port there are two points, the one on the West side running a league into the Sea, which is called Saint Matthewes point; and the other on the South-east side containing a quarter of a league, which is called the point of all the Divels. The South and South South-east, and South South-west windes doe strike into the said haven. But from Saint Matthewes Point, to the said Point of all the Divels, is very neere a league: Both these Points are dry at a low water.

CHAPTER II

Kind reception of the French by the great Sagamo of the savages of Canada; their feasts and dances; the war they carry on with the Iroquois; how and of what their canoes and cabins are made; with a description of St. Matthew's Point.

THE seven and twentieth day we sought the Savages at the Point of Saint Matthew, which is a league from Tadousac, with the two Savages whom Monsieur du Pont[1] brought with him, to make report of that

---

[16] May 24, 1603.
[17] Cedars.
[18] Sapins. Here, a variety of spruces. S.
[1] Du Pont Gravé.

which they had seene in France, and of the good entertainement which the King had given them. As soone as we were landed we went to the Caban of their great Sagamo,[2] which is called Anadabijou, where we found him with some eightie or a hundred of his companions, which were making Tabagie,[3] that is to say, a Feast. He received us very well, according to the custome of the Countrey, and made us sit downe by him, and all the Savages sat along one by another on both sides of the said Cabine. One of the Savages which we had brought with us began to make his Oration, of the good entertainement which the King had given them, and of the good usage that they had received in France, and that they might assure themselves that his said Majestie wished them well, and desired to people their Countrey, and to make peace with their enemies (which are the Irocois) or to send them forces to vanquish them. He also reckoned up the faire Castels, Palaces, Houses, and people which they had seene, and our manner of living. He was heard with so great silence, as more cannot be uttered. Now when he had ended his Oration, the said grand Sagamo Anadabijou, having heard him attentively began to take Tobacco, and gave to the said Monsieur du Pont Grave of Saint Malo, and to mee, and to certaine other Sagamos which were by him: after he had taken store of Tobacco, he began to make his Oration to all, speaking distinctly, resting sometimes a little, and then speaking againe, saying, that doubtlesse they ought to be very glad to have his Majestie for their great friend: they answered all with one voyce, ho, ho, ho, which is to say, yea, yea, yea. He proceeding forward in his speech, said That he was very well content that his said Majestie should people their Countrey, and make warre against their enemies, and that there was no Nation in the world to which they wished more good, then to the French. In fine, hee gave them all to understand what good and profit they might receive of his said Majestie. When he had ended his speech, we went out of his Cabine, and they began to make their Tabagie or Feast, which they make with the flesh of Orignac,[4] which is like an Oxe, of Beares, of Seales, and Bevers, which are the most ordinary victuals which they have, & with great store of wilde Fowle. They had eight or ten Kettels full of meate in the middest of the said Cabine, and they were set one from another some six paces, and each one upon a severall

[2] A Montagnais word, meaning Great Chief, L. The form Sagamore is usual in English writers.

[3] See note, p. 23 [133], above.

[4] Orignac, more commonly, orignal; the Algonquin name for the moose.

fire. The men sat on both sides the house (as I said before) with his dish made of the barke of a tree; and when the meat is sodden, there is one which devideth to every man his part in the same dishes, wherein they feede very filthily, for when their hands be fattie, they rub them on their haire, or else on the haire of their dogs, whereof they have store to hunt with. Before their meate was sodden, one of them rose up, and took a dog, & danced about the said Kettels from the one end of the Cabin to the other: when he came before the great Sagamo, he cast his dog perforce upon the ground, and then all of them with one voice, cried, ho, ho, ho, which being done, he went and sat him downe in his place, then immediately another rose up and did the like, and so they continued untill the meat was sodden. When they had ended their Feast, they began to dance, taking the heads[5] of their enemies in their hands, which hanged upon the wall behinde them; and in signe of joy there is one or two which sing, moderating their voice by the measure of their hands, which they beate upon their knees, then they rest sometimes, and cry, ho, ho, ho; and begin againe to dance, & blow like a man that is out of breath. They made this triumph for a victory which they had gotten of the Irocois, of whom they had slaine some hundred, whose heads they cut off,[6] which they had with them for the ceremony. They were three Nations when they went to war; the Estechemins, Algoumequins,[7] and Mountainers,[8] to the number of a thousand, when they went to war against the Irocois, whom they encountred at the mouth of the River of the said Irocois[9] and slew an hundred of them. The war which they make is altogether by surprises, for otherwise they would be out of hart; & they feere the said Irocois very much, which are in greater number than the said Mountainers, Estechemins and Algoumequins. The twenty eight day of the said moneth, they encamped themselves in the foresaid haven of Tadousac, where our Ship was; at the break of day their said great Sagamo came out of his Cabine, going round about all the other Cabins, and cried with a loud voice that they should dislodge to goe to Tadousac, where their good friends were. Immediately every man in a

---

[5] Here, apparently, in the sense of scalps.
[6] "Aux quels ils couperent les testes qu'ils avaient avec eux," etc. On the probable meaning of "testes" in this and other passages descriptive of the Canadian Indians see above, vol. I, p. 217 [105].
[7] Algonquins.
[8] The Montagnais.
[9] The Richelieu, or Sorel River.

trice tooke down his cabin, and the said grand Captain, first began to take his canoe, & carried it to the Sea, where he embarked his wife and children, & store of furs; and in like manner did well neere two hundred canowes, which goe strangely; for though our Shallop was well manned, yet they went more swift than we. There are but two that row, the man and the wife. Their Canowes are some eight or nine pases long, and a pase, or a pase & a halfe broad in the middest, and grow sharper & sharper toward both the ends. They are very subject to overturning, if one know not how to guide them; for they are made of the barke of a Birch tree, strengthened within with little circles of wood well & handsomely framed and are so light, that one man will carry one of them easily; and every Canowe is able to carry the weight of a Pipe: when they would passe over any land to goe to some River where they have busines, they carry them with them.[10] Their Cabins are low, made like Tents, covered with the said barke of a tree, and they leave in the roofe about a foot space uncovered, whereby the light commeth in; and they make many fires right in the midst of their Cabin, where they are sometimes ten housholds together. They lie upon skins one by another, and their dogs with them. They were about a thousand persons, men, women and children. The place of the point of S. Matthew, where they were first lodged, is very pleasant; they were at the bottome of a little hill, which was ful of Fir & Cypress trees: upon this point there is a little level plot, which discovereth far off, & upon the top of the said hill, there is a Plain, a league long, and halfe a league broad, covered with trees; the soile is very sandy, and is a good pasture; all the rest is nothing but Mountains of very bad rocks: the Sea beateth round about the said hil, which is dry for a large halfe league at a low water.

CHAPTER III

The rejoicing which the savages make after they have been victorious over their enemies; their disposition, suffering from hunger, ill-will; their beliefs and false ideas; they speak to devils; their clothes, and how they walk on the snow; with their marriage customs and the burial of their dead.

THE ninth day of June the Savages began to make merrie together, and to make their feast, as I have said before, and to dance for the afore-

[10] Cf. above, [vol. I] p. 167 [81].

said victory which they had obtained against their enemies. After they had made good cheere, the Algoumequins, one of the three Nations, went out of their Cabins, and retired themselves apart into a publike place, and caused all their women and girles to sit downe in rankes one by the other, and stood themseulves behinde, then singing all in one time, as I have said before. And suddenly all the women and maidens began to cast off their Mantles of skins, and stripped themselves starke naked, shewing their privities, neverlesse adorned with Matachias, which are paternosters[1] and chaines enterlaced made of the haire of the Porkespicke,[2] which they dye of divers colours. After they had made an end of their songs, they crie all with one voyce, ho, ho, ho; at the same instant all the women and maidens covered themselves with their Mantels, for they lye at their feete, and rest a short while; and then eftsoones beginning againe to sing, they let fall their Mantels as they did before. They goe not out of one place when they dance, and make certaine gestures and motions of the body, first lifting up one foote and then another, stamping upon the ground. While they were dancing of this dance, the Sagamo of the Algoumequins, whose name was Besouat,[3] sat before the said women and virgins, beweene two staves, whereon the heads of their enemies did hang. Sometimes he rose and made a speech, and said to the Mountainers and Estechemains; ye see how we rejoice for the victory which we have obtained of our enemies, ye must doe the like, that we may be contented; then they all together cried, ho, ho, ho. As soone as hee was returned to his place, the great Sagamo, and all his companions cast off their Mantels, being starke naked save their privities, which were covered with a little skin, and tooke each of them what they thought good, as Matachias, Hatchets, Swords, Kettels, Fat, Flesh of the Orignac, Seales, in briefe, every one had a present, which they gave the Algoumequins. After all these ceremonies the dance ceased, and the said Algoumequins both men and women carried away their presents to their lodgings. They chose out also two men of each Nation of the best disposition, which they caused to run, and he which was the swiftest in running had a present.

All these people are of a very cheerefull complexion, they laugh for the most part, nevertheless they are somewhat melancholy. They speake

[1] Strings of beads.
[2] Porcupine.
[3] Laverdière thinks this Besouat the same as the Tessoüat Champlain met in his exploration of the Ottawa in 1613.

very distinctly, as though they would make themselves well understood, and they stay quickely bethinking themselves a great while, and then they begin their speech againe: they often use this fashion in the middest of their Orations in counsaile, where there are none but the principals, which are the ancients: the women and children are not present. All these people sometimes endure so great extremity, that they are almost constrained to eate one another, through the great colds and snowes; for the Beasts and Fowles whereof they live, retire themselves into more hot climates. I thinke if any would teach them how to live, and to learne to till the ground, and other things, they would learne very well; for I assure you that many of them are of good judgement, and answere very well to the purpose to any thing that a man shall demand of them. They have one naughty qualitie in them, which is, that they are given to revenge, and great lyars, a people to whom you must not give too much credit, but with reason, and standing on your owne guard. They promise much and performe little. They are for the most part a people that have no Law, as farre as I could see and enforme my selfe of the said great Sagamo, who told me, that they constantly beleeve, that there is one God, which hath made all things: And then I said unto him, since they beleeve in one God onely, How is it that he sent them into this world, and from whence came they. He answered me, that after God had made all things, he tooke a number of Arrowes, and stucke them in the ground, from whence men and women grew, which have multiplied in the world untill this present, and had their originall on this fashion. I replied unto him, that this which hee said was false; but that indeede there was one God onely, which had created all things in the earth, and in the heavens: seeing all these things so perfect, without anybody to governe this world beneath, he tooke of the slime of the earth, & thereof made Adam, our first Father: as Adam slept, God tooke a rib of the side of Adam, and thereof made Eve, whom he gave him fir his companion; and that this was the truth that they and we had our originall after this manner, and not of Arrowes as they beleeved. He said nothing unto me, save, that he beleeved rather that which I said, then that which he told me. I asked him also, whether he beleeved not there was any other but one God onely. He told me, that their beliefe was, That there was one God, one Sonne, one Mother, and the Sunne, which were foure; yet that God was above them all; but that the Son was good, and the Sunne in the firmament, because of the good that they received of them; but that the Mother was naught, and did eate them, and that the Father was not very good. I shewed him his errour according to our faith, wherein he gave mee some small credit. I demanded of him, whether they had not seene, nor heard say of their ancestors, that God came into the world. He told me, that he had never seene him; but that in old time there were five men which went toward the Sunne setting, which met with God, who asked them, Whither goe ye? They said, we goe to seek our living: God answered them, you shall finde it here. They went farther, without regarding what God had said unto them: which tooke a stone, and touched two of them with it, which were turned into a stone: And hee said againe unto the other three, Whither goe yee? and they answered as at the first: and God said to them againe, Goe no further, you shall finde it here. And seeing that nothing came unto them, they went farther: and God tooke two staves, and touched the two first therewith, which were turned into staves; and the fift staied and would goe no further: And God asked him againe, whither goest thou? I goe to seek my living; stay and thou shalt finde it. He stayed without going any further, and God gave him meate, and he did eate thereof; after he had well fed, hee returned with other Savages, and told them all the former storie. He told them also, That another time there was a man which had store of Tobacco (which is a kinde of hearbe, whereof they take the smoake).[4] And that God came to this man, and asked him where his Tobacco pipe was. The man tooke his Tobacco pipe and gave it to God, which tooke Tobacco a great while: after hee had taken store of Tobacco, God broke the said pipe into many peeces: and the man asked him, why hast thou broken my pipe, and seest that I have no more? And God tooke one which hee had, and gave it to him, and said unto him; loe here I give thee one, carry it to thy great Sagamo, and charge him to keepe it, and if he keepe it well he shall never want any thing, nor none of his companions. The said man tooke the Tobacco pipe, and gave it to his great Sagamo, which as long as he kept, the Savages wanted nothing in the world. But after that the said Sagamo lost this Tobacco pipe, which was the occasion of great famine, which sometimes they have among them. I asked him whither he beleeved all this? he said yea, and that it was true. This I beleeve is the cause wherefore they say that God is not very good. But I replied and told him, that God was wholly good; and that without doubt this was the Divell that appeared to these men, and that if they

---

[4] This explanation shows that smoking tobacco was not yet familiar in France in 1603.

would beleeve in God as we doe, they should not want any thing needefull. That the Sunne which they beheld, the Moone and the Starres were created by this great God, which hath made heaven and earth, and they have no power but that which God hath given them. That we beleeve in this great God, who by his goodnesse hath sent us his deare Sonne, which being conceived by the holy Ghost, tooke humaine flesh in the Virginall wombe of the Virgin Marie, having been thirty three yeares on the earth, working infinite miracles, raising up the dead, healing the sicke, casting out Divels, giving sight to the blinde, teaching men the will of God his Father, to serve, honour, and worship him, did shed his bloud, and suffred death and passion for us, and for our sinnes, and redeemed mankinde, and being buried, he rose againe, he descended into hell and ascended into heaven, where he sitteth at the right hand of God his Father. That this was the beleefe of all the Christians, which beleeve in the Father, the Sonne, and the holy Ghost, which neverthelesse are not three Gods, but one onely, and one onely God, and one Trinitie, in the which none is before or after the other, none greater or lesse then another. That the Virgin Mary the Mother of the Sonne of God, and all men and women which have lived in this world, doing the commandements of God, and suffring martyrdome for his name sake, and by the permission of God have wrought miracles, and are Saints in heven in his Paradise, doe all pray this great divine Majestie for us, to pardon us our faults and our sinnes which we doe against his Law and his Commandements: and so by the prayers of the Saints in heven, and by our prayers which we make to his divine Majestie, he giveth that which we have neede of, and the Divell hath no power over us, and can doe us no harm: That if they had this beliefe, they should be as we are, and that the Divell should be able to doe them no hurt, and should never want anything necessary. That the said Sagamo told me, that he approved that which I said. I asked him what ceremony they used in praying to their God. He told me, that they used none other ceremonies, but that every one praied in his heart as he thought good: This is the cause why I beleeve they have no law among them, neither doe they know how to worship or pray to God, and live for the most part like brute beasts, and I thinke in short space they would be brought to be good Christians, if their Countrie were planted, which they desire for the most part.

They have among them certain Savages which they call Pilatoua,[5] which speak visibly with the Divell, which telleth them what they must doe, as well for the warre as for other things; and if he should command them to put any enterprise in execution, either to kill a French man, or any other of their Nation, they would immediately obey his commandement. Also they beleeve that all the dreames which they dreame are true: and indeede there are many of them, which say that they have seen and dreamed things which doe happen or shall happen. But to speake truely of these things, they are visions of the Divell, which doth deceive and seduce them. Loe this is all their beliefe that I could learne of them, which is brutish and bestiall. All these people are well proportioned of their bodies, without any deformitie, they are well set, and the women are well shapen, fat and full, of a tawnie colour by abundance of a certaine painting wherewith they rubbe themselves, which maketh them to be of an Olive colour. They are apparelled with skins, one part of their bodies is covered, and the other part uncovered; but in the winter they cover all, for they are clad with good Furres, namely with the skins of Orignac, Otters, Bevers, Sea-Beares,[6] Stagges, and Deer, whereof they have store. In the winter when the Snowes are great they make a kind of racket which is twice or thrice as bigge as one of ours in France, which they fasten to their feete, and so goe on the Snow without sinking; for otherwise they could not hunt nor travaile in many places. They have also a kind of Marriage, which is, that when a Maide is foureteene or fifteene yeares old, shee shall have many servants and friends, and she may have carnall company with all those which she liketh, then after five or six yeares, she may take which of them she will for her husband, and so they shall live together all their life time, except that after they have lived a certaine time together and have no children, the man may forsake her and take another wife, saying that his old wife is nothing worth, so that the Maides are more free than the married Women. After they be married they be chaste, and their husbands for the most part are jealous, which give presents to the Father or Parents of the Maide, which they have married: loe this is the ceremonie and fashion which they use in their marriages.[7]

[5] Pilotois, in Champlain's later narratives.
[6] Ours-marins, the same as loups-marins, seals.
[7] Cf. above, [vol. II] p. 130 [186].

Touching their burials, when a man or woman dieth, they make a pit, wherein they put all the goods which they have, as Kettels, Furres, Hatchets, Bowes and Arrowes, Apparell, and other goods, and then they put the corps into the grave, and cover it with earth, and set store of great peeces of wood over it, and one stake they set upon end, which they paint with red on the top. They beleeve the immortality of the Soule, and say that when they be dead they goe into other Countries to rejoyce with their parents and friends.

CHAPTER IV

The River Saguenay and its source.

THE eleventh day of June, I went some twelve or fifteene leagues up Saguenay, which is a fair River, and of incredible depth; for I beleeve, as farre as I could learne by conference whence it should come, that it is from a very high place from whence there descendeth a fall of water with great impetuositie: but the water that proceedeth thereof is not able to make such a River as this; which neverthelesse holdeth not but[1] from the said course of water (where the first fall is) unto the Port of Tadousac, which is the mouth of the said River of Saguenay, in which space are fortie or fiftie leagues, and it is a good league and a halfe broad at the most, and a quarter of a league where it is narrowest, which causeth a great currant of water. All the Countrie which I saw, was nothing but Mountaines, the most part of rockes covered with woods of Fir-trees, Cypresses, and Birch-trees, the soyle very unpleasant, where I found not a league of plaine Countrey, neither on the one side nor on the other. There are certaine hills of Sand and Isles in the said River, which are very high above the water. In fine, they are very Desarts voide of Beasts and Birds; for I assure you, as I went on hunting through places which seemed most pleasant unto mee, I found nothing at all, but small Birds which are like Nightingales, and Swallowes, which come thither in the Summer; for at other times I thinke there are none, because of the excessive cold which is there; this River commeth from the North-west. They reported unto me, that having passed the first fall, from whence the currant of water commeth, they passe eight other sauts or fals, and then

---

[1] I. e, extends only, etc.

they travaile one dayes journey without finding any, then they passe ten other sauts, and come into a Lake,[2] which they passe in two dayes (every day they travaile at their ease, some twelve or fifteene leagues:) at the end of the Lake there are people lodged: then they enter into three other Rivers, three or foure dayes in each of them; at the end of which Rivers there are two or three kinde of Lakes, where the head of Saguenay beginneth: from the which head or spring, unto the said Port of Tadousac, is ten dayes journee with their Canowes. On the side of the said Rivers are many lodgings, whither other Nacions come from the North, to trucke with the said Mountainers for skins of Bevers and Martens for other Merchandises, which the French Ships bring to the said Mountainers. The said Savages of the North say, that they see a Sea,[3] which is salt. I hold, if this be so, that it is some gulfe of this our Sea, which disgorgeth it selfe by the North part between the lands; and in very deede it can be nothing else. This is that which I have learned of the River of Saguenay.

CHAPTER V.

Departure from Tadoussac, to go to the Rapids; description of Hare Island, Isle de Coudre, Isle d'Orleans and many other islands, and of our arrival at Quebec.

On Wednesday the eighteenth day of June, we departed from Tadousac, to go to the Sault:[1] we passed by an Ile, which is called the Ile du lievre or the Ile of the Hare, which may be some two leagues from the Land on the North side, and some seven leagues from the said Tadousac, and five leagues from the South Coast. From the Ile of the Hare we ranged the North Coast about halfe a league, unto a point that runneth into the Sea, where a man must keepe farther off.

The said point is within a league of the Ile, which is called the Ile du Coudre, or the Ile of Filberds, which may be some two leagues in length: And from the said Ile to the Land on the North side is a league. The said Ile is somewhat even, and groweth sharpe toward both the ends; on the West end there are Medowes and Points of Rockes which stretch some-

---

[2] Lake St. John. Champlain used this material in his later narratives. Cf. vol. I, p. 169 [82], above; and other notes.
[3] Hudson Bay.
[1] The Sault St. Louis, the St. Louis or Lachine Rapids, just above Montreal.

what into the River. The said Ile is somewhat pleasant, by reason of the Woods which environ the same. There is store of Slate, and the soyle is somewhat gravelly: at the end whereof there is a Rocke which stretcheth into the Sea about halfe a league. We passed to the North of the said Ile, which is distant from the Ile of the Hare twelve leagues.

The Thursday following we departed from thence, and anchored at a dangerous nooke on the Northside, where there be certaine Medowes, and a little River[2] where the Savages lodge sometimes. The said day we still ranged the Coast on the North, unto a place where wee put backe by reason of the winds which were contrary unto us, where there were many Rockes and places very dangerous: here we stayed three dayes wayting for faire weather. All this Coast is nothing but Mountaynes as well on the South side as on the North, the most part like the Coast of the River of Saguenay. On Sunday the two and twentieth of the said moneth[3] wee departed to goe to the Ile of Orleans, in the way there are many Iles on the South shoare, which are low and covered with trees shewing to be very pleasant, contayning (as I was able to judge) some two leagues, and one league, and another halfe a league. About these Iles are nothing but Rockes and Flats, very dangerous to passe, and they are distant some two leagues from the mayne Land on the South.

And from thence wee ranged the Ile of Orleans on the Southside: It is a league from the North shoare, very pleasant and levell, contayning eight leagues in length. The Coast on the South shoare is low land, some two leagues into the Countrey: the said lands begin to be low over against the said Ile, which beginneth two leagues from the South Coast: to passe by the North side is very dangerous for the bankes of Sand and Rockes, which are betweene the said Ile and the mayne Land, which is almost all dry at a low water. At the end of the said Ile I saw a fall of water, which fell from great Mountaine, of the said River of Canada,[4] and on the top of the said Mountaine the ground is levell and pleasant to behold, although within the said Countries a man may see high mountaynes which may be some twenty, or five and twenty leagues within the Lands, which are near the first Sault of Saguenay. We anchored at

---

[2] Still called La Petite Rivière.

[3] July 22.

[4] I. e., from the heights overlooking the St. Lawrence. The Falls of Montmorency, so named by Champlain in honor of the Admiral of France, to whom this narrative was dedicated.

SAMUEL DE CHAMPLAIN

Quebec, which is a Strait of the said River of Canada,[5] which is some three hundred pases broad: there is at this Strait on the North side a very high Mountayne, which falleth downe on both sides: all the rest is a levell and goodly Countrey, where there are good grounds full of Trees, as Okes, Cypresses, Birches, Firre-trees and Aspes, and other Trees bearing fruit, and wild Vines: So that in mine opinion, if they were dressed, they be as good as ours. There are along the Coast of the said Quebec Diamants in the Rockes of Slate which are better than those of Alonson.[6] From the said Quebec to Ile of Coudre, or Filberds, are nine and twenty leagues.

CHAPTER VI

Point St. Croix, the River Batiscan; the rivers, rocks, islands, lands, trees, fruits, vines and the fine region beyond Quebec up to Three Rivers.

On Monday the three and twentieth of the said moneth, we departed from Quebec, where the River beginneth to grow broad sometimes one league, then a league and an halfe or two leagues at most. The Countrey groweth still fairer and fairer, and are all low grounds, without Rockes, or very few. The North Coast is full of Rockes and bankes of Sand: you must take the South side, about some halfe league from the shore. There are certaine small Rivers which are not navigable, but only for the canowes of the Savages, wherein there be many fals. Wee anchored as high as Saint Croix, which is distant from Quebec fifteene leagues. This is a low point, which riseth up on both sides.[1] The Countrey is fair and levell, and the soyles better then in any place that I have seene, with plenty of wood, but very few Firre-trees and Cypresses. There are in these parts great store of Vines, Peares, small Nuts, Cherries, Goose-beries, red and greene, and certaine small Roots of the bignesse of a little Nut, resembling Musheroms in taste, which are very good roasted and sod. All this soyle is blacke, without any Rockes, save that there is great store of Slate: The soyle is very soft, and if it were well manured it would yeeld great increase. On the Northside there is a River which is called Batiscan,

---

[5] Quebec is an Indian word, meaning narrows.
[6] Alençon.
[1] Point Platon. L.

215

which goeth farre into the Countrey, whereby sometimes the Algoumequins come downe: and another[2] on the same side three leagues from the said Saint Croix, in the way from Quebec, which is, that where Jasques Quartier was in the beginning of the Discovery which he made hereof, and hee passed no farther.[3] The said River is pleasant, and goeth farre up into the Countries. All this North Coast is very levell and delectable.

On Tuesday the foure and twentieth of the said moneth, wee departed from the said Saint Croix, where we stayed a tide and an halfe, that we might passe the next day following by day light, because of the great number of Rockes which are thwart the River (a strange thing to behold) which is in a manner dry at low water: But at halfe flood, a man may begin to passe safely; yet you must take good heed, with the Lead always in hand. The tyde floweth heere almost three fathomes and an halfe: the farther we went, the fairer was the Countrey. We went some five leagues and an halfe, and anchored on the North side. The Wednesday following wee departed from said place, which is a flatter Country then that which we passed before, full of great store of Trees as that of Saint Croix. We passed hard by a little Ile, which was full of Vines, and came to an Anchor on the South side neere a little Hill: but beeing on the top thereof all is even ground.

There is another little Ile three leagues from Saint Croix, joyning neere the South shore. Wee departed from the said Hill the Thursday following, and passed by a little Ile, which is neere the North shoare, where I saw sixe small Rivers, whereof two are able to beare Boats farre up, and another[4] is three hundred pases broad; there are certaine Ilands in the mouth of it; it goeth farre up into the Countrey; it is the deepest of all the rest which are very pleasant to behold, the soyle being full of Trees which are like to Walnut-trees, and have the same smell: but I saw no Fruit, which maketh me doubt: the Savages told me that they beare Fruit like ours.

In passing further we met an Ile, which is called Saint Eloy, and another little Ile, which is hard by the North shoare: we passed between the said Ile and the North shoare, where betweene the one and the other

---

[2] River Jacques Cartier.

[3] This is an error accounted for by Laverdière on the ground that Champlain at this time (1603) had not read Cartier's narratives of his voyages. Cartier went up the St. Lawrence as far as Hochelaga, or Montreal.

[4] The Ste. Anne.

are some hundred and fiftie paces. From the said Ile we passed a league and an halfe, on the South side neere unto a River, whereon Canowes might goe. All this Coast on the North side is very good, one may passe freely there, yet with the Lead in the hand, to avoid certaine points. All this Coast which we ranged is moving Sand, but after you be entred a little into the Woods, the soile is good. The Friday following we departed from this Ile, coasting still the North side hard by the shoare, which is low and full of good Trees, and in great number as farre as the three Rivers,[5] where it beginneth to have another temperature of the season, somewhat differing from that of Saint Croix: because the Trees are there more forward then in any place that hitherto I had seene. From the three Rivers to Saint Croix are fifteene leagues. In this River are six Ilands, three of which are very small, and the others some five or six hundred paces long, very pleasant and fertile, for the little quantitie of ground that they containe. There is one Iland in the middest of the said River, which looketh directly upon the passage of the River of Canada, and commandeth the other Ilands which lye further from the shoare, as well on the one side as on the other, of foure or five hundred paces; it riseth on the South side, and falleth somewhat on the North side. This in my judgement would be a very fit place to inhabit; and it might bee quickly fortified; for the situation is strong of it selfe, and neere unto a great Lake,[6] which is above foure leagues distant, which[7] is almost joyned to the River of Saguenay, by the report of the Savages, which travell almost an hundred leagues Northward, and passe many Saults, and then goe by Land some five or six leagues, and enter into a Lake,[8] whence the said River of Saguenay receiveth the best part of his Spring, and the said Savages come from the said Lake to Tadousac.

Moreover, the planting of The three Rivers would be a benefit for the liberty of certaine Nations, which dare not come that way for feare of the said Irocois their enemies, which border upon all the said River of Canada. But this place being inhabited, we might make the Irocois and the other Savages friends, or at least-wise under the favour of the said

---

[5] Three Rivers. The name came from the division of the St. Maurice by two islands into three streams.

[6] Lake St. Peter, an expansion of the St. Lawrence.

[7] Champlain misunderstood his Indian informants here, or else did not express himself clearly. What the Indians meant was that by the St. Maurice they could go up almost to Lake St. John and the upper waters of the Saguenay.

[8] Lake St. John.

ALGONQUIANS, HURONS AND IROQUOIS

Plantation, the said Savages might passe freely without feare or danger: because the said place of The three Rivers is a passage. All the soyle which I saw on the North shoare is sandy. Wee went up above a league into the said River, and could passe no further, by reason of the great current of water. We took a Boate to search up further, but we went not past a league, but we met a very Strait fall of water, of some twelve paces, which caused us that we could not passe no further. All the ground which I saw on the bankes of the said River riseth more and more, and is full of Firre-trees and Cypresse Trees, and hath very few other Trees.

CHAPTER VII

The length, breadth and depth of a lake, and of the rivers which flow into it; the islands in it; the soil one sees in the country; the river of the Iroquois, and the stronghold of the savages who wage war with them.

ON the Saturday following, we departed from The three Rivers, and anchored at a Lake,[1] which is foure leagues distant. All this Countrey from The three Rivers to the entrance of the said Lake is low ground, even with the water on the North side; and on the South side it is somewhat higher. The said Countrey is exceeding good, and the most pleasant that hitherto we had seen: the Woods are very thinne, so that a man may travell easily through them. The next day being the nine and twentieth of June, we entred into the Lake, which is some fifteene leagues in length, and some seven or eight leagues broad: At the entrance thereof on the Southside within a league there is a River which is very great,[2] and entreth into the Countrey some sixtie or eightie leagues, and continuing along the same Coast, there is another little River,[3] which pierceth about two leagues into the Land, and commeth out of another small Lake, which may containe some three or foure leagues. On the North side where the Land sheweth very high, a man may see some twentie leagues off; but by little and little the Mountaynes beginne to fall toward the West, as it were into a flat Countrey.

[1] Lake St. Peter. Apparently named by Champlain on this voyage, as he entered it June 29—St. Peter's Day. Its earlier name was Angoulême. L.
[2] The River Nicolet.
[3] Not clearly to be identified from this description.

The Savages say, that the greatest part of these Mountaynes are bad soyle. The said Lake hath some three fathoms water whereas we passed, which was almost in the middest: the length lieth East and West, and the breadth from North to the South. I thinke it hath good fish in it, of such kinds as we have in our owne Countrey. Wee passed it the very same day, and anchored about two leagues within the great River which goeth up to the Sault: In the mouth whereof are thirtie small Ilands, as farre as I could discerne; some of them are of two leagues, others a league and an half, & some lesse, which are full of Walnut-trees, which are not much different from ours; and I thinke their Walnuts are good when they bee ripe: I saw many of them under the Trees, which were of two sorts, the one small, and the others as long as a mans Thumbe,[4] but they were rotten. There are also store of Vines upon the bankes of the said Ilands. But when the waters be great, the most part of them is covered with water. And this Countrey is yet better than any other which I had seene before.

The last day of June wee departed from thence, and passed by the mouth of the River of the Irocois;[5] where the Savages which came to make warre against them, were lodged and fortified. Their Fortresse was made with a number of posts set very close one to another, which joined on the one side on the banke of the great River of Canada, and the other on the banke of the River of the Irocois: and their Boates were ranged the one by the other neere the shoare, that they might flie away with speed, if by chance they should bee surprised by the Irocois. For their Fort is Covered with the barke of Okes, and serveth them for nothing else, but to have time to embarke themselves. We went up the River of the Irocois some five or six leagues, and could pass no farther with our Pinnasse, by reason of the great course of water which descendeth, and also because we cannot goe on Land, and draw the Pinnasse for the multitude of Trees which are upon the bankes.

Seeing we could not passe any further, we tooke our Skiffe, to see whether the current were more gentle, but going up some two leagues, it was yet stronger, and wee could goe no higher. Being able to doe no more we returned to our Pinnasse. All this River is some three hundred or foure hundred paces broad, and very wholsome.[6] Wee saw five Ilands

---

[4] Probably butternuts.
[5] The Richelieu.
[6] Sain. Used of the sea or a river, sain means free from bars or shoals.

in it, distant one from the other a quarter or halfe a league, or a league at the most: one of which is a league long, which is the neerest to the mouth, and the others are very small. All these Countries are covered with Trees and low Lands, like those which I had seene before; but here are more Firres and Cypresses then in other places. Neverthelesse, the soile is good, although it bee somewhat sandy. This River runneth in a manner Southwest.[7] The Savages say, that some fifteene leagues from the place where we were up the River, there is a Sault which falleth down from a very steepe place, where they carry their Canowes to passe the same some quarter of a league, and come into a Lake;[8] at the mouth whereof, are three Ilands, and being within the same they meete with more Iles: This Lake may containe some fortie or fiftie leagues in length, and some five and twentie leagues in breadth, into which many Rivers fall, to the number of ten, which carrie Canowes very far up. When they are come to the end of this Lake, there is another fall, and they enter againe into another Lake,[9] which is as great as the former, at the head whereof the Irocois are lodged. They say moreover, that there is a River, which runneth unto the Coast of Florida,[10] whether it is from the said last Lake some hundred, or an hundred and fortie leagues. All the Countrey of the Irocois is somewhat Mountaynous, yet notwithstanding exceeding good, temperate, without much Winter, which is very short there.

CHAPTER VIII

Arrival at the Rapids. Description of them and the remarkable sights there, with the account given by the savages of the upper end of the great river.

After our departure from the River of the Irocois, wee anchored three leagues beyond the same, on the North side. All this Countrie is a lowe Land, replenished with all sorts of trees, which I have spoken of before. The first day of July we coasted the North side, where the wood is very thinne, and more thinne than wee had seene in any place before, and all

[7] We should say, comes from the southwest.

[8] Lake Champlain. Visited and named by Champlain in 1609. See above, vol. I, p. 213 [103].

[9] Lake George.

[10] The Hudson. Champlain uses Florida as the Spaniards used it, to describe the region now comprising the eastern and southeastern parts of the United States.

good land for tillage. I went in a Canoe to the South shoare, where I saw a number of Iles, which have many fruitfull trees, as Vines, Walnuts, Haselnuts, and a kinde of fruit like Chest-nuts, Cheries, Oakes, Aspe, Hoppes, Ashe, Beech, Cypresses, very few Pines and Firre-trees.[1] There are also other trees which I knew not, which are very pleasant. Wee found there store of Straw-berries, Rasp-berries, Goos-berries red, greene, and blue, with many small fruits, which growe there among great abundance of grasse. There are also many wilde beasts, as Orignas,[2] Stagges, Does, Buckes, Beares, Porkepickes,[3] Conies,[4] Foxes, Beavers, Otters, Muske-rats, and certaine other kindes of beasts which I doe not knowe, which are good to eate, and whereof the Savages live. Wee passed by an Ile, which is very pleasant, and containeth some foure leagues in length, and halfe a league in breadth.[5] I saw toward the South two high Mountaines, which shewed some twentie leagues within the Land. The Savages told mee, that here beganne the first fall of the foresaid River of the Irocois. The Wednesday following wee departed from this place, and sayled some five or six leagues. We saw many Ilands: the Land is there very lowe, and these Iles are covered with trees, as those of the River of the Irocois were.

The day following, being the third of July, we ranne certaine leagues, and passed likewise by many other Ilands, which are excellent good and pleasant, through the great store of Medowes which are thereabout, as well on the shoare of the maine Land, as of the other Ilands: and all the Woods are of very small growth, in comparison of those which wee had passed. At length we came this very day to the entrance of the Sault or Fall of the great River of Canada,[6] with favourable wind; and wee met with an Ile,[7] which is almost in the middest of the said entrance, which is a quarter of a league long, and passed on the South side of the said Ile, where there was not past three, foure or five foot water, and sometimes a fathome or two, and straight on the sudden wee found againe not past three or foure foot. There are many Rockes, and small Ilands, whereon there is no Wood, and they are even with the water. From the beginning

[1] The translator omitted the puzzling word pible, which, Laverdière conjectured, may stand for piboule, a kind of poplar, and érable, maple.
[2] Moose.
[3] Porcupines.
[4] Hares.
[5] The Verchères.
[6] The Sault St. Louis, or Lachine Rapids, just above Montreal.
[7] Later named, by Champlain, St. Helen's Island. See above, vol. I, p. 237 [114].

ALGONQUIANS, HURONS AND IROQUOIS

of the foresaid Ile, which is in the middest of the said entrance the water beginneth to runne with a great force. Although we had the wind very good, yet wee could not with all our might make any great way: neverthelesse wee passed the said Ile which is at the entrance of the Sault or Fall. When wee perceived that wee could goe no further, wee came to an anchor on the North shoare over against a small Iland,[8] which aboundeth for the most part with those kinde of fruits which I have spoken of before. Without all delay wee made ready our skiffe, which wee had made of purpose to passe the said Sault: whereinto the said Monsieur du Pont and my selfe entred, with certaine Savages, which we had brought with us to show us the way. Departing from our Pinnace, we were scarce gone three hundred paces, but we were forced to come out, and cause certain Mariners to goe into the water to free our Skiffe. The Canoa of the Savages passed easily. Wee met with an infinite number of small Rockes, which were even with the water, on which we touched oftentimes.

There be two great Ilands, one on the North side which containeth some fifteene leagues in length, and almost as much in breadth, beginning some twelve leagues up within the River of Canada, going toward the River of the Irocois,[9] and endeth beyond the Sault. The Iland which is on the South side is some foure leagues long, and some halfe league broad.[10] There is also another Iland, which is neere to that on the North side, which may bee some halfe league long, and some quarter broad: and another small Iland which is betweene that on the Northside, and another neerer to the South shoare, whereby we passed the entrance of the Sault. This entrance being passed, there is a kinde of Lake, wherein all these Ilands are, some five leagues long and almost as broad, wherein are many small Ilands which are Rockes. There is a Mountaine[11] neere the said Sault which discovereth farre into the Countrie, and a little River which falleth from the said Mountaine into the Lake. On the South side are some three or foure Mountaines, which seeme to be about fifteene or sixteene leagues within the Land. There are also two Rivers; one, which goeth to the first Lake[12] of the River of the Irocois, by which

---

[8] Now joined to the mainland at Montreal by the piers. L.

[9] This clause should read: "beginning at a distance of some twelve leagues in the River of Canada in the direction of the River of the Iroquois." The reference is to the Island of Montreal.

[10] Isle Perrot.

[11] Mount Royal. Now one of the most picturesque public parks in America. Cartier named the mountain Mont Royal in 1535.

[12] Chambly Basin. Reached by the St. Lambert and, after a portage, by Little River.

sometimes the Algoumequins[13] invade them: and another which is neere unto the Sault, which runneth not farre into the Countrey.

At our coming neere to the said Sault with our Skiffe and Canoa, I assure you, I never saw any streame of water to fall downe with such force as this doth; although it bee not very high, being not in some places past one or two fathoms, and at the most three. It falleth as it were steppe by steppe: and in every place where it hath some small heigth, it maketh a strong boyling with the force and strength of the running of the water. In the breadth of the said Sault, which may containe some league, there are many broad Rockes, and almost in the middest, there are very narrow and long Ilands, where there is a Fall as well on the side of the said Iles which are toward the South, as on the North side: where it is so dangerous, that it is not possible for any man to pass with any Boat, how small soever it be. We went on land through the Woods, to see the end of this Sault: where, after wee had travelled a league, wee saw no more Rockes nor Falls: but the water runneth there so swiftly as it is possible: and this current lasteth for three or four leagues: so that it is in vaine to imagine that a man is able to passe the said Saults with any Boats. But he that would passe them, must fit himself with the Canoas of the Savages, which one may easily carrie. For to carrie Boats is a thing which cannot be done in so short time as it should bee to be able to returne into France, unlesse a man would winter there. And beside this first Sault, there are ten Saults more, the most part hard to passe. So that it would be a matter of great paines and travell to bee able to see and doe that by Boat which a man might promise himselfe, without great cost and charge, and also to bee in danger to travel in vaine. But with the Canoas of the Savages a man may travell freely and readily into all Countries, as well in the small as in the great Rivers: So that directing himselfe by the meanes of the said Savages and their Canoas, a man may see all that is to be seene, good and bad, within the space of a yeere or two. That little way which wee travelled by Land on the side of the said Sault, is a very thinne Wood, through which men with their Armes may march easily, without any trouble; the air is there more gentle and temperate, and the soyle better then in any place that I had seene, where is store of such wood and fruits, as are in all other places before mentioned: and it is in the latitude of 45. degrees and certaine minutes.

[13] I. e., the Algonquins.

ALGONQUIANS, HURONS AND IROQUOIS

When we saw that we could doe no more, we returned to our Pinnace; where we examined the Savages which we had with us, of the end of the River, which I caused them to draw with their hand, and from what part the Head thereof came. They told us, that beyond the first Sault that we had seene, they travelled some ten or fifteene leagues with their Canoas in the River where there is a river[14] which runneth to the dwelling of the Algoumequins, which are some sixty leagues distant from the great River; and then they passed five Saults,[15] which may containe from the first to the last eight leagues, whereof there are two where they carrie their Canoas to passe them: every Sault may contain halfe a quarter or a quarter of a league at the most. And then they come into a Lake, which may be fifteene or sixteene leagues long.[16] From thence they enter againe into a River which may be a league broad, and travell some two leagues in the same; and then they enter into another Lake some foure or five leagues long: comming to the end thereof, they passe five other Saults,[17] distant from the first to the last some five and twenty or thirty leagues; whereof there are three where they carrie their Canoas to passe them, and thorow the other two they doe but draw them in the water, because the current is not there so strong, nor so bad, as in the others. None of all these Saults is so hard to passe, as that which we saw. Then they come into a Lake,[18] which may containe some eighty leagues in length,[19] in which are many Ilands, and at the end of the same the water is brackish[20] and the Winter gentle. At the end of the said Lake they passe a Sault which is somewhat high, where little water descendeth:[21] there they carry their Canoas by land about a quarter of a league to passe this Sault. From thence they enter into another Lake, which may be

---

[14] The Ottawa.
[15] The Cascades, Split Rock Rapid, Cedar Rapid and Coteau Rapid. The last is subdivided into two or three.
[16] Lake St. Francis.
[17] The long Sault Rapids.
[18] Lake Ontario.
[19] Lake Ontario, 197 miles long.
[20] Laverdière's text has *salubre*, wholesome, which would naturally be understood to be equivalent to "fresh." It is so translated by Otis. On the other hand, Champlain's use of the word seems to imply that he associated it with "sel," salt, and "salé," salty, and that Purchas correctly interpreted his meaning. Cf. in particular Champlain's distinct gradation on pp. 207-8, [248-49] below, of "Salubre," "Encore plus mauvaise" and "du tout salée" applied to a connected system of lakes.
[21] Niagara Falls and Rapids. Champlain misunderstood his informants.

some sixty leagues long, and that the water thereof is very brackish:[22] at the end thereof they come unto a Strait[23] which is two leagues broad, and it goeth farre into the Countrie. They told us that they themselves had passed no farther; and that they had not seene the end of a Lake,[24] which is within fifteene or sixteene leagues of the farthest place where themselves had beene, nor that they which told them of it, had known any man that had seene the end thereof, because it is so great that they would not hazard themselves to sayle farre into the same, for fear lest some storme or gust of winde should surprise them. They say that in the Summer the Sunne doth set to the North of the said Lake, and in the Winter it setteth as it were in the middest thereof: That the water is there exces-salt, to wit, as salt as the Sea water.[25] I asked them whether from the last Lake which they had seene, the water descended alwaies down the River comming to Gaschepay? They told me, no: but said, that from the third Lake onely it descended to Gaschepay: but that from the last Sault, which is somewhat high, as I have said, the water was almost still, and that the said Lake might take his course by other Rivers, which passe within the Lands, either to the South, or to the North, whereof there are many that runne there, the end whereof they see not. Now, in my judgment, if so many Rivers fall into this Lake, having so small a course at the said Sault, it must needs of necessitie fall out, that it must have his issue forth by some exceeding great River. But that which maketh me beleeve that there is no River by which this Lake doth issue forth (considering the number of so many Rivers as fall into it) is this, that the Savages have not seene any River, that runneth through the Countries, save in the place where they were. Which maketh me beleeve that this is the South Sea,[26] being salt as they say: Neverthelesse we may not give so much credit thereunto, but that it must bee done with apparent reasons, although there be some small shew thereof. And this assuredly is all that hitherto I have seene and heard of the Savages, touching that which we demanded of them.

[22] Salubre. Lake Erie is 250 miles long.
[23] Detroit River.
[24] Huron.
[25] Trés mauvaise, comme celle de ceste mer. The Indians seem to have transferred to the upper lakes information derived from others which originally referred to Hudson Bay.
[26] The Pacific Ocean.

ALGONQUIANS, HURONS AND IROQUOIS

CHAPTER IX

Return from the Rapids to Tadoussac, with the comparison of the reports of several savages as to the length and source of the great River of Canada, the number of rapids and lakes that it traverses.

WE departed from the said Sault[1] on Friday the fourth day of July, and returned the same day to the River of the Irocois. On Sunday the sixth of July wee departed from thence, and anchored in the Lake. The Monday following wee anchored at the three Rivers. This day wee sayled some foure leagues beyond the said three Rivers. The Tuesday following wee came to Quebec; and the next day wee were at the end of this Ile of Orleans, where the Savages came to us, which were lodged in the maine Land on the North side. We examined two or three Algoumequins to see whether they would agree with those that wee had examined touching the end and the beginning of the said River of Canada. They said, as they had drawne out the shape thereof, that having passed the Sault, which wee had seene, some two or three leagues, there goeth a River into their dwelling, which is on the North side. So going on forward in the said great River, they passe a Sault, where they carrie their Canoas, and they come to passe five other Saults, which may containe from the first to the last some nine or ten leagues, and that the said Saults are not hard to passe, and they doe but draw their Canoas in the most part of the said Saults or Falls, saving at two, where they carrie them: from thence they enter into a River, which is as it were a kinde of Lake, which may containe some six or seven leagues: and then they passe five other Falls, where they draw their Canoas as in the first mentioned, saving in two, where they carrie them as in the former: and that from the first to the last there are some twenty or five and twenty leagues. Then they come into a Lake contayning some hundred and fifty leagues in length: and foure or five leagues within the entrance of that Lake there is a River which goeth to the Algoumequins toward the North;[2] and another River which goeth to the Irocois,[3] whereby the said Algoumequins and Irocois make warre the one against the other. [And a little higher up on the South side of the said Lake there is another River which goeth to the

---

[1] I. e., the Sault St. Louis, or Lachine Rapids.
[2] The Bay of Quinté and River Trent.
[3] The Oswego River. S.

Irocois.[4]] Then comming to the end of the said Lake, they meete with another Fall, where they carrie their Canoas. From thence they enter into another exceeding great Lake,[5] which may containe as much as the former: They have been but a very little way in this last Lake, and have heard say, that at the end of the said Lake there is a Sea, the end whereof they have not seene, neither have heard that any have seene it. But that where they have beene, the water is not salt, because they have not entered farre into it; and that the course of the water commeth from the Sun-setting toward the East; and they knowe not, whether beyond the Lake that they have seene, there be any other course of water that goeth Westward. That the Sun setteth on the right hand of this Lake: which is, according to my judgment, at the North-west, little more or less; and that in the first great Lake the water freezeth not (which maketh mee judge that the climate is there temperate) and that all the Territories of the Algoumequins are lowe grounds, furnished with small store of wood: And that the coast of the Irocois is Mountainous; neverthelesse they are excellent good and fertile soyles, and better then they have seene anywhere else: That the said Irocois reside some fifty or sixty leagues from the said great Lake. And this assuredly is all which they have told mee that they have seene: which differeth very little from the report of the first Savages. This day wee came within some three leagues of the Ile of Coudres or Filberds.

On Thursday the tenth of the said moneth, wee came within a league and an halfe of the Ile du Lievre, or Of the Hare, on the North side, where other Savages came into our Pinnace, among whom there was a young man, an Algoumequin, which had travelled much in the said great Lake. Wee examined him very particularly, as wee had done the other Savages. Hee told us, that having passed the said Fall which wee had seen, within two or three leagues there is a River, which goeth to the said Algoumequins, where they be lodged, and that passing up the great River of Canada, there are five Falls, which may containe from the first to the last some eight or nine leagues, whereof there bee three where they carrie their Canoas, and two others wherein they draw them: that each of the said Falls may be a quarter of a league long: then they come into a Lake, which may containe some fifteene leagues. Then they passe five other Falls, which may containe from the first to the last some twenty or

---

[4] The Genesee River. This sentence was omitted by Purchas.
[5] Lake Erie.

ALGONQUIANS, HURONS AND IROQUOIS

five and twenty leagues; where there are not past two of the said Falls which they passe with their Canoas, in the other three they doe but draw them. From thence they enter into an exceeding great Lake, which may containe some three hundred leagues in length: when they are passed some hundred leagues into the said Lake, they meet with an Iland, which is very great; and beyond the said Iland the water is brackish:[6] But when they have passed some hundred leagues farther, the water is yet salter:[7] and comming to the end of the said Lake, the water is wholly salt.[8] Farther he said, that there is a Fall that is a league broad, from whence an exceeding current of water descendeth into the said Lake.[9] That after a man is passed this Fall, no more land can be seene neither on the one side nor on the other, but so great a Sea,[10] that they never have seene the end thereof, nor have heard tell, that any other have seene the same. That the Sonne setteth on the right hand of the said Lake:[11] and that at the entrance thereof there is a River which goeth to the Algoumequins,[12] and another River to the Irocois,[13] whereby they warre the one against the other. That the Countrie of the Irocois is somewhat mountainous, yet very fertile, where there is store of Indian Wheat, and other fruits, which they have not in their Countrie: That the Countrie of the Algoumequins is lowe and fruitfull. I enquired of them, whether they had any knowledge of any Mines? They told us, that there is a Nation which are called, the good Irocois,[14] which come to exchange for merchandises, which the French ships doe give to the Algoumequins, which say, that there is toward the North a Mine of fine Copper, whereof they showed us certaine Bracelets, which they had received of the said Good Irocois: and that if any of us would goe thither, they would bring them to the place, which should bee appointed for that businesse. And this is

---

[6] Salubre.

[7] Encore plus mauvaise.

[8] Du tout Salée. As noted above, this passage seems to show that Champlain attached quite the wrong meaning to the word "Salubre." Mr. Otis, taking "Salubre" as used in its proper meaning, met the difficulty by translating "encore plus mauvaise," "somewhat bad," a procedure which did more violence to Champlain's language than the supposition that he attached a wrong meaning to "Salubre."

[9] A more adequate description of Niagara than the one first obtained.

[10] Lake Erie.

[11] Lake Erie lies almost northeast and southwest.

[12] Probably Grand River.

[13] Probably Cattaraugus Creek.

[14] No doubt the Hurons. L.

all which I could learne of the one and the other, differing but very little; save that the second which were examined, said, that they had not tasted of the salt water: for they had not beene so farre within the said Lake, as the others: and they differ some small deale in the length of the way, the one sort making it more short, and the other more long. So that, according to their report, from the Sault or Fall where wee were, is the space of some foure hundred leagues unto the Salt Sea, which may be the South Sea, the Sunne setting where they say it doth.[15] On Friday the tenth of the said moneth[16] we returned to Tadousac, where our ship lay.

CHAPTER X

Voyage from Tadoussac to Isle Percée. Description of the Bay of Codfish; of Bonaventure Island; of Chaleur Bay; of many rivers, lakes and regions where there are various kinds of mines.

AS SOONE as wee were come to Tadousac, wee embarqued our selves againe to goe to Gachepay, which is distant from the said Tadousac about some hundred leagues. The thirteenth day of the said moneth we met with a companie of Savages, which were lodged on the South side, almost in the mid-way between Tadousac and Gachepay. Their Sagamo or Captaine which led them is called Armouchides, which is held to be one of the wisest and most hardy among all the Savages: Hee was going to Tadousac to exchange Arrowes, and the flesh of Orignars, which they have for Beavers and Martens of the other Savages, the Mountainers, Estechemains, and Algoumequins.

The fifteenth day of the said moneth we came to Gachepay, which is in a Bay, about a league and a halfe on the North side. The said Bay

---

[15] Champlain had probably had no opportunity to read the narratives of the explorations of De Soto and Coronado, which might have made him less ready to entertain the idea that the Pacific was within 400 leagues of the Atlantic. On the other hand, he may very likely have seen, or heard, of either the Verrazzano or Maiollo map, which divided the Western Hemisphere into three masses, introducing a great gulf from the Pacific side extending even further east than Lake Erie. See Winsor's *Narrative and Critical History*, II, 219. Cf. Lok's map of 1582, Fiske, *Old Virginia and Her Neighbors*, I, 60-61. If Champlain had seen any map of this type, the story of the Indians would seem to confirm the representation of the map. On the other hand, that so careful a man as Champlain received this impression from the Indians may explain how the men with Verrazzano received a similar impression.

[16] Friday was the 11th of July, 1603. L.

containeth some seven or eight leagues in length, and at the mouth thereof foure leagues in breadth. There is a River which runneth some thirty leagues up into the Countrie: Then we saw another Bay, which is called the Bay des Mollues, or the Bay of Cods,[1] which may be some three leagues long, and as much in bredth at the mouth. From thence we come to the Ile Percee,[2] which is like a Rocke, very steepe, rising on both sides, wherein there is a hole, through which Shallops and Boats may passe at an high water: and at a lowe water one may goe from the maine Land to the said Ile, which is not past foure or five hundred paces off. Moreover, there is another Iland in a manner South-east from the Ile Percee about a league, which is called the Ile de Bonne-adventure,[3] and it may bee some halfe a league long. All these places of Gachepay, the Bay of Cods, the Ile Percee, are places where they make dry and greene Fish.[4] When you are passed the Ile Percee, there is a Bay which is called the Bay of Heate,[5] which runneth as it were West South-west, some foure and twenty leagues into the land, containing some fifteene leagues in breadth at the mouth thereof. The Savages of Canada say, that up the great River of Canada, about some sixty leagues, ranging the South coast, there is a small River called Mantanne,[6] which runneth some eighteene leagues up into the Countreys and being at the head thereof, they carrie their Canowes about a league by land, and they come into the said Bay of Heate, by which they goe sometimes to the Isle Percee. Also they goe from the said Bay to Tregate[7] and Misamichy.[8] Running along the said coast we passe by many Rivers, and come to a place where there is a River which is called Souricoua,[9] where Monsieur Prevert was to discover a Mine of Copper. They goe with their Canowes up this River three or four dayes, then they passe three or four leagues by land, to

[1] Baye des Molues. Called by the English Molue Bay, which was corrupted into Mal-Bay.
[2] Percée Rock. A huge mass of red sandstone 290 feet high and 1500 feet long. The arch, or tunnel, is about 50 feet high. Baedeker, *Canada*, 71.
[3] Bonaventure Island.
[4] Rather, where the fisheries are carried on for dry and green fish. Green fish is fish salted, but not dried.
[5] Baye de Chaleurs. So named by Cartier in 1534 on account of the heat, L. Chaleur Bay is the modern name in English.
[6] The Matane River. There is a short portage to the upper Matapedia. S.
[7] Tracadie.
[8] Now Miramichy.
[9] Probably the Shediac. L.

the said Mine, which is hard upon the Sea shoare on the South side.[10] At the mouth of the said River, there is an Iland lying a league into the Sea; from the said Iland unto the Isle Percee, is some sixtie or seventie leagues. Still following the said coast, which trendeth toward the East, you meet with a Strait, which is two leagues broad, and five and twenty leagues long. On the East side is an Isle, which is called the Isle of Saint Laurence,[11] where Cape Breton is; and in this place a Nation of Savages, called the Souricois, doe winter.

Passing the Strait[12] of the Iles of Saint Laurence, and ranging the South-west Coast,[13] you come to a Bay which joyneth hard upon the Mine of Copper.[14] Passing farther there is a River,[15] which runneth threescore or fourescore leagues into the Countrey, which reacheth neere to the Lake of the Irocois, whereby the said Savages of the South-west Coast[16] make warre upon them. It would be an exceeding great benefit, if there might be found a passage on the Coast of Florida[17] neere to the said great Lake, where the water is salt; as well for the Navigation of ships, which should not bee subject to so many perils as they are in Canada, as for the shortening of the way above three hundred leagues.[18] And it is most certaine, that there are Rivers on the Coast of Florida, which are not yet discovered, which pierce up into the Countries, where the soil is exceeding good and fertile, and very good Havens. The Countrey and Coast of Florida may have another temperature of the season,[19] and may bee more fertile in abundance of fruites and other things, then that which I have seene. But it cannot have more even nor better soyles,[20] than those which we have seene.

[10] The Bay of Fundy.
[11] Cape Breton Island.
[12] The Strait of Canso.
[13] "La coste d'Arcadie" is the reading of the text. Arcadie is either an error of the original compositor, or perhaps a misunderstanding of the name, influenced by the recollection of the Greek Arcadia, a sort of misapprehension very common to people to-day who hear or see the name Acadia for the first time.
[14] The Bay of Fundy.
[15] The River St. John.
[16] "La coste d'Arcadie." The route would be up the St. John, down the Rivière du Loup, or the Chaudière, up the St. Lawrence, and then up the Richelieu to Lake Champlain.
[17] The eastern United States.
[18] A suggestion realized in a measure by the construction of the Erie Canal.
[19] "Une autre temperature de temps"; I. e., a more moderate climate.
[20] "Terres plus unies ny meilleures." "Unies" is "smooth" or "level."

ALGONQUIANS, HURONS AND IROQUOIS

The Savages say, that in the foresaid great Bay of Hete there is a River, which runneth up some twentie leagues into the Countrey, at the head whereof there is a Lake,[21] which may be about twentie leagues in compasse, wherein is little store of water, and the Summer it is dried up, wherein they find, about a foot or a foot and an halfe under the ground a kind of Metall like to silver, which I shewed them; and that in another place neere the said Lake there is a Myne of Copper. And this is that which I learned of the foresaid Savages.

CHAPTER XI

Return from Isle Percée to Tadoussac, with the description of the coves, harbors, rivers, islands, rocks, points,[1] bays, and shallows which are along the northern coast.

We departed from Ile Percee the nineteenth day of the said moneth to returne to Tadousac. When we were within three leagues of Cape le Vesque, or the Bishops Cape,[2] we were encountred with a storme which lasted two dayes, which forced us to put roomer with a great creeke, and to stay for faire weather. The day following we departed, and were encountred with another storme: Being loth to put roome,[3] and thinking to gaine way wee touched on the North shore the eight and twentieth day of July in a creeke[4] which is very bad, because of the edges of Rockes which lie there. The creeke is in 51. degrees and certaine minutes.[5] The next day we anchored neere a River, which is called Saint Margarites River,[6] where at a full Sea is some three fathomes water, and a fathome and an halfe at a low water: this River goeth farre up into the Land. As farre as I could see within the Land on the East shoare, there is a fall of water which entreth into the said River, and falleth some fiftie or sixtie fathomes downe, from whence commeth the greatest part of the water which descendeth downe. At the mouth thereof there is a banke of

---

[21] Lake Matapedia.

[1] Ponts, apparently for pointes. Mr. Otis has "falls" here, evidently taking points to be a mistake for saults.

[2] This cape cannot be identified. S.

[3] "Put roomer" and "put room" render the French word relâcher, to change the course and seek refuge.

[4] Anse, a cove.

[5] This latitude is too high. S.

[6] The Ste. Marguerite River, emptying into the Gulf of St. Lawrence from the north.

Sand, whereon at the ebbe is but halfe a fathome water. All the Coast toward the East is moving Sand: there is a point some halfe league[7] from the said River, which stretcheth halfe a league into the Sea: and toward the West there is a small Iland: this place is in fiftie degrees. All these Countries are exceeding bad, full of Firre-trees. The Land here is somewhat high, but not so high as that on the Southside. Some three leagues beyond we passed neere unto another River, which seemed to be very great, yet barred for the most part with Rockes:[8] some eight leagues farther there is a Point which runneth a league and an halfe into the Sea, where there is not past a fathome and an halfe of water. When you are passed this Point, there is another about foure leagues off, where is water enough. All this Coast is low and sandie. Foure leagues beyond this there is a creeke where a River entreth: many ships may pass heere on the West side: this is a low point, which runneth about a league into the Sea; you must runne along the Easterne shoare some three hundred paces to enter into the same. This is the best Haven which is all along the North shoare; but it is very dangerous in going thither, because of the flats and sholds of sand, which lye for the most part all along the shoare, almost two leagues into the Sea. About six leagues from thence, there is a Bay[9] where there is an Isle of sand; all this Bay is very shallow, except on the East side, where it hath about foure fathoms water: within the channell which entreth into the said Bay, some foure leagues up, there is a faire creeke[10] where a River entreth. All this coast is low and sandie, there descendeth [there] a fall of water which is great. About five leagues farther is a Point[11] which stretcheth about half a league into the Sea, where there is a creeke, and from the one point to the other[12] are three leagues, but all are shoals, where is little water. About two leagues off, there is a strand where there is a good haven, and a small River, wherein are three Islands, and where Ships may harbour themselves from the weather. Three leagues beyond this, is a sandie point which runneth out about a league, at the end whereof there is a small Islet. Going forward to Lesquemin, you meete with two little low Islands, and a little rocke neere the shoare: these said Ilands are about halfe a league from

---

[7] Laverdière would read: deux lieuës instead of demy lieuë.
[8] Rock River.
[9] Outard Bay.
[10] Anse, a cove.
[11] Bersimis Point.
[12] I. e., from Outard Point to Bersimis Point.

Lesquemin,[13] which is a very bad Port, compassed with rockes, and dry at a low water, and you must fetch about a little point of a rocke to enter in, where one ship onely can passe at a time. A little higher there is a River, which runneth a little way into the land. This is the place where the Basks kill the Whales;[14] to say the truth, the haven is starke naught. Wee came from thence to the foresaid haven of Tadousac, the third day of August. All these Countries before mentioned are low toward the shoare, and within the land very high. They are neither so pleasant nor fruitfull as those on the South, although they be lower. And this for a certaintie is all which I have seene of this Northerne coast.

CHAPTER XII

The ceremonies of the savages before going to war. The Almouchicois savages and their monstrous shape. Narrative of the Sieur de Prevert, of St. Malo, on the discovery of the coast of Arcadie.[1] What mines there are there; the goodness and fertility of the country.

AT our comming to Tadousac, we found the Savages which wee met in the River of the Irocois, who met with three Canowes of the Irocois in the first Lake, which fought against tenne others of the Mountayners; and they brought the heads[1] of the Irocois to Tadousac, and there was but one Mountayner wounded in the arme with the shot of an Arrow, who dreaming of something, all the other tenne must seeke to content him, thinking also that his wound thereby would mend.[2] If this Savage die, his Parents will revenge his death, either upon their Nation or upon others, or at leastwise the Captaines must give Presents to the Parents of the dead, to content them; otherwise as I have said, they would be revenged: which is a great fault among them. Before the said Mountayners set forth to the Warre, they assembled all, with their richest apparell of Furres, Beavers, and other Skinnes adorned with Pater-nosters[3] and Chaines of divers colors, and assembled in a great publike place, where there was before them a Sagamo whose name was Begourat, which led them to the Warre, and they marched one behind another, with their

---

[13] Les Escoumains, or Escoumins.
[14] More literally, "where the Basques carry on the whale fishery."
[1] See above, p. 214 [231], note.
[2] The punctuation has been changed here by inserting a period.
[3] Beads.

SAMUEL DE CHAMPLAIN

Bowes and Arrowes, Mases and Targets, wherewith they furnish themselves to fight: and they went leaping one after another, in making many gestures of their bodies, they made many turnings like a Snaile: afterward they began to dance after their accustomed manner, as I have said before: then they made their Feast,[4] and after they had ended it, the women stripped themselves starke naked, being decked with their fairest Cordons,[5] and went into their Canowes thus naked and there danced, and then they went into the water, and strooke at one another with their Oares, and beate water upon another: yet they did no hurt, for they warded the blows which they strooke one at the other. After they had ended all these Ceremonies, they retired themselves into their Cabines, and the Savages went to warre against the Irocois.

The sixt [eenth] day of August we departed from Tadousac, and the eighteenth day of the said moneth we arrived at the Ile Percee, where wee found Monsieur Prevert of Saint Malo, which came from the Myne, where he had been with much trouble, for the fear which the Savages had to meet with their enemies, which are the Armouchicois,[6] which are Savages very monstrous, for the shape that they have. For their head is little, and their body short, their armes small like a bone, and their thigh like; their legges great and long, which are all of one proportion, and when they sit upon their heeles, their knees are higher by halfe a foot then their head, which is a strange thing, and they seeme to be out of the course of Nature.[7] Neverthelesse, they be very valiant and resolute, and are planted in the best Countries of all the South Coast:[8] And the Souricois do greatly feare them. But by the incouragement which the said Monsieur de Prevert gave them, hee brought them to the said Mine, to which the Savages guided him. It is a very high Mountaine, rising somewhat over the Sea, which glistereth very much against the Sunne, and there is great store of Verde-grease issuing out of the said Myne of Copper. He saith, that at the foot of the said Mountayne, at a low water there were many morsels of Copper, as was otherwise declared unto us, which fall downe from the top of the Mountaine. Passing three or foure

---

[4] Tabagie. See note, vol. II, p. 23 [133].
[5] Matachias. See above, vol. I, p. 218 [106]. [See also vol. II, p. 163 (207)]
[6] The Indians of New England west of the Kennebec River. See above, vol. I, pp. 93, ff. [46]
[7] A description by enemies, with no basis of fact.
[8] Arcadie. Acadie, in the terms of De Monts' charter, 1603, embraced all the region from Philadelphia to Cape Breton.

leagues further toward the South,[9] there is another Myne, and a small River which runneth a little way up into the Land, running toward the South, where there is a Mountaine, which is of a blacke painting, wherewith the Savages paint themselves: Some six leagues beyond the second Myne, toward the Sea, about a league from the South Coast,[10] there is an Ile, wherein is found another kind of Metall, which is like a darke browne: if you cut it, it is white, which they used in old time for their Arrows and Knives, and did beat it with stones. Which maketh me beleeve that it is not Tinne, nor Lead, being so hard as it is; and having shewed them silver, they said that the Myne of that Ile was like unto it, which they found in the earth, about a foot or two deepe. The said Monsieur Prevert gave the Savages Wedges and Cizers,[11] and other things necessarie to draw out the said Myne; which they have promised to doe, and to bring the same the next yeere, and give it to the said Monsieur Prevert. They say also that within some hundred or one hundred and twentie leagues there are other Mynes, but that they dare not goe thither unlesse they have Frenchmen with them to make warre upon their enemies, which have the said Mynes in their possession. The said place where the Myne is, standeth in 44. degrees and some few minutes, neere the South Coast[12] within five or six leagues: it is a kind of Bay,[13] which is certaine leagues broad at the mouth thereof, and somewhat more in length, where three Rivers, which fall into the great Bay neere unto the Ile of Saint John,[14] which is thirtie or five and thirtie leagues long, and is six leagues distant from the South shoare. There is also another little River, which falleth almost in the mid way of that whereby Monsieur Prevert returned, and there are as it were two kind of Lakes in the said River. Furthermore, there is yet another small River which goeth toward the Mountaine of the painting. All these Rivers fall into the said Bay on the Southeast part, neere about the said Ile which the Savages say there is of this white Metall. On the North side of the said Bay are the Mynes of Copper, where there is a good Haven for ships, and a small Iland at the mouth of the Haven; the ground is Oze and Sand, where a man may run his ship on shoare. From the said Myne to the beginning of the mouth

[9] "Tirant à la coste d'Arcadie."
[10] "La coste d'Arcadie."
[11] Ciseaux. Here, chisels or drills.
[12] La coste de l'Arcadie.
[13] The Basin of Mines.
[14] Prince Edward's Island.

of the said Rivers is some sixtie or eightie leagues by Land. But by the Sea Coast, according to my judgement, from the passage of the Ile of Saint Lawrence and the Firme Land, it cannot be past fiftie or sixtie leagues to the said Myne. All this Countrey is exceeding faire and flat, wherein are all sorts of trees, which wee saw as wee went to the first Sault up the great River of Canada, very small store of Firre-trees and Cypresses. And this of a truth is as much as I learned and heard of the said Monsieur Prevert.[15]

CHAPTER XIII

A frightful monster, which the savages call Gougou. Our short and safe return to France.

THERE[1] is still one strange thing, worthy of an account, which many savages have assured me was true; that is, that near the Bay of Heat, toward the south, there is an island where a frightful monster makes his home, which the savages call Gougou, and which they told me had the form of a woman, but very terrible, and of such a size that they told me the tops of the masts of our vessel would not reach to his waist, so great do they represent him; and they say that he has often eaten up and still continues to eat up many savages; these he puts, when he can catch them, into a great pocket, and afterward he eats them; and those who had escaped the danger of this awful beast said that its pocket was so great that it could have put our vessel into it. This monster makes horrible noises in this island, which the savages call the Gougou; and when they speak of it, it is with unutterable fear, and several have assured me that they have seen him. Even the above-mentioned Sieur Prevert from St. Malo told me that, while going in search of mines, as mentioned in the preceding chapter, he passed so near the haunt of this terrible beast, that he and all those on board his vessel heard strange hissings from the noise she[2] made, and that the savages with him told him it was the same creature, and that they were so afraid that they hid themselves wherever they could, for fear that she would come and carry them off. What makes me believe what they say is the fact that all the savages in general fear her,

---

[15] Prevert reported much hearsay testimony in a more or less distorted form.
[1] Purchas omitted this account of the Gougou, evidently believing it, as Champlain thought likely, an idle tale.
[2] This change of gender follows the original.

and tell such strange things of her that, if I were to record all they say of her, it would be considered as idle tales, but I hold that this is the dwelling-place of some devil that torments them in the manner described. This is what I have learned about this Gougou.]

Before we departed from Tadousac, to returne into France, one of the Sagamos of the Mountayners named Bechourat, gave his Sonne to Monsieur du Pont to carrie him into France, and he was much recommended unto him by the Great Sagamo Anadabijou, praying him to use him well, and to let him see that, which the other two Savages had seene which we had brought backe againe. We prayed them to give us a woman of the Irocois, whom they would have eaten: whom they gave unto us, and we brought her home with the foresaid Savage. Monsieur de Prevert in like manner brought home foure Savages, one man which is of the South Coast,[3] one woman and two children of the Canadians.

The four and twentieth of August, we departed from Gachepay, the ship of the said Monsieur Prevert and ours. The second of September, we counted that wee were as farre as Cape Rase. The fift day of the said moneth we entred upon the Banke, whereon they use to fish. The sixteenth, we were come into the Sounding, which may be some fiftie leagues distant from the Ushant. The twentieth of the said moneth we arrived in New Haven[4] by the grace of God to all our contentments, with a continuall favourable wind.

[3] La coste d'Arcadie.
[4] Havre.

END